23 MAY 2014

26 JAN 2015

29 JUN 2017

29 MAR 2018

06 SEP 2019   – 2 NOV 2023

lo Sept

30 DEC 2022

Please return/renew this item
by the last date shown.
Books may also be renewed by
phone or the Internet.

Tel: 0161 254 7777
www.manchester.gov.uk/libraries

WORDSMITHS & WARRIORS

The English-Language Tourist's Guide to Britain

DAVID CRYSTAL

HILARY CRYSTAL

OXFORD
UNIVERSITY PRESS

OXFORD
UNIVERSITY PRESS

Great Clarendon Street, Oxford OX2 6DP,
United Kingdom

Oxford University Press is a department of the University of Oxford.
It furthers the University's objective of excellence in research, scholarship,
and education by publishing worldwide. Oxford is a registered trade mark of
Oxford University Press in the UK and in certain other countries.

British Library Cataloguing in Publication Data
Data available

ISBN 978-0-19-966812-0

Typeset by Sparks—www.sparkspublishing.com
Printed in the UK by Bell & Bain Ltd, Glasgow

CONTENTS

INTRODUCTION

'What happened here?' It's a natural question to ask when we visit somewhere for the first time. It might be the physical character of the place which prompts the question—a ruin, a wall, a statue—or a curious place name or spelling. Often we already know that something happened—a battle, a treaty, a wedding, a film—and we take pains to seek out the location.

People spend a significant part of their lives visiting places they find of particular interest. If your interest is history, you might go to battlefields. If architecture, cathedrals. If flowers, nature reserves. So, what could you visit if you have a fascination with the history of the English language in Britain? As a fairly well-travelled language enthusiast, I have often found myself in a place where the name rings a linguistic bell. Sometimes the bell rings loud and clear: so-and-so was born here, or died here, or lived here, or worked here. Sometimes it is muffled: I have a vague sense of something happening, but can't remember exactly what. And now I realize—as a result of writing this book—I've passed through places where I had no idea a linguistic bell was ringing at all.

Wordsmiths and Warriors, then, is about the English linguistic heritage of Britain as encountered through the places which shaped it. The two terms in the title overlap. In the early days of English, warriors are conspicuous, with invading regimes causing political or cultural change that had far-reaching linguistic consequences. In later days, wordsmiths predominate, with poets, commentators, translators, scholars, reformers, and enthusiasts engaging with the language, and through their work giving the language its historical character. But some warriors, such as King Alfred, were wordsmiths; and some wordsmiths, such as George Bernard Shaw, were definitely warriors, in the way they fought for a linguistic cause.

The book relates a real journey. Hilary and I went to each place ourselves, and my text reflects what we encountered on the day of our visit, conveying personal impressions as well as providing an explanation of why I chose it. Each chapter covers one topic, ordered to reflect the broad chronology of events in the history of the language. For anyone who wishes to follow in our footsteps, and visit locations that are geographically near to each other, regardless of their historical relationship, I provide a region-by-region perspective at the end of the book. I've also added a practical dimension at the end of each chapter, in the manner of a travel guide. Quite often, we found ourselves uncertain of the best way of reaching a place, or whether we could park when we got there; so I've included basic travel advice, along with postcodes for those using GPS. Needless to say, where relevant, readers should check for possible changes to opening dates and times. Many of the sites belong to heritage organizations, and we found membership of these saved us a great deal in entrance fees during our journey.

Because my purpose in writing this book was to convey a sense of place, a photographic dimension was essential—indeed, its chief motivation. Hilary took all the photographs, using a Nikon Coolpix S9100. She emphasizes that she is 'only an enthusiastic amateur' when it comes to photography, but she has a professional's eye for a good shot, and the results do everything I was hoping for. Of course, 2012 was not the best of years for photographing linguistic Britain. As I write this, I read that the summer was the wettest since records began. And the winter of 2011–12 wasn't particularly helpful either. So the pictures reflect the weather we had on the day of our visit—or weathers, in fact, for there was never any guarantee that the sun/cloud/rain which would greet our arrival at a location would still be there at our departure. And after our first encounter with a muddy field, we quickly realized that weather-proof footwear is an essential bit of kit for the English-language tourist.

This is an appropriate place, also, to acknowledge the helpfulness of the various organizations we encountered on our journey, and whose roles are reflected in individual chapters. There were a few heritage locations where we weren't allowed to take photographs, despite using all the powers of persuasion I could muster, but for the most part we found locations to be interested in our project, and more than willing to help us achieve a desired shot, and sometimes to provide relevant background not found in available published sources. Thanks, in particular, to Michael Gainey, who arranged for us to get onto the roof of the *Financial Times* building to obtain a bird's-eye view of the shape of the original Shakespeare's Globe; Dermot Gilvary, who helped me research the history of Oakham School; Richard Bailey, for advice about Bede and Lindisfarne; Iain McIntosh, for permission to use his 'Last Supper' illustration; and Allan Flack, who provided further detail to my knowledge of the find at Undley; as well as the staff at the Samuel Johnson heritage sites in Lichfield and London, at the English Department at University College London, and at the locations in Alloway,

Ayot St Lawrence, Canterbury, Chester, Dunfermline, Ely, Hampton Court, Jarrow, Lindisfarne, Lutterworth, Paston, Peterborough, Saltaire, Stratford-upon-Avon, and York. Nor should I forget the many unknown individuals we buttonholed for their local knowledge during our travels.

With locations as far apart as the south-east of Kent and the Scottish lowlands, and from the west of Wales to the East Anglian coast, we drove thousands of miles to compile this somewhat unorthodox combination of English-language history and travelogue. It has been a hugely rewarding experience, which added a sense of place to my knowledge of language topics and personalities, and I strongly recommend it as a powerful way of making language study come alive.

David Crystal
Holyhead,
September 2012

Chapter 1

Pegwell Bay

arrival

From King Vortigern's point of view, it was a bad call. The British warlord had been 'unable to prevent or repel the cruel and frequent incursions of the northern nations', according to Bede in Chapter 15 of his *Ecclesiastical History of the English Nation*. So he looked for help from abroad:

> They all agreed to call over to their aid, from the parts beyond the sea, the Saxon nation ... Then the nation of the Angles, or Saxons, being invited by the aforesaid king, arrived in Britain with three long ships, and had a place assigned them to reside in by the same king, in the eastern part of the island, that they might thus appear to be fighting for their country, whilst their real intentions were to enslave it.... In a short time, swarms of the aforesaid nations came over into the island ... and began to turn their weapons against their confederates.

The *Anglo-Saxon Chronicle* tells us that this took place in 449, and names the leaders of the incomers: Hengist and Horsa. It also reports that six years later there was a battle in which Vortigern was killed, and Hengist took over, eventually forcing the Britons out of the region.

Where did all this happen? It's the obvious starting-point for any English-language tourist. Where exactly did these Anglo-Saxons arrive? Where did they reside? The *Chronicle* gives us a number of pointers. They came to Britain 'at a place which is called Heopwinesfleot'. That's literally 'the river Heopwell', which in turn means 'the stream where hips grow'. It's called Ebbsfleet today, and the place where they landed is nearby Pegwell

Page opposite. The Hugin *Viking ship at Pegwell Bay, as it would have appeared to anyone daring to cross its path.*

Bay. It's the perfect spot, as the coastline here is the closest you can get to the European mainland. Fly over this corner of England on a clear day, and you see the curiously rounded protuberance of the north-east corner of Kent pointing towards Calais. It looks as if it has been clumsily added on to the British mainland. Which is in fact what happened.

This is Thanet—or the Isle of Thanet, as it's still called. The name is obscure, but the geological facts aren't. It was indeed an island—an ancient burial place, according to a Greek legend. *Ynys Thanatos*. Island of the dead. In Anglo-Saxon times it was separated from the rest of Kent by a wide channel. Bede is very precise about it. When he describes the arrival of Augustine in Kent in 597, he tells us:

> On the east of Kent is the large Isle of Thanet containing according to the English way of reckoning 600 families, divided from the other land by the river Wantsum, which is about three furlongs over, and fordable only on two places, for both ends of it run into the sea.

Three furlongs. That's 660 yards (600 m). Some accounts say the entrance to the channel was much wider—well over a mile. But by the 16th century the channel had silted up, and Thanet stopped being an island.

The course of the Wantsum is hard to track down today. In the north it entered the sea at Reculver, where the remains of the old Roman fort and the distinctive dual towers of St Mary's Church can be seen for miles around. At the other end, it joins the River Stour, which runs down to the south coast. It's hardly a river now—in places, more like a drainage ditch. But to my mind it characterizes the Anglo-Saxon arrival better than anything else, so I was determined to find what was left of it.

The maps I consulted proved useless. There are dozens of drainage watercourses that criss-cross this part of Kent, and any of them could have been the remains of the Wantsum. The local people we asked were aware, but vague. There was a Wantsum Walk, we were told, with waymarks. Indeed there was: we had seen one at Reculver, but it wasn't by a river. Eventually, we got lucky: the man behind the counter at the local post office in St Nicholas at Wade knew exactly where it was. On the right of the road just before it reaches the Thanet Way (the A299), he said. What he didn't say was that it was private land. We drove blithely through an open gate, and up onto a low bridge, and there indeed we found a river. That was the good news.

The bad news was that our arrival had been noticed by the local farmer, who had been working with an enormous farm vehicle in a nearby field—a tractor with long attachments that made it resemble a Star Wars ground

Left. The outline of Reculver church and fort, distinctive even on a misty day.

Bottom left. Where the Wantsum Channel used to be, as seen from Reculver fort.

Bottom right. A waymark on the Wantsum Walk.

attack vehicle rather than a piece of agricultural equipment. He obviously wondered what we were up to, and parked his vehicle across the road by which we'd entered his property. We drove up to it. There was no way past. The wheel of the tractor dwarfed our car. The banjo theme from the film *Deliverance* came into my head.

He looked down at us suspiciously. I apologized for the intrusion, and explained that we were lost English-language tourists doing research for a book about the area and trying to find the River Wantsum … I stopped there, thinking that the bit about Vortigern and Hengist and Horsa might be too much information. 'That's the Wantsum', he said, nodding towards where we'd just been, and gave us a bit more information about the river. There are indeed places where its course is confusing, it seems, and we had stumbled on one of the more distinctive stretches. He moved his tractor to let us pass. Fade out banjo.

There's no such confusion about Pegwell Bay. It's guarded by a Viking longship—a replica, but a real ship nonetheless. The *Hugin*. It was sailed from Denmark in 1949 by 53 Danes to commemorate the 1500th anniversary of the arrival of Hengist and Horsa. It landed, appropriately, at Viking Bay in Broadstairs, and was then placed on permanent display on the clifftop above Pegwell. With its bright colours, array of shields, and set of oars, from a distance it looks like a large children's toy. Stand underneath the prow and look up at the figurehead, and you get a very different impression (as on p. 4). Those longships were fearsome craft.

It's difficult to judge where the original bay shoreline was. So much of the coast has been altered by silting. In 2008, for instance, they discovered

Wordsmiths and Warriors

the remains of the original Kentish beach where the Romans landed in AD 43: it's at Richborough, which is now over two miles inland. Pegwell, by contrast, is still on the coast. If Hengist and Horsa could time-travel to the present day, they would probably recognize the line of white chalk cliffs to the east, despite the wear and tear of 1500 years of sea, wind, and weather. But they would be totally bemused by the landfill and industrial waste that covers the shoreline to the west.

As were we, to begin with, when we arrived. We walked down from the Viking ship to the shore, to be met with a huge area of concreted land, with white line markings sporadically visible between clumps of uncontrolled grass and weeds. It looked like a landing site, though hardly an Anglo-Saxon one. Then it dawned on me. It *was* a landing site. And I remembered that I'd stood there 40 years before. It was the location for the hovercraft port between England and France, operational between 1969 and 1982. The 40-minute crossing and rapid turn-around made it a popular channel-hopping choice, before the Channel Tunnel arrived, and—living in Reading in those days—we had used it once as the most convenient point of departure for a continental holiday. I realized we had just walked

The *Hugin*.

What the Anglo-Saxons
might have seen …

… and what they didn't.

through the car marshalling area to where the giant SRN4 hovercraft used
to dock.

We strolled back to the Viking ship along the hoverport approach road.
A more dramatic contrast of transport styles it is difficult to imagine. Both
are history now.

Getting there

Pegwell Bay is just off the A256, the road between Sandwich and Ramsgate. Travelling north, a brown tourist sign points ahead to Pegwell Bay Country Park. Just past the park entrance, you enter Cliffsend, and the white cliffs of Pegwell Bay are in the distance. The Viking ship is in a fenced-off green space on your right, with a small car park nearby. From the north along the A256, the ship is on the left, just past the old hoverport approach road. A brown sign saying 'Picnic Site' points to the location (postcode: CT12 5HY). A narrow path down to the bay runs from near an information panel at the edge of the site.

The road north out of St Nicholas at Wade (CT7 0PW) is actually called Wantsum Way, but it leads directly onto the Thanet Way (the A299): that does cross the Wantsum, but there's nowhere to stop. Instead, turn left into Court Road, which crosses the Thanet Way. This leads into the narrow Potten St Road. Turn left, and just after some houses the road bears to the left, with a paved path leading right, across fields, for walking only. If you take that path, you reach the Wantsum. Alternatively, take the A28 west out of the nearby village of Sarre (postcode of Sarre Mill: CT7 0JY) along the aptly named Island Road, and you cross the Wantsum almost immediately. For serious walkers, it's possible to take the Wantsum Walk between Birchington and Herne Bay via Reculver, following the waymarks; that way you walk alongside the river for a while; but it's 30 miles (48 km) in all. We did about 200 yards of it, at Reculver.

For Reculver, travelling along the Thanet Way, there's a brown tourist sign pointing to Reculver Towers & Roman Fort. From the west, turn left into Sweechbridge Road, and this leads into Reculver Lane, which takes you all the way. There's a large car park next to the King Ethelbert Inn (postcode: CT6 6SU). From the east, a similar slip-road takes you around and over a bridge, via the remarkably named Heart in Hand Road, and this leads into Sweechbridge Road.

Chapter 2

Caistor St Edmund

the earliest known English word

Rabbits were the main problem. And rabbit-hunters. Banks of stinging nettles. Roots of trees and bushes. A loose sandy soil, already deeply disturbed by ploughing and planting. All of this made the Anglo-Saxon cemetery site at Caistor-by-Norwich 'as unpropitious for archaeological investigation as could be imagined'.

So said the writers of a 1973 research report to the Society of Antiquaries of London on the excavations which took place at Caistor between 1932 and 1937. They had been carried out by a former naval officer who lived nearby, F. R. Mann, helped by the foreman labourer who had been employed on the excavations at the nearby Roman town of Venta Icenorum, about 3 miles (5 km) south of Norwich. Mann's account of his first day at the site did not augur well:

> We began digging on the 28th January 1932. The nettles by then had died down and it was possible to get a good view of the surface of the ground. We did not find this encouraging. The ground all around had all the appearance of having been thoroughly upheaved and churned up by the activities of rabbits and rabbiters. Fragments of Anglo-Saxon and Roman pottery were strewn about everywhere ...

At one spot they found a large hole dug by a rabbiter. Nearby was a broken-up urn with its contents of burnt bones scattered around. That seemed promising, so they picked out a straight line over ground that seemed to have been less disturbed, and began to dig:

Page opposite. The overgrown burial site at Caistor St Edmund.

We soon began to find urns, all of which lay over to the west part of the trench. Years afterwards, I found that, had we started our first trench a yard further to the east, we should not have found a single urn, as they had all been previously dug out.

Fortune had smiled upon them. And upon English-language scholars too, for in one of the cremation urns, later labelled N59, they made a remarkable find: on one of the objects was a runic inscription, a candidate for the oldest recorded example of a word in English.

N59 was one of a group of urns found in the south-west corner of the site. It was a piece of black ware, large and globular in shape, with a tall conical neck but lacking its rim. It was decorated with continuous horizontal lines

VENTA ICENORUM

The town is well presented on display boards. The name means 'market-place of the Iceni'. The Iceni were a client-tribe of Rome, famous for their (failed) revolt against the Romans, led by Queen Boudicca, in AD 61. The town was probably established soon after, and became an important administrative centre for the region. Between the 1st and 3rd centuries, a grid of streets was laid out, public buildings erected, and high walls built. There's no evidence of Anglo-Saxon presence during the Roman period, but after the Romans left the country in the 5th century, the site may have continued to be used as a market centre, for archaeological finds, as well as the nearby cemeteries, suggest that Anglo-Saxons were active in the area until at least the 8th century.

Today, only the outer defences of the town are clearly visible, and the knowledge of its internal layout came fortuitously as a result of an air photograph taken in 1928, which clearly showed the outlines of streets and buildings. In very dry weather some of these locations can even be seen from the walls, appearing as brownish lines in the grass. Access to the town was possible only through a gate located in the centre of each of the four walls. It's one of the few Roman sites which has not been covered over by later buildings.

They were serious about defending Caistor. As you approach the south-eastern corner from the car park, the height of the earth-covered wall (about 23 ft/7 m) is emphasized by a flight of 36 steps helpfully constructed by the Norfolk Archaeological Trust, which owns the site. A ditch runs along the outside. The scale of the site—some 35 acres (14 hectares)—took us a little by surprise. You could walk around all four sides in less than half an hour, but it would actually take a lot longer, as there are several panels to read containing information about the site, and there's a lot to see at the eastern end of the north wall, by the river Tas, where a bastion stands proud without any covering of earth.

Wordsmiths and Warriors

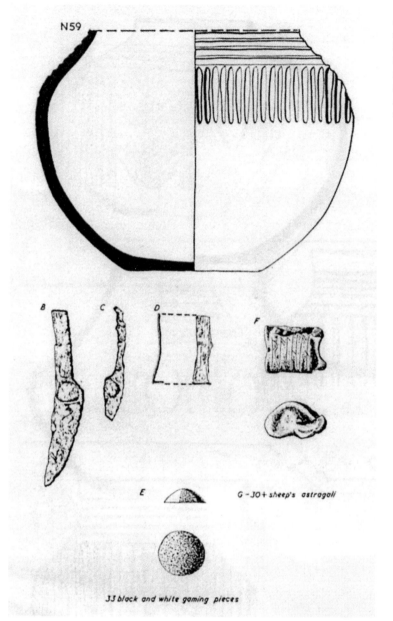

N59

B C D F

E

G - 30 + sheep's astragali

33 black and white gaming pieces

An outline of urn N59 and its contents (from the report by J. N. L. Myres and Barbara Green, *The Anglo-Saxon Cemeteries of Caistor-by-Norwich and Markshall Norfolk*, The Society of Antiquaries of London, 1973).

around the neck and a series of continuous vertical lines on the shoulder. It contained some burnt bones, a corroded iron knife, half of a pair of iron shears with the tip of the blade missing, a miniature pair of bronze tweezers, 33 gaming pieces (11 black, made possibly of black shale, and 22 white, made probably of bone), and 35 or more ankle-bones from sheep or roe deer (it was impossible to be sure of the exact number, as some were fragments). One of these ankle-bones was different—larger, dark brown, and

Caistor St Edmund

15

The Caistor astragalus, showing the runic letters.

polished—and it was on this item that someone had carved a sequence of runes.

The letters read as follows:

ᚱᚠᛇᚻᚨᛏ

r a i h a n

Various interpretations have been proposed. It could be a proper name: this piece belonged to someone called Raiha. It could be a word referring to the rune-master who did the inscribing, the 'cutter' or 'colourer', for the earlier root of the word, *rei*, could mean 'cut' or 'coloured'. However, the most likely gloss is the name of the animal to which the ankle-bone belonged: 'roe-deer'.

The bone in question is technically referred to as an *astragalus*—the anatomical name for the lower part of the ankle joint found in several species, including humans. Astragali were often used in ancient rituals and in gaming, and some of the games that were played then are still played today, going under such names as knucklebones or jackstones. In one game, the bones were thrown into the air and had to be caught on the back of the hand. In another, the sides of the bones were given different values, and

Wordsmiths and Warriors

a group of them were thrown onto a surface—just as we do with modern dice. It's impossible to say what sort of game this particular astragalus was used for, but the fact that it was given a name at all suggests it had a very special status—perhaps a king in a primitive version of chess, or the quarry in a game of chase. 'Hunt the roe' we might call it today.

Visitors to Caistor are more likely to be interested in the Roman town of Venta Icenorum than in the Anglo-Saxon cemetery. Not so, English-language tourists. Indeed, to find the cemetery, you have to turn your back on the Roman town—literally. We stood in the entrance to the car park and looked across the road. We could see the cemetery site on the brow of a low hill, marked by a cluster of trees about 1100 ft (335 m) away, to the south-east of the Roman eastern wall. A gate led to a broad greensward walkway up the hill, alongside a field where we are asked not to feed the horses because they are on a special diet. It takes only a few minutes to get to the top, where there's a marker with the archaeological site number on it (County Monument 234) and a brief description of the cemetery. Urn N59 was found in the south-west corner of the site, so its location was on our immediate left as we approached the trees.

They ask you not to walk across the cemetery area. Not that you would want to: the land has been left to return to its natural state, and the rough ground bemoaned by the original excavators looks just as unwelcoming now. But it's easy to walk all the way round the cemetery. The site is smaller than we were expecting. And higher, too. Although we describe it as a low hill, it's a great deal higher than the surrounding flat Norfolk landscape. We looked north across the Roman town. The tower of the medieval parish church of St Edmund, in the south-east corner, was just visible among the trees. The height is important. As the burial site description says: 'The site was located on high ground to shorten the spirits' journey to the heavens'.

The relationship between the town and the cemetery remains unclear. The area seems to have been part of the town as originally laid out, because several remains of Roman buildings, refuse pits, and artefacts have been found there, and streets from the town centre passed nearby. But when the main part of Caistor was fortified in the 3rd century, this area was left outside the walls, and at some point was made available for Anglo-Saxon use as a cemetery.

There has been much speculation about the character of the people who were buried there. Were they German mercenaries brought in to protect the town, who were then buried according to their own traditions? Were they inhabitants of a village which grew up to provide services for the Romans? The archaeological facts show this to be one of the few Roman sites in Britain where Roman military equipment, Romano-Saxon pottery,

The burial site, showing the side of the cemetery where Urn N59 was found.

Looking towards Venta Icenorum from the burial site.

and Germanic cremation urns have been found in such close association. The Caistor cemetery remains enigmatic, along with its solitary English word.

Getting there

Leave the A47 at the junction with the A140, and turn south, signposted towards Ipswich, but don't follow the main road. Turn sharp left into a minor road (Markshall Farm Road) signposted towards Caistor St Edmund. A sign says it is unsuitable for long vehicles, which indeed it is. When you reach Caistor, turn right into Stoke Road. A sign tells you that the Roman town is half a mile ahead. You pass Caistor Hall (built in 1612), now a hotel, and soon see the Roman town car park on your right (postcode: NR14 8QN). Cross the road, walk through the gate and up the hill, and you're there.

The burial urns from the site are on display in the Norwich Castle Museum, Castle Hill, Norwich, NR1 3JU.

Chapter 3

Undley Common

the first recorded English sentence

Fields, fields, and more fields. When you visit Undley Common in Suffolk, near the county boundary with Norfolk and Cambridgeshire, there's little to catch the eye apart from the farmland. Large, straight-sided fields used for mixed farming, separated by a track or an occasional low hedge. Sporadic trees that look as if they don't want to be there. A few farm buildings and houses. The chances of finding anything of historical linguistic interest in such a huge expanse of agricultural terrain seem remote.

But in 1981 a farmer working in one of these fields found something a few inches down in the soil. He thought it was a coin, but it turned out to be a bracteate. The name comes from Latin *bracta*, meaning a flat piece of metal, usually gold or silver, which has been beaten thin to form a coin, medal, or other ornament. This one had a stamped design in the centre and what appeared to be lettering around the edge—but letters unlike anything he had seen before.

The object is now known as the *Undley bracteate*, and it is lodged safely in Room 41 of the British Museum. It has been dated to AD 450–80. The find is of huge significance in the history of the English language for it is the first time we see what seems to be a sentence written in Old English. No wonder the farmer couldn't decipher the writing. The letters are runes.

The bracteate was of sheet gold, weighing 0.08 oz (2.24 g), and with a diameter of 0.9 inches (2.3 cm)—about the size of a British 10 pence piece. A ribbed loop shows that it was intended as a pendant, probably worn around the neck. The design is on one side only, and was modelled on an ancient Roman coin; the back is plain. In its amazing artistic detail,

Page opposite. One of the many fields at Undley Common.

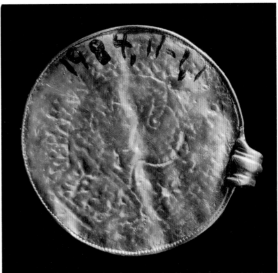

it's clearly the work of a master craftsman. We see a helmeted head with wide eyes gazing to the right. The jaw is fringed—probably the representation of a collar rather than a beard. Beneath is a wolf suckling twins—the story of Romulus and Remus in Roman mythology. The carving is really detailed—we even see some strokes for the fur. Behind the head is an eight-pointed star and a circle, and we can just see the edge of a second star and circle behind the spirals in gold wire attached to the loop. A decorative V pattern runs all the way round the edge of the bracteate. But it is what lies within this edging that has fascinated English-language students.

The runes are in the Anglo-Frisian alphabet, which is slightly different from other runic alphabets of the time. In particular, the rune representing the 'o' is the earliest example we have of this letter-shape in England. So either this alphabet developed in the Frisian region, in the south of Scandinavia, and the bracteate was brought to East Anglia by a settler from there, or the alphabet developed in England and the bracteate was manufactured locally.

The runes have been carved as reverse images, forming three blocks, each block separated by a tiny circle. The sequence of runes begins to the right of the spirals, and reads from right to left. The first six have been written as three groups of two, presumably because the rune-master wanted to be sure he had enough space for the whole transcription. Turned into Roman letters, and with the runes shown right way round, the text reads as follows:

Wordsmiths and Warriors

ᚷᛇᚷ · ᛗᚨᚷᚨ · ᛗᛇᛞᚢ
gægogæ   mægæ   medu

With so little evidence to go on, the translation is very uncertain. There's general agreement about the second and third words. *Medu* is the origin of *meed* (i.e. 'reward'). *Mægæ* was a 'relative' or 'kinsman', and the word-ending suggests the interpretation 'to a kinsman'. It's the first word that poses the problem. It might be a magical chant or battle-cry. A similar expression, *gagaga*, was found on a spear-shaft discovered at Kragenhul in Denmark. Magical or ritual syllables were often used repetitively in this way. On the other hand, people have looked for a more orthodox meaning. Bengt Odenstedt from the University of Umeå in Sweden proposed a widely quoted translation. He took the *go* of *gægogæ* to be from the same root as Old English *goian* 'lament, groan'—a word which was also used for dogs and wolves to mean 'howl'. Based on that, and the possibility that the word-ending might represent a female (i.e. the wolf) and the prefix might add some sort of agentive or intensifying force, he ended up with 'this howling she-wolf is a reward to my kinsman'. It's a possibility, but we need to find evidence of similar forms in Old English before it becomes a probability.

Undley is near Lakenheath in Suffolk, and a turning off the Undley Road is signposted Undley Common. It looks unpromising, for it's simply a wide farmland track, but after a few buildings the fields open up before you, in all directions. It's then that you realize just how fortuitous the bracteate find was. We drove a little way along the lane, not expecting to see anything special. It ended abruptly, among some buildings, and we had to do a bit of awkward reversing. A local man saw our difficulty, and asked if we were lost. We said we were hoping to find Mr Flack—the name of the farmer, according to the British Museum records, who had found the bracteate. 'Which one?' asked the man, 'the father or the son?' The father, we said. (It was most likely to have been him, given that the find had been made 30 years before.) And then, one of those special moments that all researchers hope for. The man nodded over my shoulder. 'Well, there's the son coming along now', and sure enough, there he was, walking along the lane. We checked we'd got the right Mr Flack. He pointed out his father's bungalow, and phoned him to warn him of our impending arrival. A few minutes later, we were getting the story of the find from the farmer's mouth.

Allan Flack had been well aware of the archaeological potential of his land, and went about with a metal detector in the back of his tractor. He was surprised by the tiny object's shine and brightness, and thought at first it would make a nice necklace for his wife. But after showing it to a local amateur archaeologist, well known in the online metal-detecting world as 'Roman Ron', it soon became apparent that he had found something special. The news spread—with unwelcome results. For some time his farmland was inundated with treasure-seekers, harming the crops and with no interest in reporting any finds to the authorities. To avoid further unwanted attention, Mr Flack has never told anyone of the exact place he found the bracteate, and we respected his attitude, deciding that this would be one place in this book where the photograph would *not* be the actual location of the event (p. 20). It is, however, a picture of one of the fields at Undley Common. It clearly shows the odds against finding a tiny object in this vast expanse of flat fenland. This is one of dozens of fields of a similar size in this part of Suffolk.

Surprisingly, very little else has been discovered from the Anglo-Saxon period in the area—only an axe-head and a couple of swords, perhaps relics from a nearby cemetery. We might expect there to be more. The landscape would have attracted settlers, because the soil is good, much better than the fenland to the west and the dry sandy soils to the east. In Anglo-Saxon times, there would have been water and marshland everywhere, with occasional 'islands' of chalk offering dry settlement. Several place names in the area reflect this state of affairs, such as Thistley Green, Holmsley Green, Littley Field—the *-ey* ending being the Old English word for 'island'. Undley was another.

'Undl's ey'. The origins of the *Undl* part are unclear. *Undela* was an Anglo-Saxon name, so it could simply be 'Undela's island'. However, *un-dæl* in Old English meant 'undivided', so the name could refer to some sort of administrative arrangement for this piece of land. And not far away was a tribe of Middle Angles known as the *Undalum* or *Undele* (they gave Oundle in Northamptonshire its name), who might also have passed through the area. So it may have been a tribal name.

The best way of finding Undley is first to find Lakenheath. You can't miss that, because for miles around there are signs pointing to the RAF airbase there—a base which also hosts a unit of the US Air Force in Europe: the Statue of Liberty Wing. Lakenheath. It's a name which in Old English also reflects the waterlogged character of the terrain. The *heath* element isn't what we might expect. It doesn't mean 'heath'. In Old English a *hyð* or *hið* was a 'landing-place'—we see it also in such names as Hythe and Rotherhithe. Lakenheath was earlier *Lacingahið*—probably, 'the landing-place of Laca's people'. It might have been 'the landing-place of the people by a lake or stream', but I think that is less likely; with so much water around, such a name wouldn't have distinguished this island from the many others. Today, it's the landing-place of F-15 Eagle fighter planes.

Wordsmiths and Warriors

Getting there

Lakenheath is especially noticeable if you approach the village from the south, from the A11. As you head along the A1065 towards Brandon the airbase signs and buildings are everywhere, and as you turn left onto the B1112 through Eriswell you pass a series of entrances (some inviting, some prohibiting) before you reach Lakenheath. Turn left onto the Undley Road, just before the High Street. If you're travelling south from Brandon along the A1065, you turn right at the sign to Lakenheath, and after driving through the High Street you see Undley Road on your right. It's a long, straight road—typical of many roads in the fenland—and after a few hundred yards there's a small signpost pointing left to Undley Common.

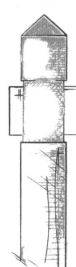

Chapter 4

Jarrow

Bede and the origins of English

'Did he work hard?' The question came from a 6-year-old, dressed in a monk's habit. He was one of a group of 30 children on a school trip to the Anglo-Saxon monastery site of St Paul's Church in Jarrow. When we arrived, they were already packed tight into the end of the chancel, each one duly habited, and listening with rapt faces as their guide told them all about Bede and his times. The lady volunteers looking after the church said another school group was due later that morning. The costumes were evidently in great demand.

As the children de-habited, we listened to their excited chatter. Several of the questions had a linguistic slant. 'How did he write?' 'Did he have paper?' A visit to the nearby Bede's World would answer these questions. Among the museum's artefacts is a stylus, which could be used to write in wax or to draw straight lines on vellum, guiding the writing of the scribes. And there's a replica of the huge Codex Amiatinus, a single-volume Latin Bible made around 700. The original was sent to Italy as a gift to the Pope, and is named after the abbey at Monte Amiata where it was placed in the 9th century. It's now in Florence.

Another question from a tiny monk: 'What did he eat?' The reconstruction of an Anglo-Saxon farm at Bede's World shows the vegetables, herbs, animals, and fish that the monks would have known. The farm animals have been bred to resemble those found in Anglo-Saxon times. Two Dexter oxen have been named, period-appropriately, Oswin and Edwin. The farm is called *Gyrwe*, the Old English name for Jarrow—pronounced roughly as 'yeerway'. It's an atmospheric place, with three full-size timber

Page opposite. The eastern end of St Paul's Church, showing the Anglo-Saxon church. The monastery site has changed a lot in recent years. Trees have grown quite high along the hillside leading down to the Don, so that the unimpeded view of the church along with the ruins on one of the official postcards is now totally lost.

The habits awaiting their next group of small wearers.

buildings—though these are dwarfed by the enormous riverside development next door, with its electricity pylons, cranes, storage tanks, and container ships.

St Paul's Church is just a couple of minutes' walk down the hill from the museum, through a children's grassy playground. You can't miss it: just look for the largest pylon. The ruins behind the church, on the land as it falls away to the River Don, locate the monastery where Bede spent most of his life. There were originally two churches on the site, later linked by a tower. The one to the west of the tower was demolished, and the area today provides St Paul's with its nave. It's the church to the east, now forming the chancel, which has features surviving from Bede's time. The Latin dedication stone is original. An ancient chair, known as 'Bede's chair', rests against a wall. Large corner stones from the 7th-century building can be seen, and there are three original windows in the south wall. The pieces of

Wordsmiths and Warriors

Above. Gyrwe, with modern Jarrow behind.

Left. The Norman tower through the medieval wall.

The Latin dedication stone, now placed above the chancel arch. It's sculpted in bold Roman capital letters, with some words abbreviated:

DEDICATIO BASILICAE
SCI PAVLI VIIII KL MAI
ANNO XV ECFRIDI REG
CEOLFRIDI ABB EIVSDEM
Q ECCLES DO AVCTORE
CONDITORIS ANNO III

'The dedication of the basilica of St Paul on the ninth day before the kalends of May in the fifteenth year of King Ecgfrith and the fourth year of Abbot Ceolfrith, founder by the guidance of God of the same church'

That would be 23 April 685. It's the earliest such stone to be found in an English church. Bede would have seen it every day.

BEDE'S BONES

Bede has to play second fiddle at Durham, which is officially the shrine of St Cuthbert. But the Galilee Chapel is an effective setting for his remains, which have been placed in an altar tomb of blue marble, with two tall candles on each side. On the top is a simple Latin inscription:

HIC SUNT IN FOSSA BEDAE VENERABILIS OSSA

Here in this tomb are the bones of the Venerable Bede

In the wall recess behind the tomb is a quotation from his commentary on the Book of Revelation, in Latin and English, in large gold letters on a wooden frame:

Christ is the morning star
who when the night
of this world is past
brings to his saints
the promise of
the light of life
& opens everlasting day

Wordsmiths and Warriors

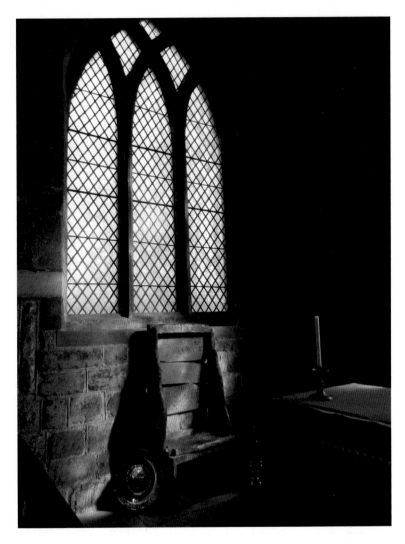

coloured soda-lime glass forming the small circular central window were found during excavation—the oldest stained glass found in Europe, so they say.

Almost everything we know about Bede (c.672–735)—Bæda, in Old English—comes from some autobiographical remarks in his major work, *Historia Ecclesiastica Gentis Anglorum*, 'The Ecclesiastical History of the English People'. This was an ambitious 400-page treatment organized into five books, and the reason that he is regularly described as 'the father of English history'. At the very end of the fifth book he gives us a list of his writings, and tells us:

> Bede, servant of Christ and priest of the monastery of the blessed apostles Peter and Paul which is at Wearmouth and Jarrow . . . was born

in the district around this monastery. When I was seven years of age my
kinsmen gave me into the care of the most reverend abbot Benedict, and
later of Ceolfrith, to be educated. From then on I have spent all my life in
this monastery, devoting myself entirely to the study of the scriptures.
And while observing monastic discipline and singing daily office in the
church, my chief delight has always been to learn or to teach or to write.

And write he did. He is the author of over 60 works on history, geography, and science, as well as of biblical commentaries, lives of the saints,
hymns, and poems. The English-language tourist will take special note of
his books on orthography, metrics, and figures of speech, but will probably
spend most time reflecting on his account of the origins of English in the
'Ecclesiastical History'. It is a summary which has been reported in virtually every history of the language.

Bede's aim was to tell the story of how Christianity arrived in Britain,
but in so doing he became the first to give an account of the island's history,

and he is the earliest literary source we have for the linguistic events which shaped the nation (Chapter 1). In his opening chapter he tells us:

> This island at present … contains five nations, the English, Britons, Scots, Picts, and Latins, each in its own peculiar dialect cultivating the sublime study of Divine truth. The Latin tongue is, by the study of the Scriptures, become common to all the rest.

He reports the arrival of the Anglo-Saxons in AD 449, and describes where they came from:

> Those who came over were of the three most powerful nations of Germany—Saxons, Angles, and Jutes. From the Jutes are descended the people of Kent, and of the Isle of Wight, and those also in the province of the West-Saxons who are to this day called Jutes, seated opposite to the Isle of Wight. From the Saxons, that is, the country which is now called

Old Saxony, came the East-Saxons, the South-Saxons, and the West-Saxons. From the Angles, that is, the country which is called Anglia, and which is said, from that time, to remain desert to this day, between the provinces of the Jutes and the Saxons, are descended the East-Angles, the Midland-Angles, Mercians, all the race of the Northumbrians, that is, of those nations that dwell on the north side of the river Humber, and the other nations of the English.

Even though there are real problems interpreting exactly what Bede meant, it is clear that Britain was multiethnic and multilingual from the outset. For those who marvel at the diversity of accents and dialects in Britain, the source of the variation lies here.

The archaeologists must have had a marvellous time working on this site. Viking raids beginning in 794 burned the monastery, and it ceased to function until some rebuilding took place in the 11th century. There are thus medieval as well as Anglo-Saxon foundations and remains, and the original wall-lines have been carefully picked out in the grounds. English-language tourists should ignore the cobbled paths, which show the later period of construction. The walls of the buildings Bede would have known are demarcated by pathways laid out in flat stone slabs. The original floors lie about 2 ft (60 cm) below the present ground level.

Bede's monastery was unusual, as it was 'one monastery in two places' (as its founder, Benedict Biscop, put it)—the first foundation at Wearmouth, and the

The cobbled pathway in the foreground marks the line of the medieval monastery walls. The flat paving stones running towards the walls show the location of Anglo-Saxon walls. The building here would probably have been a large hall with a dormitory above. At the east end (to the left in this picture) there was a suite of two small rooms, probably a small oratory and an adjoining monk's cell. It is a plausible candidate for Bede's death-bed.

second a year later at Jarrow, seven miles distant. There's no record of how Bede might have moved between the two locations, but tradition points to Jarrow being his home. This is where he was buried—though not for long. In 1022 his bones were removed by a Durham cleric and taken to Durham Cathedral, where they lay for a while alongside the coffin of Saint Cuthbert. In 1370 they were placed in a separate shrine in the Galilee Chapel of the cathedral.

The 'Ecclesiastical History' is over 400 pages. It would take a scribe several months to copy it out. We know that several copies were made. And Bede wrote over 60 books. Our 6-year-old's question is easily answered. Yes, he did.

Getting there

These sites are most directly accessed from the A19. From the north, after you pass through the Tyne Tunnel, turn left onto the A185 signposted Jarrow, left again at the roundabout (with a tourist sign to Bede's World) and then left into Church Bank. At the top of the hill you see parking signs left and right to Bede's World (postcode: NE32 3DY); the car park on the left is very much larger. From the south, turn right at the roundabout just before you enter the tunnel.

If you want to visit St Paul's first, you turn right before going up the hill. You can park right outside the church, or turn left at the end of the side road, where there is a parking area next to the river (post-code: NE32 3DZ).

For Durham Cathedral, leave the A1(M) at junction 31 (from the south) or 32 (from the north) and follow the signs to the city centre. Prince Bishop car park is immediately in front of you. Signs point you towards the cathedral (where parking is permit-restricted), so the postcode is not much help (DH1 3EH). Turn right immediately inside the door for the Galilee Chapel. But don't expect to take photographs. Cameras are not allowed, as we discovered on our visit, and we could get no immediate dispensation even after a visit to the Chapter Office to plead a special case. So we can give you no picture of Bede's tomb in this book. You will however find one on the Durham Cathedral website.

Chapter 5

Lindisfarne

glossaries and translations

The isle is full of noises. We were reminded of Caliban's words, in Shakespeare's *The Tempest*, as we entered the priory ruins at Lindisfarne, off the coast of Northumberland. We were greeted by a weird distant howling, too resonant and deep to be birds, too plaintive and drawn-out to be hounds. The man on duty at the entrance explained: grey seals, in large numbers, calling across the sand banks between the island and the mainland. Their main breeding-ground is further out to sea, among the Farne Islands, but our man told us that many are now found nearby. We got the impression that he wasn't entirely enamoured of the seal calls. When several start vocalizing at once, the effect is ghostly and unsettling. I expect you get used to it, if you live there.

Most people visit Lindisfarne to see the impressive remains of the 12th-century priory, established by monks from the cathedral city of Durham, the 13th-century St Mary's Church, and the 16th-century Castle—the most prominent feature on the island, easily visible from the train between Newcastle and Edinburgh. But English-language tourists will be interested in an earlier period, when the first Irish missionaries, led by St Aidan, were invited here by King Oswald of Northumbria in AD 635. The island grew in fame when it became the home of St Cuthbert, and acquired the name of Holy Island. After his death, his body was placed in the abbey church, and Lindisfarne became the most important pilgrimage centre in the north of England. The monastery became a centre of learning, and in its scriptorium, in the first quarter of the 8th century, were created the Lindisfarne

Page opposite. The iconic 'rainbow arch' at Lindisfarne Priory, a rib from the vault over the church crossing, a lone survivor of a tower collapse in the 18th century.

Lindisfarne Castle, a mile distant from the abbey ruins.

Gospels, widely held to be the most beautiful illuminated manuscript to survive from the Anglo-Saxon period.

Its 258 vellum pages contain the Latin text of St Jerome's translation of the four Gospels. Each Gospel opens with a full-page portrait of the evangelist and a large intricately painted initial letter, and the decoration continues on a smaller scale throughout. The illumination is breathtaking in its ornateness, colour, and complexity, but what has made this text of special interest to those who study the history of the English language is revealed in the last sentence of a closing paragraph to the work. It was added by a scribe, probably during the third quarter of the 10th century. He tells us his name:

> Eadfrith, Bishop of the Lindisfarne Church, originally wrote this book, for God and for Saint Cuthbert and jointly for all the saints whose relics are in the island. And Ethelwald, Bishop of the Lindisfarne islanders, impressed it on the outside and covered it, as he well knew how to do. And Billfrith the anchorite forged the ornaments which are on it on the outside and adorned it with gold and with gems and also with gilded-over silver, pure metal. And Aldred, unworthy and most miserable priest, glossed it into English between the lines with the help of God and Saint Cuthbert.

This is the fullest account we have from Anglo-Saxon times of the making of a book: who wrote it, bound it, and decorated it. Aldred carried out his task probably in the third quarter of the 10th century—but not in Lindisfarne. The monastery had been raided and sacked by Vikings in 793. Soon after, the monks left the island, taking St Cuthbert's remains and the Gospels with them. They wandered through the country for seven years before settling at Chester-le-Street in County Durham.

Glosses are an important source of information about the earliest state of English. A collection of Latin words is given a translation into Old English, presumably to help monks and others whose command of Latin was not very good. Some glossaries have just a few hundred words; others have many thousands. Some are simply lists, much like a modern bilingual dictionary. Others are glosses of continuous text. The Lindisfarne Gospels are of the latter type. The glosses follow the Gospel text, in tiny writing above the Latin words, with occasional marginalia. It was an intricate and painstaking task.

Aldred's work is often called a 'translation'—'the earliest translation of the Gospels in English', some books say—but it is actually little more than a crib to the Latin text. It follows the word order of the Latin text, and interprets Latin idioms literally. If the glosses are separated from their Latin original, we don't get a very comprehensible version of the Gospels. And we certainly don't get a sense of Anglo-Saxon sentence structure or

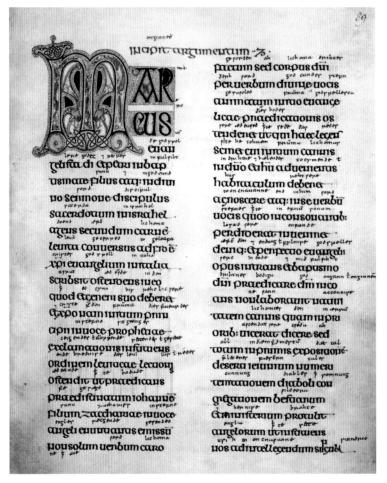

A detail from the Lindisfarne Gospels—the preliminary page to the Gospel of Saint Mark—showing Aldred's glosses.

idiomatic expression—unlike the impression we get from the glosses in Ælfric's Colloquy (Chapter 10). On the other hand, Aldred isn't entirely slavish in his glossing, and is clearly trying to find equivalents that will be meaningful to the English reader. He sometimes adds English words that are not in the Latin, for clarity, or varies the word order to reflect Old English. For example, the phrase *filii david* ('the son of David') is usually glossed as *sunu dauides*, following the Latin, but occasionally we see *dauides sunu*, showing English word order. And alternative English words are occasionally offered for a single Latin word. Aldred's work is neither a full translation nor a mechanical gloss, but something in between.

The Latin text of the Gospels would have been copied out in the scriptorium of the original monastery at Lindisfarne. Archaeology (and a comment by Bede) suggests that there were very few buildings on the original site, but whatever was there has long been covered by later works. There are traces of pre-Norman activity in and around St Mary's, which may well have been built on the site of the first church. The location of the scriptorium is unknown, but—of several possibilities—local experts think a likely site, a little way from the church, is now the lower garden of the Manor House Hotel. So we went there.

A stone from the Anglo-Saxon period built into the wall of St Mary's Church.

But not for long. Time was passing, and the tide was rising. Lindisfarne really is an island, accessible only twice a day. As Bede put it, in his *Ecclesiastical History* (Book 3, Chapter 3):

The lower garden of the Manor House Hotel. The wall beyond the trees is the presbytery (on the left) and nave (on the right) of the old priory church.

Wordsmiths and Warriors

Which place, as the tide flows and ebbs twice a day, is enclosed by the waves of the sea like an island; and again, twice in the day, when the shore is left dry, becomes contiguous to the land.

For centuries the pilgrims' route to Holy Island was difficult, crossing sand and mud flats, with uncertain weather and tides. Today, there's a mile-long tarmacked causeway and ample warning of the high tides that cover the road and make the island inaccessible. It's one of the first things you see when you arrive in the village. 'Don't risk it' is the clear message, on a sign showing a half-submerged car. We didn't. There are many things I will do for linguistic research, but joining the Farne Island seals isn't one of them.

Don't risk it!

Getting there

Lindisfarne is signposted from the A1, midway between Newcastle and Edinburgh. Turn at the Lindisfarne Inn, pass through the tiny village of Beal and you reach the causeway across to the island. It's about 1.5 miles. Whether walking or driving, you need to check the tide times in advance, either at local accommodation sites or online such as

http://www.northumberlandlife.org/holy-island/

leaving a good half an hour to allow for unexpected fluctuations in tide level due to weather conditions. Tide tables are also displayed at each end of the causeway. On reaching the island, there's a large car park on the left at the entrance to the village. It's a short five-minute walk to the Priory (postcode: TD15 2RX). The car park in the village centre is for buses and disabled only.

The manuscript of the Lindisfarne Gospels is at the British Library in London (Cotton MS Nero D.iv). Photographic copies have also been made, and one can be seen at Lindisfarne. Online illustrations can be seen at

http://www.bl.uk/onlinegallery/sacredtexts/lindisfarne.html

Chapter 6

Ruthwell

the finest runic inscription

It's the size of the cross that strikes you, when you enter Ruthwell church. I'd seen pictures of it often enough. It's an obligatory illustration in any account of the early history of the language, simply because it carries the longest and most impressive runic inscription in Old English. But the pictures don't give you a proper sense of scale, and often miss out on the colour of the sandstone—light grey, but often with a pink or beige sheen as it picks up the colour of the walls. The full size of the cross is impossible to show in a single photograph, for the top reaches into the dome of the apse while its base descends some six feet below floor level. You miss this when you see the cross at a distance. It's almost 18 ft (5.5 m) high.

The cross dates from the early 8th century, at a time when Ruthwell was part of the kingdom of Northumbria, and we did feel we were going back in time as we left the main road and threaded our way along narrow lanes towards the coast of Dumfries and Galloway in south-west Scotland. It's easy to take a wrong turning, for the road winds unexpectedly, with side paths leading to farms or country houses. If you do get lost, be prepared for an unexpected pronunciation when you ask the way. Although many people follow the spelling these days, and say 'ruth-well', an older pronunciation is locally common: 'ruthell' or 'rithell' with the *th* sounded as in *the*, or dropped altogether, so that the name comes out as 'riwell'. (Southwell in Nottinghamshire works in a similar way: 'suthell'.) An even earlier spelling of *Rivall* suggests the pronunciation 'rivell', though this seems to have disappeared now.

Page opposite. The Ruthwell Cross in situ. We are looking at the south face.

The cross as we see it today shows signs of its controversial history. It was first raised as a preaching cross, on a route between northern England and south-west Scotland. When the church was established at Ruthwell, it was located in the grounds, where it stayed until the 1640s. It then fell foul of the post-Reformation climate of the time. The general assembly of the Church of Scotland passed an 'Act anent [relating to] the demolishing of Idolatrous Monuments', and the figures on the cross were seen in that light. The minister at Ruthwell obeyed the law, and took the cross down, but sympathetically, so that large chunks remained intact, scattered throughout the church and churchyard. In the early 19th century a new minister, Henry Duncan, took on the task of reconstruction, finding the pieces that now form the vertical column. The cemented joins are clearly visible. The cross-beam was missing, so a new piece was created in an attempt to suit the style, and some plain stones were added to form the base. It was brought into the church in 1887, to give it protection from the weather, but its height meant that a special space had to be built—the pit and the semi-circular apse. Enclosed by a simple iron balustrade, it is now the focal point of the church behind the altar and close to the pulpit. It is a preaching cross again.

At first glance, it is the set of figurative reliefs that catch the attention. These are the largest carvings to be found on any surviving Anglo-Saxon cross, and chiefly show various scenes from the New Testament. English-language tourists, however, will have their eyes drawn to the four edges of the cross, where the inscriptions are. One series is in Latin; the other is in runes—an unexpected occurrence on a Christian cross, given the pagan associations of runes in early Anglo-Saxon times.

Ruthwell Church.

The text of the runic inscription is familiar. It corresponds to a section from the first half of the 156-line Old English poem, *The Dream of the Rood* (*rood* is from the Anglo-Saxon word for 'cross'), written in the Northumbrian dialect of the time. The narrator recounts a dream in which he sees Christ's cross triumphant, high in the sky, adorned with gold and jewels. He hears it speak. It tells the story of how it was made, how it felt during the crucifixion, and what happened to it afterwards, and explains the significance of the event. The narrator then reflects on the meaning of the vision for himself and for all people.

As an illustration, this is the dramatic final statement (lines 44–56) of the Cross's account, translated here showing the two-part metrical lines, but lacking the alliteration which links the parts together in Old English.

> As a cross was I set up. I lifted up the great king,
> The Lord of heaven. I dared not bow down.
> They pierced me with bloody nails. My wounds can still be seen,
> Open wounds of hatred. Nor dared I harm any of them.
> They mocked us both together. I was all bedewed with blood,
> Shed from the man's side, after he had sent forth his spirit.
> Many things on the hill I have endured,
> Cruel experiences. I saw the God of hosts
> Cruelly stretched out. Darkness had
> Covered with clouds the Lord's body,
> The bright radiance. A shadow went forth,
> Dark beneath the clouds. All creation wept,
> Lamented the King's death. Christ was on the cross.

That last sentence is one that can be seen on the Ruthwell Cross. To locate it, you first have to think of the four sides of the cross as facing north, south, east, and west. The south side is in front of you as you face the altar. The runic text is in four sections, two on the east face and two on the west. One sequence of letters runs across the top and down the north-east and north-west borders, while the other runs down the south-east and south-west borders. The combination of weathering and damage means that several parts of the inscription have been lost, though some letters have been retrieved using drawings of the runes made by scholars in earlier centuries. The transcription of the runes on the west side comes from an edition of the poem by Bruce Dickins and Alan Ross. For example, across the top and down the south-west border side we see the following sequence:

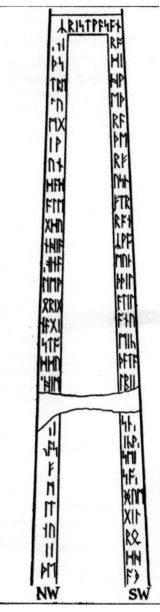

NW   SW

Left. The runic inscriptions
on the north-west
(to the left) and
south-west borders.

Right. The runes of the
Ruthwell Cross, from the
edition of *The Dream of the
Rood* by Bruce Dickins and
Alan Ross (Methuen, 1934).

k r i s t   w æ s   o n   r o d i

ᛣᚱᛁᛋᛏ ᚹᚫᛋ ᚩᛏ ᚱᚩᛞᛁ

'Christ was on the cross'

The history of the Ruthwell Cross is all around the church. One of the wall
panels lists the costs involved in removing and re-erecting the cross and

refurbishing the chancel area between 1885 and 1887. The total bill came to £361.3s.10d—£361.20 in decimal money—and equivalent to around £30,000 today. Another acknowledges the work of Mr J. W. Dodds, who designed the machinery needed to move the cross from the grounds into the church. He was paid £12.10s. Worth every penny, for a cross that has been described (in 1884, by George Stephens, professor of Anglo-Saxon at Copenhagen University) as 'the finest runic cross in the world'.

Getting there

Leave the A74(M) at junction 22, and take the A75 signposted to Dumfries. After about eight miles you'll see a sign left to Cummertrees and Ruthwell. This is a single-lane road, almost a track in places, hedge-lined and winding, taking you through farmland. Make sure you keep to the 'main' road—there are places where the road seems to go straight ahead, but it's actually a side turning. After a couple of miles you see the whitewashed walls of Ruthwell Church ahead on your right. There's a parking area just before you reach it, in front of the old manse (postcode: DG1 4NP). If the church is closed, a notice on the church gate gives details of the keyholder.

If you'd rather drive along a better class of road, keep going a little further along the A75 and take the B725 left signposted Clarencefield. After a mile or so you pass under the bridge of Ruthwell Station. Turn left onto the B724, pass through Clarencefield, and turn left after a few hundred yards. Ruthwell Church is then a short way along on your left.

Chapter 7

Stourton and Edington

King Alfred and the birth of English

King Alfred the Great looks down from his tower in the grounds of the Stourhead estate (now part of the National Trust) near Warminster in Wiltshire. An inscription tells us why he is there, but there's something missing.

> ALFRED THE GREAT
> A.D. 879 on this Summit
> Erected his Standard
> Against Danish Invaders
> To him We owe The Origin of Juries
> The Establishment of a Militia
> The Creation of a Naval Force
> ALFRED The Light of a Benighted Age
> Was a Philosopher and a Christian
> The Father of his People
> The Founder of the English
> MONARCHY and LIBERTY

… and of the English language? 'Founder' is going a bit far, but certainly, without Alfred, this book today would have been written in a modern dialect of Norse.

Page opposite. King Alfred's Tower, showing the triangular structure.

The Alfred statue and inscription at the front of the tower.

'Light of a Benighted Age' hints at the reason. Alfred was keenly aware of the way the Viking invasions had virtually destroyed education in England. Sometime in the early 890s he wrote a preface to a translation of Gregory's *Cura Pastoralis* ('Pastoral Care'), in which he identified the problem:

> It has very often come into my mind what learned men there once were throughout England, from both sacred and secular offices, and what happy times there were throughout England … and how people abroad looked to this country for learning and instruction, and how we should now have to get it from abroad, if we were to have it. So completely had it declined in England that there were very few people on this side of the Humber who could understand their service-books in English or translate even one written message from Latin into English, and I think there were not many beyond the Humber either. So few they were that I cannot think of even a single one south of the Thames when I came to the throne.

That was the problem. This is his solution:

> we translate certain books, which it is most needful for all men to know, into the language that we can all understand, and make it happen—as we very easily can with God's help, if we have peace—that all young people who are now freemen in England, those that have the means, should devote themselves to study while they have nothing else to do, until the time that they know how to read written English well.

The results of Alfred's enthusiastic language planning were remarkable. Almost all surviving prose texts during the late 9th century and throughout the 10th were written in the dialect of English that was used by Alfred and his scribes. Today we call it West Saxon, and for well over a century it became the most widely used form of the English language. If the Normans had lost at Hastings (Chapter 13), it might well have remained so. As it is, much of our knowledge of Old English comes from writings which, directly or indirectly, we can trace back to Alfred's initiative. He deserves his tower, for linguistic and literary reasons alone.

The tower is there to remember a battle, not a language, but none of Alfred's reforms could have taken place if he had not defeated the Vikings. At the beginning of 878, this prospect seemed unlikely. The invaders had achieved a series of victories across the south of England.

Wordsmiths and Warriors

Only Alfred's kingdom of Wessex continued to resist, and even that was in danger. Alfred himself had been forced to seek refuge at Athelney in the Somerset marshland (where the legendary cake-burning incident took place). Then, according to the Anglo-Saxon Chronicle, he planned a new campaign:

> in the seventh week after Easter he rode to Egbert's Stone, to the east of Selwood, and there came to meet him all the men of Somerset and Wiltshire and that part of Hampshire which was on this side of the sea, and they received him warmly. And one day later he went from those camps to Iley Oak, and one day later to Ethandun; and there he fought against the entire host, and put it to flight.

A few weeks later, after laying siege to the Vikings at Chippenham and starving them into submission, Alfred received the Danish king Guthrum and his surviving nobles at Aller, near Athelney, where they became Christians, and plans for a peaceful division of England into English and Danish areas began to be made.

According to tradition, Egbert's Stone was somewhere near where Alfred's Tower now stands. The tower is an amazing folly, by any standards. It was planned by the banker Henry Hoare II, designed by Henry Flitcroft, and completed in 1762. Hoare's original inspiration was the four-sided St Mark's Tower in Venice, but in the end a triangular redbrick building was constructed, with round projections at each of the three corners. Its height is 162 ft/49 m. The walls are 33 inches (84 cm) thick. Someone has calculated that the tower contains 1.2 million bricks. A website <http://www.alfredstower.info/> reports that the bricklayers used no scaffolding, but sat upon the rising walls as they were built. Amazingly, given the precarious method of construction, there are no reports of any deaths.

A spiral staircase of 205 steps, occasionally illuminated by light from the small windows, leads to a platform behind a crenellated parapet. Expect views + vertigo. It's thought that the tower was built at the point where the boundaries of Somerset, Wiltshire, and Dorset meet, with one base in each county, and even though boundaries have changed somewhat, the three-county views are spectacular.

The top 10 metres (33 ft) of the tower has newer bricks, for the old ones had to be replaced when an American military plane crashed into the top in 1944, killing all five members of the crew. It might seem impossible for a plane to come upon such an obstacle, but during World War II an airfield had been built at Zeals, just south of Stourton. The tower was on its flight-path, and there was thick fog that day.

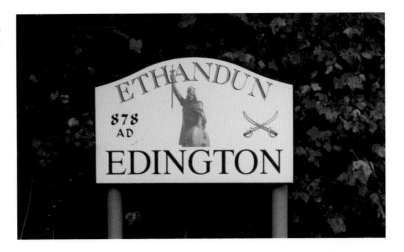

Zeals is an interesting name. It comes from the Old English word for 'sallow', a type of willow tree: *sealh*, here used in the plural. To have an English place name beginning with *z* is unusual. There are less than a dozen in the whole of Britain. It reflects the local 'Zummerzet' pronunciation.

Alfred's statue is facing south-east, but when he and his troops left Egbert's Stone they travelled north-east, and met the Vikings at Ethandun, some 15 miles away. The place is called Edington today, and although there is another Edington further west and an Eddington further east, the present-day Wiltshire village is in no doubt that this was the site of the famous battle, as its welcome sign makes clear. The year was indeed 878, not 879 (as recorded on Alfred's Tower).

It's difficult to disagree with the village's claim when you see the battle location, an Iron Age hillfort at the western edge of the Salisbury Plain chalk escarpment. It's 738 ft (225 m) high and an obvious defensive position. The site is also the home of a famous landmark on the steep western slope of the ridge: the Westbury White Horse. It was originally cut into the chalk, but is now concreted over, safeguarding its future but, when seen close up, reducing its aesthetic appeal. The symbolic value of the white horse is very great, for it is associated with the first Anglo-Saxon invaders (Chapter 1), who are said to have fought under a white horse banner; but records of this particular horse date only from the 18th century.

The fort is known as Bratton Camp, or Bratton Castle, and is enormous, covering an area of 23 acres (9.3 ha), with two circuits of ditch and bank. It's a steep and slippery path up to the ramparts, along small steps cut into the chalk, and signs warn you to be careful, but once at the top it's obvious that no enemy would dare attack from the north. They would be seen approaching for miles. Alfred, knowing the area, attacked from the south-west, where the ground rises more gently.

Opposite top The Westbury
white horse.

Opposite bottom View from
Bratton Camp, looking north.
The red object is part of a
child's sledge, presumably
left behind after a snowfall.

Wordsmiths and Warriors

A 6 ft standing stone, erected in 2000, guards the entrance to the site.
There are two plaques, one on each side of the stone. The first records that
this is a sarsen stone, like those found at Kingston Deverill to the south-
west—another contender for the location of Egbert's Stone. The other
reads (with an aberrant comma):

TO COMMEMORATE
THE BATTLE OF ETHANDUN, FOUGHT IN THIS VICINITY
MAY 878 AD
WHEN KING ALFRED THE GREAT, DEFEATED
THE VIKING ARMY, GIVING BIRTH TO
ENGLISH NATIONHOOD

… and, once again, with just a little poetic licence, to the English language.

Getting there

There's good signage to the Stourhead estate at Stourton, near Warminster in Wiltshire (postcode: BA12 6QD) from the main roads. You can walk up to the tower from the house, but it's a couple of miles. By road, you leave the A303 at Mere and go north along the B3092, past Stourton, then bear left along Tower Road to the appropriately named Kingsettle Hill. There's a small car park, and just across the road an entrance into a field. An information panel provides some basic background. Turn right, and the tower rises in front of you. Opening times are given on the National Trust website at

http://www.nationaltrust.org.uk/stourhead/

For Edington, coming through Westbury from the west along the B3098, there's a sign on the right to Bratton Camp and also the White Horse. If you approach Westbury from the east, along the B3098 through Edington village, there's no road sign; but just past The Duke At Bratton you turn left up Castle Road, which narrows to become Portway (postcode: BA13 4SP). Beware horses, walkers, and joggers. At the top of the hill, turn right at the signpost saying Byway, and a car park is ahead.

Chapter 8

Maldon

the ultimate warrior wordsmith

The question I wanted to answer was: could it really have happened? Could two armies, facing each other across a river, have exchanged harangues as recorded in the Anglo-Saxon poem, 'The Battle of Maldon'? Could they even have heard each other?

The poem has been called (by E. V. Gordon, who edited it for the Methuen Old English Library) 'the greatest battle-poem in the English language', and few other texts from the period equal it in stature. Only 325 lines have survived. The beginning and end of the poem have been lost. But we are lucky to have anything at all, for the original manuscript was destroyed in a fire during the 18th century. Fortunately, someone had earlier made a transcription, which provides the text we know today. And thanks to the detail provided by the poet, we have a rare opportunity to locate the exact site of an Anglo-Saxon battle.

According to the calendar of Ely Abbey, the battle took place on 10th August 991. It was the beginning of a new era. After the successful campaigns of King Alfred against the Vikings (Chapter 7), England had a peaceful time during the first half of the 10th century. But in the 980s Viking raids began again in the south and east. Maldon was an important commercial port in those days, with a royal mint, and was a strategically significant point of entry for hopeful invaders.

One of the texts of the Anglo-Saxon Chronicle recounts what happened in 991:

Page opposite. The Byrhtnoth Monument, with the town of Maldon in the background.

In this year Olaf came with 93 ships to Folkestone, and ravaged round about it, and from there went to Sandwich, and so from there to Ipswich, and overran it all, and so to Maldon. And Ealdorman Byrhtnoth came against him there with his army and fought against him; and they killed the ealdorman there and had control of the field.

The 68-year-old Byrhtnoth (the name is found in various spellings, such as Brihtnoth) was the regional commander (or ealdorman) of the Essex area. The plaque next to his statue in Maldon tells us that he was 'the leading military figure of his time' and 'the principal voice in rejecting the policy of appeasement which dominated the court of King Ethelred in the closing years of the 10th century'. If anyone was going to defeat the Vikings, it was going to be him.

The poem tells us that the armies faced each other at 'Panta stream'. Today this is the River Blackwater, though the name Pant is still used for the river from its source to Braintree in Essex. Where on the river, exactly? Various places have been suggested for the Viking landing, but the most likely is at Northey Island, in the estuary two miles south-east of the town. The poet's account of the battle gives us two crucial pieces of information. There was a 'bridge' (that is, a causeway) between the armies, where we read (at line 64—I have modernized the Old English letters):

> Ne mihte thar for watere werod to tham othrum:
> Thar com flowende flod after ebban.

> 'One troop might not come to the other because of the water;
> in that place the flood came flowing after the ebb-tide.'

The Vikings were on the island. The Anglo-Saxons were on the mainland shore. Evidently a high tide had covered the causeway, so there was a shouted exchange. The Viking spokesman asks for tribute, to avoid a battle, but Byrhtnoth angrily replies:

> Gehyrst thu, salida, hwat this folc segeth?
> Hi willath eow to gafole garas syllan,
> Attrynne ord and ealde swurd ...

> 'Do you hear, pirate, what this army says?
> They will give you spears as a tribute,
> deadly sword-point and ancient swords.'

The causeway to Northey Island, a few hours after high tide. The wet ground shows how far the water rises.

And when the tide goes out, that is what they do.

The Vikings try to cross the causeway, but are forced back. Then Byrhtnoth makes his fatal mistake. In his 'pride' (according to the poet) he invites the Vikings across the causeway, anticipating that a decisive victory will stop these raids once and for all. It is the wrong decision. He is killed. Some of his followers fly the field, and his most loyal retainers fight to the death. It must have been a ferocious battle. In one account the Vikings are said to have suffered such severe losses that they hardly had enough men to man their ships.

The poem feels as if it was composed soon after the battle. The poet was probably not there: 'I heard', he says at one point, about the feats of one of the nobles, Eadweard. He doesn't spend much time describing the way the battle went. Rather, his aim is to present the heroic state of mind of the English combatants. He gives us in full Byrhtnoth's exhortations to his followers, and the speeches of his loyal retainers who choose to fight on, despite hopeless odds. One of them, Byrhtwold, is given a speech which sums up the heroic ideals of the time:

> Hige sceal the heardra, heorte the cenre,
> Mod sceal the mare, the ure magen lytiath.

> 'Courage must be the more resolute, heart the bolder,
> spirit shall be the greater, as our might lessens.'

They are two of the most famous lines of the poem.

So: 'Do you hear, pirate, what this army says?' Could Byrhtnoth have been heard by the Viking messenger? At full tide today, the distance between the firm ground on the mainland and the island is about 220 yds (200 m), which would challenge even the strongest voice. But studies have shown that the sea level has changed dramatically in the past thousand years. What are mud flats now would have been dry land in the 10th century, and the distance between the island and the mainland about half what it is today. A powerful voice would have had no trouble carrying over such a distance. I have such a voice. On the wind-free day we visited, a shout from the edge of the present causeway easily carried across the 'bridge'.

No archaeological finds from the battle have been made, because much of the site is now below sea level or under the landfills and flood protection mounds behind the sea wall. The site is most probable but not definitive,

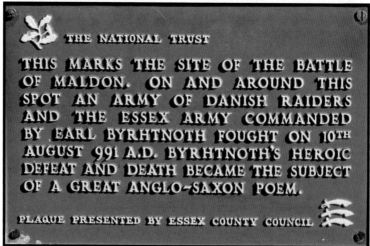

THE NATIONAL TRUST

THIS MARKS THE SITE OF THE BATTLE OF MALDON. ON AND AROUND THIS SPOT AN ARMY OF DANISH RAIDERS AND THE ESSEX ARMY COMMANDED BY EARL BYRHTNOTH FOUGHT ON 10TH AUGUST 991 A.D. BYRHTNOTH'S HEROIC DEFEAT AND DEATH BECAME THE SUBJECT OF A GREAT ANGLO-SAXON POEM.

PLAQUE PRESENTED BY ESSEX COUNTY COUNCIL

Top. The uninspiring approach to the battle site.

Bottom. The official plaque on the rusting gate.

Wordsmiths and Warriors

and little attention is drawn to it. Behind a floodbank, beneath a lone tele-graph pole, there is only a small sign on a rusting gate.

Indeed, for a long time there was little to see in Maldon related to the battle. A memorial window in St Mary's Church, near Hythe Quay. A statue of Byrhtnoth at the entrance door of All Saints' Church in the High Street. Times have changed. In 2006 an imposing statue of the ealdorman, created by local sculptor John Doubleday, was erected at the end of the promenade. The warrior has his sword raised and is looking down the

The 'GRACE' side of the Byrhtnoth plinth—shields and swords above, prayer at a church below.

river towards the causeway. It is cast in bronze, and nine feet high (2.7 m). Around the base is a series of scenes depicting Anglo-Saxon life and the battle, along with the words 'Grant O Lord thy grace'—an adaptation of a fragment of Byrhtnoth's prayer as he lies dying. This is my translation of the full prayer, as told by the poet (line 173):

> I give thanks to thee, God of nations, for all the benefits I have met with in this world. Now I have, merciful God, the greatest need, that you should grant my spirit favour, that my soul might journey to thee, into your keeping, prince of angels, may journey in peace. I beseech you that the fiends of hell might not harm it.

The height of the statue is appropriate. In the history of Ely Abbey, it is recorded that the monks there took Byrhtnoth's body from the battlefield and buried it in their church. His head had been cut off and taken away by the invaders, so they replaced it with a round lump of wax. The remains were reburied in the Norman Cathedral in 1154, discovered in the 18th century, and placed in Bishop West's chapel (Chapter 11). The antiquaries of the time reported a huge skeleton lacking a head, and it was estimated that Byrhtnoth was 6 ft 9 inches (2.05 m) in height. With a voice to match this physique, the Vikings would have had no problem hearing him at all.

Wordsmiths and Warriors

Getting there

The site at Northey Island, now a nature reserve, is owned by the National Trust. If you enter Maldon from the south, along the B1018, you turn sharp right at the roundabout as you approach the town, signposted Promenade Park, into Limebrook Way. If you turn right at the next roundabout, you enter Mundon Road. A few hundred yards along is a left turn (just opposite a bus-stop) into a private lane (South House Chase), which runs past South House Farm to a small parking area next to the sea wall. This floods at high water, and it's difficult to park on Mundon Road in any case, so the recommended approach is on foot along public rights of way from Maldon.

To do this you need to start in Promenade Park. Instead of turning right at Mundon Road keep straight ahead into Park Drive, and the Park is a little way along on the right, by the Leisure Centre (postcode: CM9 5JQ). There's a large car park. If you are starting from the town centre, it's a short walk down hill to the riverside, the promenade (with the Byrhtnoth Monument), and the Park entrance.

From the Park to Northey Island is just over two miles. You walk along the river past the recycling centre, a landfill site, and fields, and along the flood bank. You will see Northey Island ahead of you, and—if low tide—the causeway. It's possible to walk across at low tide, but contact the warden and consult tide tables before doing so, to avoid being cut off. The approach to the causeway carries a caution: 'Warning, dangerous tides. You should make an appointment with the warden.' and there is a website address:

http://www.nationaltrust.org.uk/northey-island/

The Maldon manuscript is in the Bodleian Library (MS Rawlinson B.203).

Chapter 9

Winchester

the first standard English

Driving into Winchester from the north, along the old London Road, the place names give you clues about what to expect. You pass through the suburb of Abbotts Barton. Abbotts Road is on your right. Then, Edington Road, on your left. I would have expected that to be a major thoroughfare, given the proud history of the name (Chapter 7), but it's a small private road and a cul-de-sac. The next on the left takes you down to Saxon Road, with the King Alfred pub. You pass Nuns Road and then Monks Road, and end up in King Alfred Place, part of which is Alswitha Terrace. Alswitha was Ealhswith in Anglo-Saxon times—the wife of Alfred the Great. And in front of you is what remains of Hyde Abbey—a gate-house. This is as near as you can get to an above-ground memorial of the famous scriptorium that influenced the character of English in later Anglo-Saxon times.

A scriptorium was the writing-area in a monastery—the place where manuscripts were created, copied, and illuminated. It was sometimes a separate room, but often the monks wrote on desks in window recesses in the corridor around the cloisters, as at Chester (Chapter 16). Writing might also be carried on in the monks' individual cells. The Winchester scriptorium was renowned for the quality of its output. It began in the centre of the city, where a church had been built in the 7th century. Alfred had planned a 'New Minster' on land right next to the 'Old Minster', but died in 899 before the work began. His son, Edward the Elder, completed the project, and was present at its dedication in 903. Later in the century,

Page opposite. The entrances to the gate-house of Hyde Abbey.

Benedictine monks arrived and established a monastery there—it was the first cathedral in England to house a monastic chapter—and it was in their scriptorium that they began to develop the distinctive form of manuscript production now known as the 'Winchester style'.

The 200 years following the reign of King Alfred saw the emergence of Wessex as the dominant and eventually unifying force in English politics, and this inevitably resulted in an increased status for the dialect of this area, West Saxon. Writing in English had been given a huge boost through Alfred's deep desire to see the vernacular language used in Britain (Chapter 7). The practices of the monks at Winchester—especially following Æthelwold, Bishop of Winchester (963–84)—began to influence the way scribes wrote elsewhere. It took a while, but by the second half of the 10th century most of the surviving manuscripts contain West Saxon spellings, words, and grammatical constructions.

There's no sign of the old scriptorium now. In the later part of the 11th century the Normans demolished the minsters and built a new cathedral on the site. Today, only a hint of the old buildings remain, in the churchyard just north of the present cathedral, outlined on the ground in brick. But as a result of the reconstruction, the monastery attached to the old church had to move. Henry I ordered a new abbey to be built on meadowland to the north of the city walls, in the area known as Hyde—an interesting name, probably from *hide*, an old measure of land, based on the amount of ground needed to support a family (usually, what could be ploughed in a year). It would have been around 120 acres (50 ha), plenty of space for an abbey. The monks moved there in 1110, reinterring the bodies of King Alfred, Alswitha, and Edward in the new abbey church near the altar—a location now somewhere underneath the western edge of the car park at the Riverpark Leisure Centre.

An outline of Hyde Abbey has been superimposed onto an aerial photograph of this part of Winchester in an information panel inside the gatehouse at King Alfred Place. It was indeed an extensive development. No mention is made of a scriptorium, but it would probably have been in the cloisters at the centre of the monastic compound, just north of present-day King Alfred Terrace. The gate-house, providing access to the inner courtyard of the monastery, was some distance away, and was built much later, in the 15th century. The entrances—one for horses and carriages, one for pedestrians—were on the side away from the road. It is built of flint, with a stone dressing, and the roof is modern tiling. A simple plaque on the roadside wall remembers Alfred, Alswitha, and Edward.

The location of Hyde Abbey in Winchester.

Little else survives. Adjoining the gateway to the west are the remains of an old cart shed, partly 12th century, converted into a day room for flats in a sheltered housing development. There are remnants of walls nearby. East of the gateway is a footbridge over a small stream: the arch is also 12th century. Fragments of the abbey buildings are preserved in St Bartholomew's Church on the other side of King Alfred Terrace. And there is a book.

It's called the Liber Vitae of Newminster and Hyde, dating from around 1031. A *liber vitae* (or 'book of life') was essentially a listing of those involved

in a religious community, the idea being that if their names were entered in such a book on earth they would also appear in the corresponding heavenly book which would be opened at the Day of Judgement (as described in Revelation 20). The Hyde copy was begun by a monk and priest of the New Minster, Ælfsige, in 1031, and there were several later additions. Apart from its obvious historical interest, the text gives us valuable information about the naming practices of the time.

I find the bynames especially intriguing. I can see why Ælfstan was called Claudus ('the lame'). He would want to be distinguished from Ælfstan Niger ('the black'). And similarly there is a transparency behind Osmær Nanus ('the dwarf'), Lyfingc Calvus ('the bald'), and Stephanus Decrepitus ('the feeble'). But why was Wulfgar called Agnus ('the lamb')? And why Rodbertus Losenge? A *losenger*, in early Middle English, was a false flatterer, a lying rascal, but such an appellation would hardly qualify Rodbertus for a place in the book of eternal life. Perhaps he simply had a diamond-shaped face.

Getting there

Leave the A33 at the B3047 (the old London Road). It becomes Worthy Road after a while, because it leads to the 'Worthies' (a name that meant an enclosure or homestead)—the villages of Headbourne Worthy and Kings Worthy. Keep an eye open for Edington Road and then Arthur Road, where you turn left. Alternatively, take the next left into Hyde Street, which leads down to King Alfred Place (postcode: SO23 7DQ).

If you're travelling from the city centre, go north along Jewry Street, following the sign which says 'Local traffic only'. At the traffic lights, Hyde Street is in front of you, but you can't drive across. Instead, turn left, and at the major crossroads turn right (signposted Basingstoke M3, Newbury, and Andover). Worthy Lane (the beginning of the B3047) is then the second on the right.

Beware: don't turn right at the Hyde Street traffic lights, even though you may have noted, a little way along North Walls, a turning on the left called Hyde Abbey Road. This is a dead end. We know. We tried it.

The Hyde Liber Vitae is in the British Library, manuscript BL Stowe 944. A good selection of pictures can be seen at

http://www.bl.uk/catalogues/illuminatedmanuscripts/record.asp?MSID=94&CollID=21&NStart=944

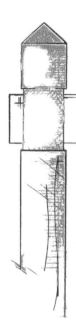

Chapter 10

Cerne Abbas

Ælfric and the first English conversation

Mention Cerne Abbas in Dorset to most people, and they think of a naked and well-endowed male giant carved into the chalk on the side of a hill. That's where all the tourist signs point: To the Giant. View the Giant. The village even has a Giant Inn. But nothing points to the linguistic giant of Cerne Abbas.

This was Ælfric (pronounced [alfritch]), who lived from about 955 to about 1010. He became a Benedictine monk at Winchester, where he must have done well, for when a new monastery at Cerne was established in 987 he was sent there as a teacher. He stayed until 1005, when he left to become abbot of Eynsham, near Oxford.

He was without doubt the greatest vernacular prose writer of his time. His works include two series of homilies, lives of the saints, and three texts to help students learn Latin: a Grammar, a Glossary, and also a Colloquy—the work for which he is most famous in the history of the English language. A colloquy was a dialogue between a teacher and his pupils, designed as an instructional technique in monastic schools to help students improve their conversational Latin. It was written originally in Latin, but someone (probably not Ælfric himself) has inserted an English translation in tiny writing above the Latin words in the manuscript. It is thus the first recorded example we have of an English conversation.

Here's a translation of the opening into modern English:

Page opposite. The abbot's hall at Cerne Abbey.

The Cerne Giant.

Pupil: We children ask you, O teacher, that you teach us to speak [Latin correctly], because we are unlearned and we speak corruptly.

Teacher: What do you wish to talk about?

Pupil: What do we care what we talk about, as long as the speech is correct and useful, not idle or base.

Teacher: Are you willing to be beaten while learning?

Pupil: We would rather be beaten for the sake of learning than not to know it. But we know that you are kind, and do not want to inflict a beating on us unless we force you to it.

It has a question/answer style, designed to elicit vocabulary, as this extract shows, where the pupil has to role-play being a hunter:

Teacher: Do you know how to do anything?

Pupil: I do have a calling.

Teacher: Which?

Pupil: I'm a hunter.

Teacher: Whose?

Pupil: The king's.

Teacher: How do you carry out your work?

Pupil: I knot myself a net and set it up in a convenient place, and get my hounds to chase wild deer until they come unawares into the net and get ensnared, and I slay them in the net.

Wordsmiths and Warriors

The opening page of the Colloquy, showing the interlinear translation (British Library Cotton Tiberius Aiii).

It's a lively and realistic exchange, with the pupils doing most of the talking. It was very different from the pedestrian teaching exercises of the day, and it gives a sense of what an Anglo-Saxon conversation would have been like in 10th-century Cerne, in the days before it acquired its Abbas ('abbey') suffix.

The name *Cerne* has attracted several imaginative explanations. Some have linked it to a Celtic horned god, Cernunnos. And the 12th-century chronicler William of Malmesbury suggested that it derived from words supposedly used by St Augustine during a mission to this part of England. Apparently the people rebuffed Augustine and his followers, fastening cow-tails to their garments and chasing them away. But Augustine made a prophecy: 'I see God who shall give us grace and impart to these deluded people a change of heart'. The conversion did eventually take place, and

The gate into Cerne Abbey.

(according to William) the people, regretting their earlier bad behaviour, decided to use the opening word of the prophecy (*Cerno*, 'I see') along with the Hebrew word for God (*El*) as a new name for their settlement. Over time, *Cernel* then became *Cerne*.

The real etymology is less fanciful. *Cerne* means no more than 'rocky stream', referring to the river that runs by the village. There are several other 'cerne' names around the country, such as *Cerney* in Gloucestershire and the *Charn* river in Berkshire. A similar word, *carn*, meaning 'rock', is found in Welsh.

Little is left of the abbey today, and you have to search for it; but Cerne Abbas is small enough for this not to be a problem. The landmark is the 14th-century church of St Mary the Virgin in Abbey Street, the commercial centre in medieval times, and well worth a visit in its own right to see its wall paintings and texts. We found the entrance to the abbey grounds at the top of the street, along a path and through a narrow gate. It felt like entering a secret garden, and in a sense it is, for the land is now part of the imposing Abbey House. It's a building film buffs might recognize, for it was used as Squire Western's house in the 1963 film of Henry Fielding's *Tom Jones*.

Nothing remains of the original abbey buildings. There's a surviving monastery guest house, but it's 15th century. A wall plaque recounts major events in Cerne's history. A few years after Ælfric wrote his Colloquy, the site was plundered and burnt by King Canute—though following his later conversion to Christianity he became a staunch supporter of the abbey. Its status grew, and it attracted royal visits, including King John in *c.*1200 and Henry III some 50 years later. Margaret of Anjou, the wife of Henry VI, stayed here with her son in 1471, the very day her Lancastrian cause was lost at the Battle of Barnet.

The most striking feature of the site is the stone-vaulted porch of the abbot's hall, with its double oriel window, surrounded by elaborate carvings. Ælfric wouldn't have known it, for that too is medieval, but it marks the place where he probably lived and worked. Also surviving is part of the gate-house, which houses a series of panels about the history of the site. Ælfric stars in one of them, along with his Colloquy—a rare example in Britain of a language writer being publicly acknowledged.

The panel doesn't mention the title by which he was later known, to distinguish him from several other people with the same name: Ælfric the Grammarian. People are recalling his translation of the Latin Grammar, when they describe him in this way. But from an English language point of view, we would do better to call him Ælfric the Conversationalist. Or simply, Ælfric the Giant.

Getting there

Cerne Abbas is to the right of the A352 travelling north between Dorchester and Sherborne. Turn at the Royal Oak pub, and you're in Abbey Street. At the top of the street, on the right just past a duck pond, is the gate which leads you into the grounds (postcode: DT2 7JQ).

Chapter 11

Ely

Wulfstan and Old English style

It's a commonplace of necrology that you never know who you're going to end up lying next to. For the English-language tourist, nowhere is this more apparent than in Ely Cathedral, Cambridgeshire. We went there looking for Wulfstan—and had a second encounter with Byrhtnoth (Chapter 8).

Wulfstan was Archbishop of York in the early 11th century, having previously been Bishop of London. He is famous for his homilies, which illustrate the way Old English had developed into a highly sophisticated medium of prose expression. Indeed, prose is hardly the word, for when we read Wulfstan we see a highly crafted rhetorical style, with balanced constructions, formulaic expressions, and pairs of words linked by alliteration and often rhyme. It feels as if we're reading poetry.

There's an example below. It's taken from his most famous homily, composed in 1014, with the Latin title *Sermo Lupi ad Anglos*—'Homily of Wolf to the English'. Wolf was what he called himself—short for *Wulf-stan*, 'wolf-stone'. It must have been a bit like Pope Francis writing an encyclical and calling himself Frank.

The homily pulls no punches. Wulfstan is haranguing the people for their wickedness. The Danish invasions, which had harassed the English for decades, he believes are a punishment from God for their sins. And he lists them:

Page opposite. Ely Cathedral.

Ac wearð þes þeodscipe, swa hit þincan mæg, swyþe forsyngod þurh mænigfealde synna and þurh fela misdæda: þurh morðdæda and þurh mandæda, þurh gitsunga and þurh gifernessa, þurh stala and þurh strudunga, þurh mannsylena and þurh hæþene unsida, þurh swicdomas and þurh searacræftas, þurh lahbrycas and þurh æwswicas, þurh mægræsas and þurh manslyhtas, þurh hadbrycas and þurh æwbrycas, þurh siblegeru and þurh mistlice forligru …

And the people, as it can seem, became very corrupted through numerous sins and through many evil deeds: through deadly sins and through crimes; through greed and through gluttony; through theft and through robbery; through slave-trafficking and through pagan vices; through deceits and frauds; through violations of human law and God's law; through attacks on kinsmen and homicides; through harming those in holy orders and through adultery; through incest and through manifold immoralities …

It's easy to imagine the cumulative impact of these rhythmical couplings on a congregation. The effect simply wouldn't have been the same if he had simply given a long list. It's the sonic pairings that make the difference: *gitsunga* and *gifernessa*, *mægræsas* and *manslyhtas*, which is why I include the Old English here. The translation can only hint at these.

Living in the north, his vocabulary shows many influences of the earlier Viking presence in this region. The area is full of Danish place names (Chapter 33), and we see Old Norse loan words in his writing, such as *bonda* for 'husband', *laga* for 'law', and *þræl* for 'servant'. Several other Old English words are known only from Wulfstan's writings or the work of those influenced by him. *Sibleger* 'incest' is an example. *Werewolf* is another.

I can't think of anyone better to show off the power of Old English prose than Wulfstan (though Ælfric is a close second, Chapter 10). He died at York in 1023, and—following his wishes—his body was taken for burial to the Benedictine monastery at Ely. So the cathedral, on the site of the monastery, is the obvious place for a linguistic pilgrimage. But when we entered it we encountered a problem. There were memorial windows all around—over 70 of them—but he wasn't in any of them. On the other hand we did find Byrhtnoth, the leader at the Battle of Maldon.

In fact we found two Byrhtnoths. The north-east window in the Octagon of the cathedral tells the Anglo-Saxon story, including the founders of the monastery, and each personality has a panel. The first abbot is there, appointed by King Edgar in 970, and he is called Byrhtnoth—spelled Brithnoth in his panel, and distinguished from his neighbour by the appellation Brithnoth ABBAS ('abbot'). The leader at Maldon is there because he was a great benefactor of the monastery. The story goes that he visited it before setting out to do battle with the Danes, giving it several manors on condition that, if he fell in battle, the monks should bring his body to Ely for burial—which they duly did. He is named as Brithnoth MILES ('soldier') in his panel.

But there is no Wulfstan. Yet he had to be here somewhere. And eventually we found him, in the south-east corner of the cathedral, in a small chapel, panelled with tabernacle-work and crowded with figures, dedicated to Bishop Nicholas West, Bishop of Ely in the time of Henry VIII.

The two Brithnoths—Abbas on the left, Miles on the right.

REQUIESCANT

WLSTANUS ARCHIEP'US EBOR OBIIT A.D.MXXIII.

OSMUNDUS EP'US E SUEDIA OBIIT CIRCA A.D.MLXVII.

ALWINUS EP'US ELMHAMENSIS OBIIT A.D.MXXIX.

ÆLFGARUS EP'US ELMHAMENSIS OBIIT A.D.MXXI.

EDNOTHUS EP'US DORCESTRENSIS CÆSUS A DANIS A.D.MXVI.

ATHELSTANUS EP'US ELMHAMENSIS OBIIT CIRCA A.D.DCCCCXCVI.

BRITHNOTHUS NORTHUMBRIÆ DUX, PRÆLIO CÆSUS A DANIS A.D.DCCCCXCI.

The sculpted figures and ornaments have been severely defaced, probably at the time of the Reformation. But the memorial we were looking for is intact and its text very readable.

Bishop West's tomb is on the right, and above it are seven niches, each containing an inscription. A Latin text reads:

> Beneath are buried the bones of seven men who served well the people of Ely. Preserved piously in the abbey church; solemnly transferred to the cathedral church in 1154; afterwards enclosed in the north wall of the recent choir; finally each was placed in its own coffin in the chapel on 31st July 1771. May they rest in peace.

And there, in the leftmost niche, is Wulfstan, with a Latin inscription which translates: 'Archbishop of York (Eboracum), died AD 1023'. The Latin in the rightmost niche tells us: 'Brithnoth, Duke of Northumberland, killed in battle by the Danes AD 991'. The Northumberland title seems wrong, as Byrhtnoth was Earl of Essex, but there was probably some connection with the north for which we have no record.

There's nothing more to say about Wulfstan at Ely; but there's a lot more to say about Byrhtnoth. According to the *Liber Eliensis* ('Book of Ely', c.1170), the Danes cut off Byrhtnoth's head and carried it away with them, and the monks buried him with a ball of wax in its place. When his tomb was opened in 1769, preliminary to moving the remains to Bishop West's

Wordsmiths and Warriors

chapel, one of those present sent a letter to the Society of Antiquaries, in which this story seemed to be confirmed:

> there were no remains of the head, though we searched diligently, and found most, if not all his other bones almost entire, and those remarkable for their length … It was observed that the collar-bone had been nearly cut through, as by a battle-axe, or two handed sword.

So there we are: an exemplar of late Old English prose style bookending five Anglo-Saxon bishops (Osmund, Alwin, Ælfgar, Ednoth, Athelstan) along with a headless general. We encountered some unexpected juxtapositions during our tour, but none to beat this one.

Getting there

Ely is on the A10 between Cambridge and King's Lynn, and the cathedral is shown on the brown tourist signs (postcode: CB7 4DL). There's a short-stay car park in St Mary's Street just round the corner from the main entrance.

After entering the Cathedral, you find Bishop West's Chapel by walking through to the very far end, on the right. Look up left as you pass the central Octagon, and you'll see the Byrhtnoth window.

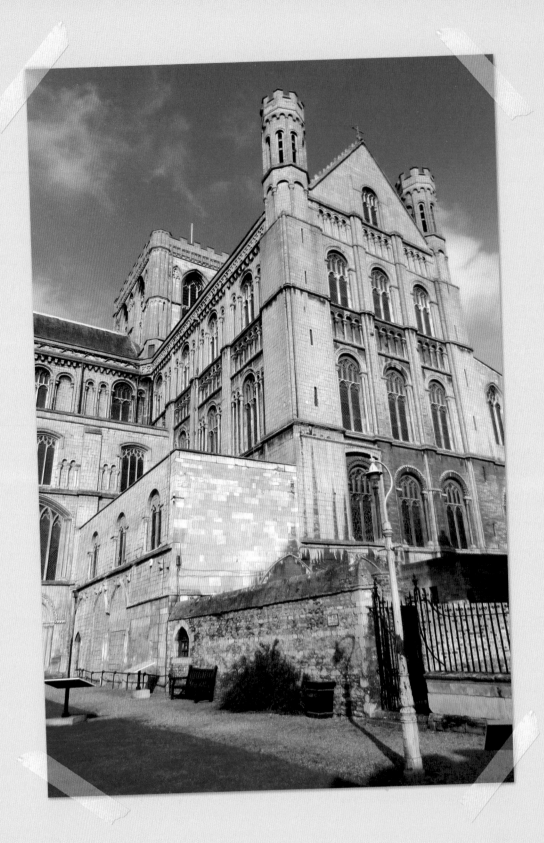

Chapter 12

Peterborough

the Anglo-Saxon Chronicle

Peterborough in Cambridgeshire is one of those place names that keep turning up in the early history of English. It's because of the Anglo-Saxon Chronicle—the remarkable effort by an unknown number of scribes writing over several generations to record, year by year, the main events of their era in their own language (as opposed to in Latin, which was the usual medium for historical documentation at the time). Their output, thought of as a single book, is the first major work of English prose. No account of the history of English is possible without frequent reference to its contents. And no self-respecting English-language tourist could make a journey around England without visiting one of the places where it was written.

But which place? The *Chronicle* was first compiled in Wessex in the south of England at the end of the 9th century during the reign of King Alfred (Chapter 7). Copies were then made of the original manuscript and sent to monasteries in different parts of the country, where scribes independently kept them up to date. The original manuscript is lost, but nine versions do survive, in whole or in part, associated chiefly with Winchester, Abingdon, Worcester, Canterbury, and Peterborough. It's Peterborough, in Northamptonshire, which has special significance, which is why we went there.

The *Peterborough Chronicle* is special because it goes on for much longer than the others, and bridges the gap between the period we call Old English and the one we call Middle English. It received its name because it was first copied in the Benedictine monastery at Peterborough in 1121, probably to

Page opposite. The abbey cloister area beneath the south wall of Peterborough Cathedral.

replace a manuscript destroyed in a devastating fire five years earlier. The copyist updated the text, and various scribes kept it going until 1131. Then there was a gap of 23 years. This covered the reign of Stephen I, whose seizure of the throne in 1134 heralded an anarchic period in English history. After his death in 1154, the *Chronicle* was immediately updated to that year—probably the work of a single continuator making a personal effort. Six annals were added recording the events of the time, one of which (for the year 1137) is a famous description of the torments and misery which had affected everyone:

> I do not know how, nor am I able, to describe all the atrocities and all the cruelties that they inflicted upon the unhappy people of this land. It lasted for the nineteen years that Stephen was king, and always it was worse and worse.

And he describes in graphic detail the torturing, plundering, and taxing that took place.

That gap of 23 years proved to be of immense significance for English linguistic studies. The *Peterborough Chronicle* entries up to and including 1131 were written in Old English; but the later entries are so different in spelling, grammar, and vocabulary that they have to be considered an early example of Middle English. The later text has fewer inflectional endings on words, for example, and the word order is much more modern. It's also the earliest text we have in the East Midland dialect, from which modern standard English would later develop. Nowhere else is the transition between Old and Middle English so visible.

Some physical finds from the period are visible too. The first church on the site was actually a 7th-century Celtic abbey, from which several artefacts have survived, including a stone grave marker from the year 870. The *Peterborough Chronicle* recounts what happened that year at Medehamstede (the former name of Peterborough):

> The Danes ... came to the monastery at Medeshamstede and burned and demolished it, and slew the abbot and monks and all they found there, reducing to nothing what had once been a very rich foundation.

The abbot's name was Hedda, and the stone has come to be called the Hedda Stone.

Page opposite. The Hedda Stone behind the high altar The holes in the stone show places for carrying rods.

Below. The year on the Hedda Stone. The origin of the date is unclear: it would have been in Roman numerals if it had really been carved in 870. Arabic numerals didn't become common in Europe until the 13th century.

ABBOTS OF MEDESHAMSTEDE, LATER PETERBOROUGH	
c.655-674	Saxulf
675-c.709	Cuthbald
pre-716	Egbald
?	Pusa
758-789	Bothwin
c.789-823	Beonna
c.852	Ceolred
?-870	Hedda
971-992	Aldulf
992-1005	Kenulf
1005-1042	Aelfsige
1042-1052	Earnwig
1052-1066	Leofric
1066-1069	Brand
1069-1098	Turoldus of Fecamp
1099-1103	Godric
1103-1105	Matthias
1105-1114	Ernulf
1114-1125	John de Sais
1128-1133	Henri d' Angely
1133-1155	Martin de Bec
1155-1175	William de Waterville
1177-1193	Benedict
1193-1201	Andrew
1201-1214	Acharius
1214-1222	Robert of Lindsey
1222-1226	Alexander of Holderness
1226-1233	Martin of Ramsey
1233-1245	Walter of St Edmunds
1246-1249	William of Hotot
1249-1262	John de Caux
1262-1274	Robert of Sutton
1274-1295	Richard of London
1295-1299	William of Woodford
1299-1321	Godfrey of Crowland

A new church was consecrated in 972, as part of a Benedictine abbey, which in turn was replaced by the cathedral in the early 12th century. 2018 is the 900th anniversary. It's in the scriptorium of this abbey that the *Chronicle* would have been copied. And it's the abbot of the time, Martin de Bec, who presumably gave the task his blessing. He was really special, according to the report of the year 1137. Having described the horrors of the time, the chronicler goes on to say:

During all those evil days, abbot Martin governed his abbacy under great difficulties for twenty and a half years and eight days. He provided everything necessary for the monks and the visitors and was liberal in alms-giving . . .

Another 200 words of praise follow, before the writer concludes: 'He was a good monk and a good man, and therefore he was loved by God and by good men.' And without him, there might have been no *Peterborough Chronicle*.

I know it's difficult to imagine, but some people believe that there are more important things in heaven and earth than English philology. And as the *Chronicle* is a tiny drop in the ocean of history that comprises this cathedral, I wasn't expecting to see any reference to it as we walked around. However, I was wrong. A series of exhibition panels in an aisle presented the history of the place, and in one of them there was a monk at his desk, with the *Chronicle* proudly identified in the adjoining caption.

All I had to do now was find the scriptorium. We left the cathedral by the side door and came into the grounds of the old abbey, nestling in the shadow of the south wall. A notice told us that this is where the cloisters were, so the scriptorium is likely to have been nearby. Two gardeners were trimming the grass edges, talking in a richly colourful local accent that was curiously reminiscent of earlier centuries of English. It was as close as I was going to get.

The list of abbots, located behind the choir-stalls on the north side of the cathedral. Martin de Bec is the one English-language tourists should look out for.

Wordsmiths and Warriors

Getting there

The A15 from the north, and the A47 and A605 from the west, all lead to the city centre. The cathedral is well represented on brown tourist signs (postcode: PE1 1XS). It's very difficult to park on roads right by the cathedral. The best bet is to aim for one of the larger car parks near the centre, such as the multi-storey Queensgate car park on the A15 (postcode: PE1 1NT). From here there's an underpass beneath the large roundabout which brings you out at the entrance to Cowgate, leading into Church Street and then into Cathedral Square. For cathedral opening times, see

http://www.peterborough-cathedral.org.uk/

It has a sensible policy of permitting photography upon purchase of a permit.

The manuscript of the *Peterborough Chronicle* is at the Bodleian library in Oxford: MS. Laud Misc. 636.

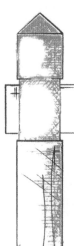

Chapter 13

Battle and Normans Bay

the French connection

It's 1066 that gets all the publicity. Driving along the A21 towards the Sussex south coast, we passed a sign: Welcome to 1066 Country. The theme permeates the region. There's the 1066 Country Walk, if you're up to it (it's 30 miles/50 km), from Pevensey to Rye via Battle. On the High Street in Battle there's The 1066—a pub. That's all as it should be. Without the Battle of Hastings, there'd be no reason for the English-language tourist to visit here at all.

It's said to be the most famous battle fought on English soil. Duke William of Normandy's defeat of King Harold on 14 October 1066 marked the end of Anglo-Saxon England. From a linguistic point of view, it led to a seismic shift in the character of English. Around 30,000 words entered English from French during the early Middle Ages. French scribes made fundamental changes in the way English was spelled. New styles of writing appeared in such areas as law, architecture, and literature, reflecting a French cultural vision. It was a pattern of influence which would continue. Today, only some 20 per cent of English vocabulary retains its original Germanic character.

The basic facts about the battle are well known. I learned them, as I suppose British children still do, in primary school. King Edward the Confessor had died in January 1066, leaving no heir. Earl Harold of Wessex was immediately consecrated king in Westminster Abbey in London. But there were others who laid claim to the English throne. In September 1066 Harold defeated the Norwegian claimant, Harold Hardrada, at the Battle

Page opposite. The imposing gate-house entrance to Battle Abbey. It was built in 1338, replacing an earlier one. Only the west range, seen here to the left of the present-day entrance, incorporates parts of the original gate-house.

of Stamford Bridge in Yorkshire. His army then rapidly journeyed south to face William.

Harold arranged his army of foot-soldiers as a shield-wall in an east–west line on the ridge of Senlac Hill, just north of Hastings. The Norman army of archers, infantry, and cavalry approached across the valley to the south. There were probably between 5000 and 7000 men on each side. William of Poitiers, who later became King William's chaplain, noted the contrast between the two sides: 'It was a strange kind of battle, one side attacking with all mobility, the other withstanding, as though rooted to the soil.' The first Norman attack was beaten back, but renewed assaults over several hours were finally successful. At least twice the Normans pretended to flee, tempting some of the English to follow them. Then, in the last charge of the day, Harold was killed—one of those historical events that stays in a child's mind—by an arrow in his eye.

William gave thanks for his victory by establishing a Benedictine abbey on the hilltop at the northern part of the battlefield. Despite considerable demolition and decay over the centuries, there's a great deal still to be seen,

Wordsmiths and Warriors

in addition to the site of the battle itself. The battlefield, now a broad green field falling away from the abbey, is surprisingly compact: it takes only half an hour to walk all the way round it. Within the abbey ruins, the high altar of the abbey church was built on the place where Harold is thought to have fallen. It's marked by a plaque in the ground now.

So where did the Normans land? This has been the subject of great debate. Proposals have been made for locations anywhere between Pevensey and Bulverhythe. The place that is called Normans Bay is in the middle. The name (its apostrophe on signs comes and goes like the tides) is a bit of a tourist trick. It was founded on a small shingle island in the marshes, and has now become a holiday village, surrounded by caravan sites and other amenities. Its shingly beach has built up over the centuries, the pebbles brought in from erosion further along the coast. In 1066 the beach area would have been sea, and the original shore would have been much further inland—as far as the tiny village of Hooe, which was on the coast a millennium ago, and is now two miles from the sea. At nearby Ninfield, just three miles south-west of Battle, there's a Standard Hill, where William is reputed to have raised his standard. Turn in almost any direction, in this part of East Sussex, and you see some sort of echo of those days. It's all 1066 country now.

The Harold memorial, with the remains of the monastic dormitory in the background. The plaque reads: 'The traditional site of the high altar of Battle Abbey founded to commemorate the victory of Duke William on 14 October 1066. The high altar was placed to mark the spot where King Harold died.'

The present-day broad expanse of Normans Bay. Groynes try to prevent the movement of the shingle. The tall building on the beach is a Martello Tower (No. 55), renovated since 2004 and now a private house. Hastings is in the distance.

Getting there

Senlac Hill is easy to find, as it's one of Britain's major tourist attractions. From the A21, follow the A2100 south into Battle, and the abbey is dead ahead. Turn right just before the abbey gate, and there's a car park on the left. The battle site is inside the abbey (postcode: TN33 0AD). For opening times, see the English Heritage website:

http://www.english-heritage.org.uk/daysout/properties/
1066-battle-of-hastings-abbey-and-battlefield/history/

Ninfield is on the A269, south-west of Battle, on the Bexhill Road.

Normans Bay is quite tricky to get to. From Hastings, take the A259 towards Pevensey, and at Pevensey Roundabout turn left to Pevensey Bay and then left again at the traffic lights (signposted to Beachlands) along Coast Road. Immediately after you pass the end of the 30 mph limit, there's a wide path to the right leading to the beach, and roadside car parking is possible on the left. The road into the village of Normans Bay is a private road (postcode: BN24 6PS).

If you travel from the east along the B2182 out of Hastings, past Cooden Beach Golf Course, you pass a left turn into Normans Bay: this is the other end of the private road. The train station is a few yards along this road. From there, it's a short walk along Coast Road to the beach. The Martello Tower is a good landmark.

Chapter 14

Bourne

Orrm and English spelling

Another day, another abbey. I often felt like that, on our linguistic tour, and wondered sometimes whether our photographic records would ever show more than a series of churches. But I had no choice. For well over 700 years, the written history of English was, quite literally, in the hands of the monks. And at the end of the 12th century, in the hands of one monk in particular, Orrm, whose masterwork, the *Orrmulum*, holds a unique place in the history of English. It was going to be another abbey—but one with a difference.

His name—he calls himself both Orrm and Orrmin—suggests he was of Scandinavian descent. The name meant 'serpent' in Old Norse, and we see it again in the Great Orme at Llandudno in North Wales. He tells us in his opening lines that he and his brother Walter are both canons following the rule of 'Sannt Awstin'—Saint Augustine. Canons were priests who lived a religious life within a closed community but also carried on the kind of outreach (preaching, visiting the sick, teaching, and so on) associated with parish work. And we can see this practical intent in the *Orrmulum*.

His idea was to provide a helpful collection of homilies for use in church, based on the Gospel readings throughout the year. He has a table of contents listing Latin texts for 243 homilies, but only about an eighth of these have survived—if indeed they were all completed. It was an immensely ambitious undertaking: the surviving English text is 10,220 full poetic lines. If he did complete it along the lines of what remains, the whole work would

Page opposite. The parish church of St Peter and St Paul, from the south, otherwise known as Bourne Abbey.

have been three quarters of a million words. The original manuscript shows a process of revision which suggests a period of writing of at least 20 years, and on linguistic grounds a date of around 1180.

Why are linguists so interested in Orrm? He was, in brief, the first English spelling reformer, and his system of spelling tells us a great deal about how English was pronounced at the time. It has many features, but the most noticeable one is the way he shows the difference between long vowels (as in *seat*) and short vowels (as in *sit*) by doubling the following consonant when the vowel is short. So, instead of *sit*, he would write *sitt*. We see the principle in practice when he tells us in his Preface:

ROBERT DE BRUNNE

Bourne is associated with a second famous linguistic personality: the translator Robert Mannyng, usually known as Robert de Brunne (i.e. Bourne), who wrote in the early 14th century. He was probably born here, and the town and abbey claim him as their own; but he makes it clear in the prologue to his long (12,000-line) morality poem, Handlyng Synne, begun in 1303, that he was a Gilbertine monk (not an Augustinian) who spent fifteen years at the Gilbertine mother-house in Sempringham, some nine miles north of Bourne. In the introduction to his *Chronicle of England*, completed in 1338, he says he wrote it in 'þe hous of Sixille'—modern Sixhills—to the north of Sempringham. On the other hand, he dedicates his prologue

| To alle Crystyn men vndir sunne, | To all Christian men under the sun |
| And to gode men of Brunne | And to the good people of Bourne |

so plainly Bourne was still very much in his mind, and perhaps he did indeed spend time there.

Either way, he is an important voice in the movement of the time to provide people with writing in English (rather than in French or Latin). And not just a formal, clerical, or legal English. He wants a down-to-earth vernacular that everyone will understand, as he makes clear at the beginning of his *Chronicle*:

Haf I alle in myn Inglis layd	I've set down everything in my English
In symple speche as I couthe,	In simple language as much as I could,
þat is lightest in mannes mouthe.	That is easiest in a man's mouth.

In his desire to tell a good story in the most direct way, he anticipates Chaucer. And he provides a second good reason to visit Bourne.

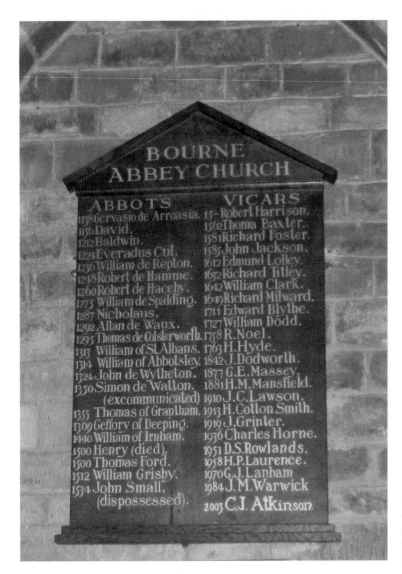

The list of abbots. Gervasio, the abbot of Arrouaise, is named as the founder, but the first local abbot was David in 1156.

þis boc is nemmnedd Orrmulum
Forrþi þatt Orrm itt wrohhte

'This book is called Orrmulum because Orrm wrote it.' We can see immediately that *boc* was pronounced 'bohk' not 'bokk', and that the first part of *nemmnedd* was pronounced 'nem' and not (as it would be today) 'name'. He applies the principle throughout the whole work, relaxing it in just a few places—*fox*, for example, is spelled as it is today, and not as *foccs*. It's an amazing linguistic creation, even though it never caught on. Nobody had

A banner displaying the two names of the church.

done anything like it before, and nobody would try to reform English spelling so fundamentally for another 300 years.

But where did he write it? That's what the English-language tourist wants to know. And this is where we have to turn detectives. The dialect spellings, grammar, and vocabulary of the *Orrmulum* indicate an origin in the East Midlands, and to Lincolnshire in particular. Orrm uses lots of Scandinavian loan words, for example, which are typical of writings coming from this region. And when we look in closer detail, the spellings suggest the south of the county rather than the north. That's important, for there are two places in Lincolnshire where Orrm could have worked: in the north, at Elsham Priory, near Brigg, between Scunthorpe and Grimsby—almost in Yorkshire; and to the south-west, at Bourne Abbey, a few miles north of Peterborough.

We know that in 1138 the lord of the manor at Bourne, Baldwin FitzGilbert, invited canons of the Arrouaisian order to found an abbey in his town. The first abbot is named as Gervasio of Arrouaise, the mother-house in northern France which was the centre of a form of Augustinian rule that founded several abbeys in the 12th century. This gives plenty of time to develop a community of canons by the time Orrm was writing—according to the Bourne Abbey records, perhaps as many as 12. By contrast, the priory at Elsham wasn't founded until 1166, and was intended as a hospital for the poor, with just one or two canons to support it. This seems an unlikely environment for an intellectual exercise of the order of magnitude that we see in the *Orrmulum*.

And one thing more. As part of his dedication, Orrm specifically mentions St Peter, the first patron saint of Bourne, and—along with St Paul, added after the Reformation—the name of the parish church as it is today. All this was enough—as lawyers say—to take a view. We went to Bourne.

The 12th-century church is still there, though much altered. The nave is the oldest part, dating from the foundation. Orrm would have worked in the monastic buildings nearby, which in the Augustinian tradition were always built to the north of the church. When the monastery was dissolved in the reign of Henry VIII, these buildings were demolished. A new vicarage covers part of the ground now. But the open grassy space between that building and the boundary wall alongside Church Walk is very likely to have been where Orrm painstakingly worked out his system of English spelling.

Wordsmiths and Warriors

The site of the monastic foundation, to the north of the abbey church.

Getting there

From the north, you approach Bourne along the A15. About a mile into the town there is a junction with four-way traffic lights. About 200 yards on the left past the junction is a lane signposted to the 'Abbey Church'. A short way along the lane you turn right into Church Walk, where it's possible to park (postcode: PE10 9UQ).

From the south along the A15, carry straight over the roundabout towards the town centre. After almost a mile, you see the Memorial Gardens on the left, and the sign to Abbey Church on your right.

Chapter 15

Areley Kings

Layamon's English Chronicle

Whatever else you might expect a hermit monk to do, living in a cave on a river bank, writing a historical survey of Britain isn't one of them. But this is what Layamon did, in the early years of the 13th century, in a work that has come to be called *Layamon's Brut*—a name that refers to the legendary founder of Britain, Brutus of Troy. It is a remarkable 16,096 lines, the longest piece of writing in English to have survived from this period and the first attempt at a history in English since the Anglo-Saxon Chronicle (Chapter 12).

Layamon begins his account with the landing of Brutus, and ends it with the death of King Cadwallader in AD 689. It includes an account of the arrival of the Anglo-Saxons in Britain and is famous for a long section (taking up almost half of the history) telling the story of King Arthur. King Lear and King Cymbeline are in it too.

The chronicle is told poetically, in a style which is partly Anglo-Saxon and partly French. The lines are split in two, linked by alliteration (an Old English verse technique) and often by rhyme. The poem uses a Germanic vocabulary that would soon fall out of use in English, to be replaced by words from French; but it already contains over a hundred of these new French words. Layamon was writing just at the point when Old English was transmuting into Middle English. His *Brut* simultaneously reflects the language of the past and points to the language of the future.

It is one of those rare pieces of writing from the Middle English period where the author has actually told us exactly where it was written. The poem begins by the author naming himself:

Page opposite. The main entrance to Layamon's Caves.

An preost wes on leoden Laȝamon wes ihoten . . .
A priest was on earth Layamon was named . . .

and he then gives us the crucial geographical information:

He wonede at Ernleȝe at æðelen are chirechen
he dwelt at Ernley at noble a church

Vppen Seuarne-staþe sel þar him þuhte
upon Severn bank good there to him it seemed

On-fest Radestone þer he bock radde . . .
Hard by Redstone where he book read . . .

. . . that is, the Gospel or church service book.

His name looks strange when you see it written in its original Middle English form, for it uses a letter long lost in English writing, and today called a 'yogh'. The letter had various sounds, and has come down to us in his name as a 'y'. The original pronunciation of the first *a* of *Layamon* would have been like the sound in modern English 'ah', though today people pronounce it as in 'lay'.

Where is Ernley? The name has developed into Areley (pronounced 'ah-lee'), and the village which has grown up on the north bank of the Severn is today called Areley Kings. *Ernley* probably comes from Anglo-Saxon *earn* 'eagle' + *leah* 'clearing', or it might simply refer to a river name. It is one of many *-ley* names in England which describe a clearing in the forest in terms of who or what was found there. We find *King* or *Kings* attached to the name from as early as the 14th century, showing that the place had special status as part of a royal manor. Local people today always include the *Kings* element when they talk about where they live, as they need to distinguish the name from nearby Upper Areley and Areley Common.

Areley Kings is just outside Stourport in Worcestershire, and we approached it from the town. Imagining a medieval priest–scholar, we were anticipating a peaceful village location. But there was a visual gauntlet to run past first, as we crossed the bridge out of Stourport. The last thing we were expecting to see was a local theme park—the colourful and popular Treasure Island amusement park, complete with Ferris wheel, helter-skelter, and all sorts of slides, rides, and stalls. But the turning to Areley Kings, a quarter of a mile further on, brought a reassuring contact with Layamon's world. A quiet road winds up a hill, and at the top there's a cluster of old

and new houses, including a timber-framed black-and-white 16th-century village hall (now Church House). Next to it is the Norman church of St Bartholomew, whose chancel dates from the 12th century. That was our goal. From the churchyard you can look down through the trees to the Severn, just as Layamon said you could.

Layamon is well remembered inside the church. He was its first known priest, and he has an elegant memorial window, set deep into one of the walls. It looks old, and probably is, for the wall is very thick at this point. The words in the window read:

LAYAMON SON OF LEOVENATH
PRIEST OF ERDLEY C. 1200

A memorial tablet next to the window, erected in 1884, states, somewhat misleadingly, 'He was the earliest writer in the English language'.

The most important feature is the baptismal font, which was made in the Norman style during a period of church renovation in 1885. The two base stones and part of the shaft are much older, for they were discovered in fragments under the floor of the nave during the renovation, and they provide an important bit of evidence for the presence of Layamon at the church. Around the base there is an inscription, found when a thick layer of paint and whitewash had been removed:

The inscription on the base of the Layamon font. The Y in his name has been obliterated, following repairs to a fracture in the stone.

TEMPORE LAYAMANNI SANTI

'in the time of the blessed Layamon'. However, the date of the carving is unclear. The style of the lettering suggests a much later date than the Middle Ages.

Layamon is remembered in the village too. One of the dwellings is called Layamon House. Across the main road, going down towards the river, we went through a new estate past Layamon Walk. The road is called Hermitage Way, and there's also a Redstone Lane. A path leads along the river's edge, next to a caravan park, to a series of caves cut into a red sandstone cliff known as Redstone Rock. The locals we spoke to called them Layamon's Caves.

The caves date from the Stone Age, and in the Christian era became used as a hermitage. The river-crossing at this point was important, as it was on the main route between North Wales and London. A ford allowed travellers to cross when the river was low; otherwise you needed a ferry. The hermits were on hand to offer blessings and prayers for passers-by in return for alms. Layamon may have been one of them.

The cave complex is huge, and housed several people—though it can never have been a comfortable location, always at risk from Severn flooding. The caves face north onto the river, and postcard photographs taken years ago, some of which can be found on the Internet, give you the impression that you get a good view from the south bank. Don't believe them. We did, walked for half an hour, and then found that trees and undergrowth totally obscure the view from the south.

We had to walk along the north bank to see the caves clearly, and to get a real impression of their size. The entrance cavities are enormous. Unfortunately, the complex internal excavations aren't visible from outside, and there's no way in. A high fence capped with razor wire surrounds them. Signs say KEEP OUT and DANGER OF DEATH. Being English-language tourists, we respected the words.

According to those who *have* explored them, a passageway at the east end runs parallel to the cliff face, leading to a series of cells. There are chambers at different levels within the rock. One functioned as a chapel, with an altar; another as a refectory; and there were dormitories and living areas. Some of the larger spaces have fireplaces. It must have been a strange sight, seeing smoke emerge from the chimney-hole at the top of the cliff.

Local historians report that the caves provided a habitation for poor people until the middle of the 19th century—and the cave-dwellers didn't always get a good press. As early as 1538, the Bishop of Worcester, Hugh Latimer, wrote to Thomas Cromwell, the chief minister of Henry VIII, describing them as 'an hermitage in a rock by Severn, able to lodge 500 men, and as ready for thieves and traitors as true men. I would not have hermits masters of such dens, but rather than some faithful man had it'. A lot had changed since Layamon's time.

Above. The cave complex looking north-west. Some of the small holes would have been used to provide support for the wooden frameworks of cliffside dwellings.

Right. An unenclosed cavity at the eastern end of the complex conveys, thanks to this nearly six-foot tall stand-in, a sense of scale.

Wordsmiths and Warriors

Getting there

Stourport is a couple of miles west of the A449 between Worcester and Kidderminster, and is easily reached from the M5. You wind your way around the one-way system until you reach the southbound A451 (Dunley Road) in the direction of Great Witley. Cross Stourport Bridge, passing the amusement park, and after about a quarter of a mile there is a right turn (Areley Lane) with a brown signpost saying Saint Bartholomew. Take the first left up Rectory Lane, and you find the Church at the top on the right (postcode: DY13 0AR). There is car parking outside.

To find the caves, start at Stourport Bridge (there's a large car park at Riverside), and go down the steps on the north side onto a riverside path. It's about a 25-minute walk along the path, past Redstone Caravan Park, to the caves. At the eastern end of the complex there are steps taking you to the top of the cliff, where a narrow path takes you above Stourport Caravan Park and eventually to the housing estate at Redstone Lane. A section of this path is part of the Geopark Way.

Two manuscripts of *Layamon's Brut* survive, both held in the British Library in London. The earlier text is Ms Cotton Caligula A.IX (*c.*1225); the later, showing several modernizations, is Cotton Otho C XIII (*c.*1250). A reproduction of a page from the *Brut* is shown in my *Evolving English* (British Library), p. 81.

Chapter 16

Chester and Berkeley

Higden, Trevisa, and the rise of English

In the preface to the King James Bible of 1611, there's a brief historical account of those who have translated the scriptures into local vernacular languages. After mentioning Saint Jerome, Bede, King Alfred, and other famous names, we read: 'even in our King Richard the second's days, John Trevisa translated them into English.' At which point, most people would have to ask 'Who he?'

His name reflects his probable birthplace: John of Trevisa—or Trevessa, as it's also spelled. It's a Cornish name, from *tref* ('farmstead, village') and *isel* ('low down'), a tiny hamlet in the parish of St Enoder, a few miles south-east of Newquay. Today we find it only in the name of a property, Trevessa Farmhouse, where it's said he was born, in about 1342. There's nothing to see there now, as the original house has long been buried under an 18th-century building. Just pretty country lanes and fields. Very isolated. And it poses the question: how did a lad from such an out-of-the-way place become a major literary figure of the 14th century?

The story starts with Ranulph Higden, a Benedictine monk at the monastery of St Werbergh in Chester, Cheshire. Very little is known about him. He was born in about the year 1280, perhaps in the west of England, and took his monastic vows at Chester in 1299. He's the author of a historical work called the *Polychronicon*, a 'chronicle of many ages'—as many as he could imagine, in fact, for it begins at the creation of the world. Its Latin title reads:

Page opposite. The entrance to Berkeley Castle.

Polychronicon (sive Historia Polycratica) ab initio mundi usque ad mortem
regis Edwardi III in septem libros dispositum

Or: 'from the beginning of the world to the death of King Edward III, arranged in seven books'. The same number as the days of creation.

The book was one of those which caught the attention of Lord Thomas de Berkeley, the fifth baron of Berkeley Castle in Gloucestershire. Berkeley was a kind of medieval Alfred (Chapter 7), with ambitious plans to have important Latin works translated into English, and he chose Trevisa to do the job. Why him? Presumably because of a connection through patronage. An earlier head of the Berkeley family—Lord Thomas's grandfather—was lord of the manor to which Trevessa belonged. Another Berkeley was briefly Bishop of Exeter. And the Berkeleys also had links with Oxford University. Someone must have noticed the young man and been impressed by his potential, for we find John Trevisa in the records of Exeter College, Oxford from 1362, dutifully paying his fees, and later at Queen's College, where he's likely to have been involved in the bible translation project led by Wycliffe, who was also there (Chapter 26).

At some point in the 1370s, probably 1374, he became chaplain to Lord Thomas, and was appointed vicar of the local church, St Mary the Virgin. When he actually arrived there isn't known. The record of vicars in the church gives his dates as 1368–1402 (the year of his death), but the earlier date is a guess, for we don't know the year his predecessor died either. What we do know is that Trevisa was in Berkeley in 1388 and 1389, because there are records saying he was involved in a quarrel over a church appointment at Westbury. It must have been quite a fight, according to a petition of complaint to the king (here translated from the French):

John Trevysa and John Poleyn, his maintainer, on the 16th day of February in the twelfth year of the reign of our said lord the king [Richard II, 1389] did raise the whole country for fifteen leagues around by sounding horns, as though against enemies of the king and his realm, with persons to the number of three hundred or more armed and arrayed in warlike fashion with habergeons, pikes, swords, bucklers, drawn bows and arrows, in the manner of insurrection, and came to the said church of Westbury to the stall where the said prebendary is, and there did beat and mistreat one Robert Banak, his vicar, occupying the aforesaid stall adorned for divine service, and from there they did drag him by the legs and feet up to the door of the same church, tearing his clothes, and with drawn daggers and bare swords placed against his

The minster church of
St Mary the Virgin.

sides and his back so that he was placed in great fright and peril of his
life...

Not the sort of thing one tends to associate with the cerebral task of
translation!

Whatever the date of his arrival in Berkeley, Trevisa is quite specific
about when he finished his translation of the *Polychronicon*, as he concludes
the work with these words:

> This translation is ended in a Thursday, the eighteenth day of April,
> the year of our Lord 1387... the year of my lord's age, sir Thomas lord of
> Berkeley, that made me make this translation, five and thirty.

He could never have anticipated its subsequent popularity. Over 100 copies of the manuscript survive today, showing that it was widely read. William Caxton printed an edition in 1482. Other writers added continuations, and it remained in use as an authority into the 17th century. For those interested in the history of English it continues to be read today, because of the insight it gives into the way the language was evolving during the Middle Ages.

Towards the end of the book, Higden reviews the language-teaching situation in England after the Norman Conquest. Things are not looking good for the future of English, he says, for two reasons (I've translated from the Middle English of the original):

> Children in school, contrary to the usage and custom of all other nations, are compelled to abandon their own language and to carry on their lessons and their affairs in French, and have done so since the Normans first came to England. Also the children of gentlemen are taught to speak French from the time that they are rocked in their cradle, and learn to speak and play with a child's trinket; and rustic men will make themselves like gentlemen, and seek with great industry to speak French, to be more highly thought of.

But when Trevisa translates this passage, he adds a paragraph of his own:

> This practice was much used before the first plague [the Black Death of 1349], and has since been somewhat changed … so that now, AD 1385, the ninth year of the reign of the second King Richard after the Conquest, in all the grammar schools of England, children abandon French, and compose and learn in English, and have thereby an advantage on the one hand, and a disadvantage on the other. The advantage is that they learn their grammar in less time than children used to do. The disadvantage is that nowadays children at grammar school know no more French than their left heel, and that it is a misfortune for them if they should cross the sea and travel in foreign countries, and in other such circumstances.

Times have changed. And indeed, when he was writing, English was consolidating its status as a national language. We see it, slowly but surely, becoming a part of official English life.

In 1344 we find the first known instance of a petition to the Crown to be written in English. In 1356 the mayor and aldermen of London order that proceedings in the sheriff's courts should be in English. And in 1362 there's the famous Statute of Pleading, in which the king wills that all pleas 'shall be pleaded, counted, defended, answered, debated, and judged in the English language'. The parliamentary clerk actually mentions that English was used in the opening speech to parliament that year, and repeats the mention in relation to the next two parliaments. It was clearly something out of the ordinary. The parliamentary rolls for the previous two years haven't survived, unfortunately, so this is the first official record we have of English being used in this way. It was a significant moment, with England having recently ended a long war with France. Using the vernacular was a statement which would be noted abroad as well as at home.

John of Trevisa's fame arose from where he worked, so a visit to Berkeley Castle is likely to be more meaningful than one to a country lane in Cornwall. He is said to be buried in the church, near the tomb of his probable first patron, which is in the south aisle. It's not clear where he would have worked inside the castle—possibly in the Morning Room. That's the place where he's remembered, anyway, for around the timbered ceiling, built around 1340, are painted a few verses from the Book of Revelation, translated from Latin into Norman French. It's just possible to make out a few words, and a helpful transcript aids the visitor. The Castle brochure says that this is a translation by Trevisa, but that is highly unlikely, as everything we know about him indicates his skills and motivation were from Latin into English.

Ranulph Higden is commemorated colourfully in a window at Chester Cathedral, where he is buried. The old Saxon church of St Werburgh, and the Benedictine abbey founded in 1092, is remembered in the name of the street outside the cathedral, and the window is in one of the walls of the scriptorium, adjoining the monastic cloisters. A monk writing in Latin hardly seems to be a candidate for visitation by an English-language tourist, but—as book dedications often say—without whom …

The Higden window at
Chester Cathedral

The location of the scriptorium at Chester Cathedral.

Wordsmiths and Warriors

Getting there

The entrance to Chester Cathedral is on St Werburgh Street (postcode: CH1 2HU), which is off Northgate Street. The nearest car park is on Princess Street, the other side of Northgate Street. On entering the cathedral, turn left out of the nave, and the scriptorium corridor with Higden's window is in front of you, adjoining the cloister garden. For opening times, see the website at

http://www.chestercathedral.com

For Berkeley, travelling north, take the M5 from Bristol to junction 14, signposted Berkeley, turn right onto the A38 to Gloucester then left at Berkeley Heath onto the B4066. If travelling south from Birmingham on the M5, leave at junction 13 signposted A419 to Stroud and Dursley, then right at the roundabout signed Berkeley and left at the A38 to Berkeley Heath. As you approach Berkeley along Canonbury Street, the entrance to the castle is on the left, just after the 30 mph signs (postcode: GL13 9PJ), with car parking outside. For St Mary's Church, continue into Berkeley, turn left into the High Street, and the church is on Church Lane, a few hundred yards on the left (postcode: GL13 9BJ). There's limited parking on the roadside. Opening times for the Castle are given at

http://www.berkeley-castle.com/visit.php

It's important to check, as it's often closed to visitors.

For Trevessa, from the south leave the A30 at the junction signposted to Newquay A3076 and St Newlyn East. At the roundabout, don't follow the A3076 but take the next turn, an unmarked country road. The privately owned house, also a listed building (postcode: TR8 5AN), is about a mile along the road on the left, just past a farm.

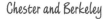

Chapter 17

Rhuddlan

the English language in Wales

In 2005 I travelled all over Wales making a programme for the BBC on the English accents and dialects of the country, as part of the BBC's ambitious *Voices* project—a nationwide investigation of English dialects in the UK. It was called *The Way That We Say It*. What struck me more than anything else was the remarkable variety of the accents we encountered—the heavily Welsh-influenced tones of the west and north-west, the accents reminiscent of Somerset in the southern valleys, of Herefordshire in the eastern marches, and of Lancashire along the northern coast, and the fascinating linguistic mix of 'little England beyond Wales' in the south-west peninsula (Chapter 18). Welsh English is a reality today. It's not as distinctive as Scots (Chapter 43), but it has a comparably long history, and it forms an important strand in the history of English in Britain.

It's usually difficult to pinpoint a moment when one language decisively influences the future of another, but in the case of English in Wales there is no problem. Which is why we went to Rhuddlan, in Denbighshire—a castle town just to the south of Rhyl. It's pronounced 'rhith-lan', with the 'th' voiced, as in *the,* and it means 'red bank' in Welsh. It was here, in 1284, that the Statute of Rhuddlan was signed, imposing English law on the Welsh. It created new counties out of the old region of Gwynedd—including Anglesey, where Hilary and I live. A new administration of English sheriffs and bailiffs was introduced. And one of the consequences was the banning of Welsh as a language for official purposes.

Page opposite. Norman soldiers still guard the entrance to Rhuddlan High Street.

The Statute remained in force for 250 years. Then in 1535–6 the status of English in Wales was confirmed by the Laws in Wales Act, whose twentieth clause stated (I have modernized the spelling):

> That all Justices, Commissioners, Sheriffs, Coroners, Escheators, Stewards, and their Lieutenants, and all other Officers and Ministers of the Law, shall proclaim and keep the Sessions Courts, Hundreds, Leets, Sheriffs Courts, and all other Courts in the *English* Tongue;
>
> and all Oaths of Officers, Juries and Inquests, and all other Affadavits, Verdicts and Wagers of Law, to be given and done in the *English* Tongue;
>
> and also that from henceforth no Person or Persons that use the *Welsh* Speech or Language, shall have or enjoy any manner Office or Fees within this Realm of *England*, *Wales*, or other the King's Dominion, upon Pain of forfeiting the same Offices or Fees, unless he or they use and exercise the *English* Speech or Language.

And that's how it stayed, for over 400 years, until, in 1967 and 1993, two Language Acts formally recognized the need to revitalize Welsh in Wales.

The Statute was signed on a site where the medieval court building, known as the Parliament House, stands today. A plaque on its gable wall states:

> THIS FRAGMENT
> IS THE REMAINS OF THE BUILDING
> WHERE KING EDWARD I HELD HIS PARLIAMENT
> A.D. 1283
> IN WHICH WAS PASSED THE STATUTE
> OF RHUDDLAN
> SECURING TO THE PRINCIPALITY OF WALES
> ITS JUDICIAL RIGHTS AND INDEPENDENCE.

The text sounds very positive, and indeed the Statute was welcomed by the Welsh gentry at the time, as it seemed to provide them with an equality with their peers across the border that had previously been missing. But for 'rights and independence' read 'duties and subservience'. The long-term consequences for Welsh were devastating, and it's only thanks to a lively 20th-century activism that the language has survived. English, on the other hand, grew to become the language of power in Wales.

Why was Rhuddlan chosen for the Statute? The town is on a hill overlooking the river Clwyd (pronounced 'kloo-id'), which a thousand years

The parliament building with its memorial plaque.

Rhuddlan Castle from across the River Clwyd.

ago emptied into the sea in a wide expanse of marshland estuary. This was the lowest fording-place into the western half of North Wales, and its strategic position made it a battleground from Anglo-Saxon times, when Offa of Mercia fought the Welsh. The Norman invasion of England (Chapter 13) was quickly followed by incursions into Wales, and the first castle at Rhuddlan was built there in 1073, at Twt Hill ('look-out hill'), just south of the present town. Its motte can still be seen.

A conveniently passing herd of cows show the relatively small size of the Norman motte at Twt Hill compared to Edward's massive fortress. The site may also have been where Llewelyn ap Gruffydd had his palace.

Further conflict between the English and the Welsh led to the campaign in 1277 by Edward I to ensure Welsh submission. A series of new castles was the outcome, first in July at Flint and a month later at Rhuddlan, designed by the leading military architect of the time, Master James of St George. Rhuddlan was modelled on the fortresses of the Holy Land, which Edward knew from his time in the Crusades. It was completed in 1282, a new town created, and the river Clwyd straightened so that the castle could receive supplies by sea.

The castle must have been a fearsome sight to medieval eyes. It's impressive still. The hilltop position makes it visible for miles around, and from its ramparts there's a commanding view of the Vale of Clwyd to the south and the river running north towards the coast. Its presence was decisive. The Welsh under Llewelyn ap Gruffydd—the 'last leader', as he's often called—were defeated the following year, and the Statute of Rhuddlan was the result.

The day we visited Rhuddlan, the local primary school, which is situated midway between the two castle sites, was holding its summer fete. We had heard the music as we went around the castle, and we saw the colourful scene as we walked towards Twt Hill. The grounds were filled with excited children and their parents and friends. A group of them started singing 'Here comes the sun', and to our delight the sun did indeed then appear —a rare phenomenon in the summer of 2012, as many of the photographs in this book illustrate. The children were into castles too—but of the bouncy kind.

Looking west from the ramparts, showing the castle's dominating position over the Vale of Clwyd and the river route to the coast.

Getting there

Travelling west along the A55, leave at junction 27 (St Asaph) and take the A525 north. At the roundabout, turn right, crossing the bridge over the River Clwyd into the town centre. Halfway up the High Street, there's a right turn into Parliament Street (Stryd y Senedd); the Parliament building is on the corner. Continue along this street to the castle entrance at the end of Castle Street, where there is a car park (postcode: LL18 5AD). For opening times, see the website at

http://cadw.wales.gov.uk/daysout/rhuddlancastle

Travelling east along the A55, leave at junction 24 signposted Rhuddlan, and follow the A547 to the roundabout, then go straight over into the town centre.

For Twt Hill, turn right outside the castle entrance into Hylas Lane (Lôn Hylas), and a few yards along on the right there is a footpath leading past the local primary school. At the end of this path is a gate into a field, and the motte is immediately in front of you.

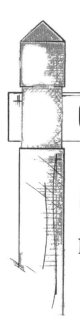

Chapter 18

Manorbier

little England beyond Wales

Of all the places I visited in Wales, when researching the programme for the BBC *Voices* project (Chapter 17), the most interesting was an area in south-east Pembrokeshire and south-west Carmarthenshire that has long been described as 'little England beyond Wales'. It earned its name for being an area that managed to preserve a distinctive English language and culture, despite being as far away from the border with England as it's possible to get. In Welsh they call it Sir Benfro Saesneg—'English-speaking Pembrokeshire'.

The name is an old one, but it's first recorded in William Camden's *Britannia* in 1607. In his section on Pembrokeshire he writes (in Latin: this translation is by Philemon Holland, with modernized spelling) of the area that the British—that is, the Welsh—call *Anglia Transwalliana*:

> That tract was inhabited by Flemings out of the Low-countries, who by the permission of King Henry the First were planted here when the Ocean, by making breaches in the banks, had overwhelmed a great part of the said Low-countries. These are distinctly known still from the Welsh, both by their speech and manners, and so near joined they are in society of the same language with Englishmen, who come nighest of any nation to the low Dutch tongue, that this their little country is termed by the Britons Little England beyond Wales. (... *ut haec eorum regiuncula a Britannis Anglia Transwallina nuncupetur.*)

Page opposite. Manorbier Castle, looking across the Bristol Channel.

He stresses the close relationship between Flemish and English. But English settlers also came to the area, and although there must have been a long period of bilingualism, eventually English became the dialect norm.

Why were the Flemings there? Camden quotes the early 12th-century chronicler William of Malmesbury, who lived at the time all this happened. In his *Gesta regum Anglorum* ('The deeds of the English Kings') he talks about William II and Henry I (reigned 1100–35):

> Many a time and often King William Rufus had but small success against the Welsh men.... But King Henry, who now reigneth, a man of an excellent wit, found means to frustrate all their devises, by placing Flemings in their Country, who might be always ready to repress and keep them in.... And resting in the end upon this good and wholesome policy for to take down and abate their swelling pride, he brought over thither all the Flemings that dwelt in England. For a number of them who in those days, in regard of his mother's kindred by her father's side, flocked thither, were closely shrouded in England, in so much as they for their multitude seemed but densome [overpopulated] unto the realm. Wherefore he sent them altogether with their substance, goods, wives, and children unto Ross a country in Wales, as it were into a common avoidance [draining], thereby both to purge and cleanse his own Kingdom, and also to quail and repress the rash boldness of his enemies there.

His mother's kindred? Henry I's mother was Matilda of Flanders.

A little later, Giraldus Cambriensis also reported the event in Chapter 11 of his *Itinerary through Wales*:

> The inhabitants of this province derived their origin from Flanders, and were sent by King Henry I to inhabit these districts; a people brave and robust, ever most hostile to the Welsh.

The antagonism seems to have lasted. George Owen, writing a *Description of Pembrokeshire* in the early 17th century, draws attention to the mutual antagonism, which is reflected in a clear linguistic divide:

> you shall find in one parish a pathway parting the Welsh and English, and the one side speak all English, the other all Welsh, and differing in tilling and in measuring of their land, and divers other matters.

He frequently refers to the physical separation as a *landsker*—from Old English *land-scearu* meaning a 'land boundary'—and in the 20th century this term came to be applied to the linguistic frontier between Welsh (to the north) and English (to the south): the Landsker Line. When we visited, people still talked about the 'up aboves' and 'down belows'.

The line has shifted a bit over the centuries, and the boundary is not always easy to define, but its impact is evident in the distribution of Welsh vs non-Welsh place names—though many of the English ones now have Welsh glosses. It's a long Line, from St Bride's Bay in the south to Carmarthen Bay in the west. For the serious walker, the Landsker Borderlands Trail is a waymarked footpath—all 58 miles (94 km) of it.

The castles dominate the region—over 50 of them, built during the 11th and 12th centuries to 'quail and repress', such as Pembroke, Haverfordwest,

Top. Dinefwr Castle, Carmarthenshire.

Bottom. Laugharne Castle, Carmarthenshire, with boats 'tilting and riding' (Chapter 54) in a low channel. The large artificial flowers adorning the castle walls are not medieval.

Gerald's description of Manorbier (*Itinerary*, Book 1, Ch 12):

It is excellently well defended by turrets and bulwarks, and is situated on the summit of a hill extending on the western side towards the sea-port, having on the northern and southern sides a fine fish-pond under its walls, as conspicuous for its grand appearance, as for the depth of its waters, and a beautiful orchard on the same side, inclosed on one part by a vineyard, and on the other by a wood, remarkable for the projection of its rocks, and the height of its hazel trees. On the right hand of the promontory, between the castle and the church, near the site of a very large lake and mill, a rivulet of never-failing water flows through a valley, rendered sandy by the violence of the winds. Towards the west, the Severn sea, bending its course to Ireland, enters a hollow bay at some distance from the castle; and the southern rocks, if extended a little further towards the north, would render it a most excellent harbour for shipping . . .

and Dinefwr. The southernmost was Laugharne. I was going to Laugharne anyway (Chapter 54), but which one to choose to represent the others? There was a linguistic reason for going first to Manorbier.

This was the birthplace of Giraldus Cambriensis—or Gerald of Wales, Gerald the Welshman (Gerallt Cymro), Gerald de Barry... He is known under several names, and had an ancestry that was both Welsh and Anglo-Norman. His kaleidoscopic career followed paths in the church, the court, and international politics (from diplomat to outlaw), but it is his work as a prolific chronicler and ethnographer that attracts linguists. He travelled the length and breadth of Ireland and Wales, and his detailed account of the journeys (written in Latin) provide unsurpassed detail about medieval life and times in these countries—and a number of comments about language.

Linguistic points keep cropping up in his two books on Wales—Welsh words are glossed, names have their etymology explored, distinctive songs are described. And he shows himself to be a philologist in spirit—though 500 years before that profession emerged in Europe. Indeed, he's sometimes been called 'the father of comparative philology'. In his *Description of Wales* (Book 1, Ch 15, translation by Richard Colt Hoare), he observes that 'almost all words in the British [i.e. Welsh] language correspond either with the Greek or Latin'. And he reflects, in *Itinerary through Wales* (Book 1, Ch 8): 'It is remarkable that so many languages should correspond in one word', and he illustrates from the words for *salt* in the languages he knows, including Greek, British, Irish, Latin, and French. He can't explain it other than ascribing the similarities to divine providence. 'If a scrupulous inquirer should ask my opinion of the relation here inserted, I answer with Augustine, "that the divine miracles are to be admired, not discussed"'.

He has things to say about English too (in *Description of Wales*, Ch 6):

> in the southern parts of England, and particularly in Devonshire, the English language seems less agreeable, yet it bears more marks of antiquity (the northern parts being much corrupted by the irruptions of the Danes and Norwegians), and adheres more strictly to the original language and ancient mode of speaking; a positive proof of which may be deduced from all the English works of Bede, Rhabanus, and king Alfred, being written according to this idiom.

He also reports, in a preface to *The Conquest of Ireland*, that he had been told by Walter Mapes, Archdeacon of Oxford, that he should get his works translated into 'the vulgar tongue', because few people understand Latin. This everyday tongue, however, was French. It would be some centuries before English was thought to be a medium for scholarly exposition.

Manorbier is an unusual castle in some ways, combining defensive and manorial functions, but it's in a striking position, overlooking the Bristol Channel, with wooded hills on each side, and the surrounding beaches and countryside have made this part of Pembrokeshire a popular tourist destination. Gerald—albeit biased—called Manorbier 'the pleasantest spot in Wales'. As we walked around, we learned that we had seen it before without realizing it, for it provided the exteriors for the 2003 film *I Capture the Castle*, and acted as Cair Paravel in the BBC adaptation of *The Chronicles of Narnia*. In one of the corridors we came face to face with an image of Aslan. And as we visited nearby Dinefwr Castle, we encountered Dr Who's Tardis. Our journey was becoming surreal.

Above and right.
The 17th-century mansion in
Dinefwr Park, with (evidently)
a time-lord choosing 2012 to
visit the Dinefwr Festival.

Wordsmiths and Warriors

Getting there

Travelling west along the A40, leave at St Clears and follow the A477 then the A478 towards Tenby. You pick up the A4139 around the edge of the town, signposted Pembroke, and a few miles along take the left turn on the B4585 down the hill into Manorbier (postcode: SA70 7SY). There's a car park below the castle, just above the beach. Walk up the hill towards the village, and you'll see a side entrance to the castle on the left. Alternatively, the front entrance to the castle is easily visible further up the hill from the centre of the village. For opening times (usually March to September), see the website at

http://www.manorbiercastle.co.uk/map.html

For Dinefwr, travelling west along the A40 towards Carmarthen, there's a brown tourist sign pointing left to Llandeilo and Dinefwr Park. Entrance to the Park is half a mile along the road, past the White Hart Inn, on the right. The postcode is SA19 6RT, but the website says not to trust it! Plenty of car parking space, but if on the field near the mansion it can be muddy. For opening times, see

http://www.nationaltrust.org.uk/dinefwr

For Laugharne, see Chapter 54.

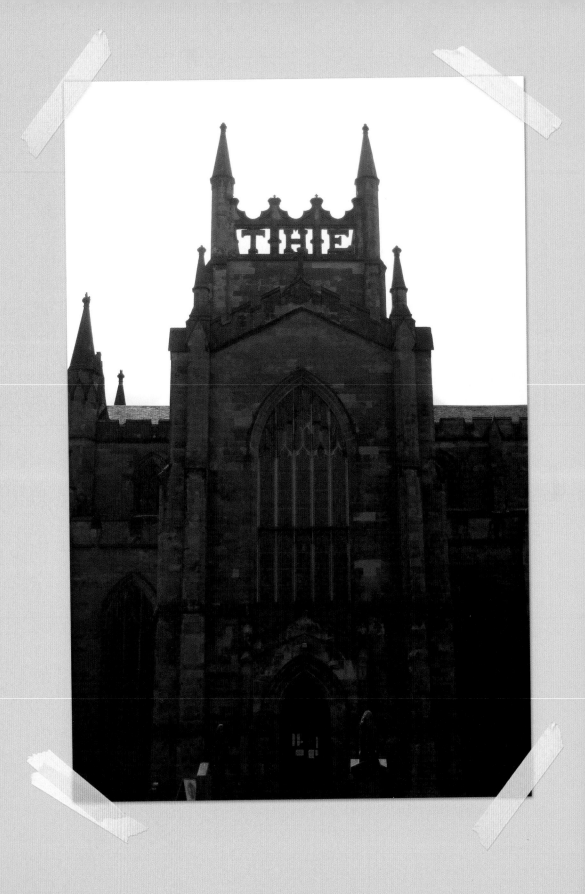

Chapter 19

Dunfermline

the birth of Scots English

At first, it looks like a monument to the definite article. As we approached Dunfermline Abbey from the High Street, there it was, an imposing THE gracing the top of the abbey church tower in large stone letters. It was only after we rounded the corner, and looked at the tower from other angles, that I realized what we were looking at: seen in sequence, the four sides of the crown of the tower read KING ROBERT THE BRUCE. The memorial reflects the discovery in 1818 of his bones during the construction of the new abbey church, and their reinterment in the centre of the building.

The Bruce is the most famous of those buried in the Abbey, but linguistically he has to take second place to King Malcolm III, who was king of Scotland between 1058 and 1093, and his second wife, Margaret (c.1045–1093), who became Saint Margaret of Scotland after her canonization in 1249. Malcolm had moved his royal court to Dunfermline from Perthshire, so that for a while the town was the country's capital. His name will be familiar to anyone who has seen Shakespeare's *Macbeth*. The play tells a very different story from what is historical fact, but the names of the monarchs are the same: Duncan (1034–40) and Macbeth (1040–57), were both grandsons of Malcolm II, and Malcolm III was the son of Duncan.

But it's Margaret who is the key player in the English-language story. She was an English princess of the House of Wessex, the granddaughter

Page opposite. Dunfermline Abbey church tower, from the High Street.

King Robert ... Bruce.

of Edmund II (Ironside) of England and the sister of Edgar the Atheling. After the Norman Conquest, she and other members of her family were forced to flee, and they took refuge in Scotland at Malcolm's court. Malcolm already spoke English, for he had been an exile in England during the reign of Macbeth, and his marriage to Margaret in *c*.1070 gave the language considerable prestige in what was a predominantly Gaelic-speaking region.

The English linguistic presence was consolidated when Margaret invited Benedictine monks from Canterbury to establish a priory at Dunfermline. Most new townships in this part of Scotland were given English names, as were the children of Margaret and Malcolm—solidly Anglo-Saxon names for the four eldest—Edward, Edmund, Ethelred, and Edgar—followed by Alexander, David, Matilda, and Mary. English became a lingua franca among the new trading settlements (or *burghs*) in the region, and these quickly grew in size, thanks to the steady number of refugees escaping from William the Conqueror's disestablishment of the Anglo-Saxon nobility, and the arrival of many Flemish and Scandinavian immigrants. By the 13th century, English had become the dominant language in the Lowland south and east, and it gradually replaced French and Latin as the language of commerce, the court, the law, and the parliament.

The dialect of English that emerged was very different from anything to be found south of the River Tweed. Its character can be seen in one of the earliest epic poems, John Barbour's *The Bruce*, written in 1375. Spellings that would eventually be viewed as distinctively Scottish are already present, such as *ane* for 'one' and *richt* for 'right', and we see local words such as *gang* 'go' and *mekill* 'great'. The language was still being called *Inglis* 'English' at the time. The term *Scottis* 'Scots' or 'Scottish' doesn't appear with reference to English (as opposed to Gaelic) until the end of the 15th century.

Without Margaret, none of this might have happened, so a visit to her locations is a must for any English-language tourist. The road from Edinburgh to Dunfermline (*dun—fiar—linne*, 'the tower by the crooked stream') has several memorials. She arranged for a ferry to transport pilgrims across the Firth of Forth (hence the town of Queensferry, near the Forth Road Bridge). Legend has it that she rested against a huge roadside stone on her way to Dunfermline in 1069, and paused at the same spot on other occasions. Another tradition says that this was

Saint Margaret's Stone is 8 ft 6 in (2.6 m) long × 4 ft 7 in (1.4 m) high × 1 ft 6 in (0.5 m) deep. The cup-shaped markings in the sandstone block are probably the result of weathering. The inscription reads:

ACCORDING TO TRADITION
MARGARET
AFTERWARDS QUEEN OF
MALCOLM CANMORE
RESTED ON THE ABOVE
STONE A.D. 1069
WHEN ON HER WAY TO
DUNFERMLINE

where she would sit to help people who would come to her with their troubles. In the course of time, the stone became a shrine, and when the road was widened in 1856 it was carefully removed for safe keeping. An information board on a wall in Saint Margaret's Cave tells you that it can now be seen in the grounds of the Carnegie Business Campus off the Queensferry Road, but this is ambiguous, as it's actually in the approach road to the Pitreavie Business Park on the other side of the road from the main campus. It looks rather incongruous, turned into a bench seat next to double-yellow lines, but its sheer size and weathered surface make it evocative still.

Saint Margaret's Cave is another odd location: in a corner of a car park near the town centre. This was the place where, according to ancient tradition, Margaret would go to pray. It was located at the bottom of a glen not far from the royal court, near a stream, and until recently could be accessed directly. But in 1962 the town council decided to infill the glen for a much-needed car park. The cave might have been completely buried, but a local outcry resulted in the construction of a tunnel access. Sections of Arnico piping were installed from the car park down to the cave—now 56 ft (17 m) below the surface—and a small entrance hut was built at the top. Information panels along the tunnel walls tell the story of the cave. At the bottom there's a statue of Margaret at prayer in her alcove, and an accompanying chant echoes along the tunnel. There are 87 steps down. And up.

The entrance to Saint Margaret's Cave, in the corner of Glen Bridge car park.

Wordsmiths and Warriors

Only fragments of the foundations of the royal court remain: 'Malcolm's Tower' in Pittencrieff Park—locally known as 'The Glen'. What dominates Dunfermline is the abbey church, with its linguistically crowned tower, next to the ruins of the abbey, built in her honour by her youngest son, who became King David I of Scotland in 1124. From the higher parts of the town, on a clear day, it's possible to see Edinburgh Castle. And this is the other important visit to make, when following in the footsteps of Margaret, for this is where Malcolm and Margaret lived in their later years. At the very top of the castle, overlooking the city, is a tiny building, said to be the oldest building in Edinburgh, known as Saint Margaret's Chapel. It can hold only around 20 people, and its narrow doorway causes a crush when tourist numbers build up.

Our arrival in Dunfermline brought us one unexpected linguistic encounter; our visit to Edinburgh gave us another. Every week of the year, flowers are placed in the chapel by members of the St Margaret's Chapel Guild—but only if their name is Margaret. I don't know of anywhere else in Britain that confers such an onomastic privilege on a name-bearer.

Above. Saint Margaret's Chapel interior is only 28 ft (8.5 m) long and 10 ft (3 m) wide. It was the only building left to stand after the capture of the Castle by the Earl of Moray in 1314. Restoration took place in stages in the 1850s and 1930s.

Overleaf. Stained-glass windows of Scottish saints and heroes, including this one of Margaret, were installed in the chapel in 1922.

Dunfermline

Getting there

From Edinburgh, cross the Forth Road Bridge and follow signs into Dunfermline along M90, then A823(M). After this becomes the A823 (Queensferry Road), turn left at a roundabout signposted Business Centre, and Saint Margaret's Stone is immediately on your right. You can't park right by it, but there are several office car parks nearby (ask permission first) as well as on the other side of the roundabout along Carnegie Avenue. It's 1.5 miles (2.4 km) south-east of the town.

For Saint Margaret's Cave, follow the A823 north round the edge of the town, under a railway bridge and into St Margaret's Drive. The signs point you to the town centre and station. Keep in the left-hand lane, signed towards the A907 (W) and East Port. Turn left at the round-about, but not sharp left towards the town centre along East Port; take the second left, along Carnegie Drive (the A907), past Debenhams. Follow the Tourist Information signs all the way around the north of the town until you see one pointing left towards a short-stay car park. This is Chalmers Street, and you take the first left into the Glen Bridge car park, which is where the entrance to Saint Margaret's Cave can be seen (postcode: KY12 8DF). Opening times for the Cave were 11 a.m. until 4 p.m., when we visited, with a closure from 12.30 to 1.

For the Abbey, turn left outside the Cave and up the St John's Vennel steps. Turn right into Bruce St, cross the High St and the Abbey is ahead of you (postcode: KY12 7PE). For opening times, see

http://www.dunfermlineabbey.co.uk

(The street name *vennel* is found in the burghs of Scotland and parts of north-east England and N. Ireland: it's from French *venelle*, 'alley'.)

Saint Margaret's Chapel is a part of Edinburgh Castle, entrance at the top of the Royal Mile (postcode: EH1 2NG). Queues for tickets to enter the Castle can be very long, especially at peak tourist times, but if you are a member of English Heritage, Historic Scotland, Cadw, or associated organizations, you can bypass the main queue and get your free ticket in the Information Centre. As you walk up the hill into the Castle under the Argyle Tower, turn sharp left up the Lang Stairs; turn right at the top, and the Chapel is in front of you, next to the huge cannon known as Mons Meg. For opening times, see

http://www.edinburghcastle.gov.uk

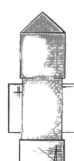

Chapter 20

Talbot Yard, London SE1

Chaucer and Middle English

At the beginning of the Prologue to his *Canterbury Tales*, Geoffrey Chaucer tells us where his band of pilgrims met:

Bifil that in that seson on a day,	*bifil*: it happened
In Southwerk at the Tabard as I lay	
Redy to wenden on my pilgrymage	*wenden*: go
To Caunterbury with ful devout corage,	*corage*: desire
At nyght was come into that hostelrye	
Wel nyne and twenty in a compaignye,	
Of sondry folk, by aventure yfalle	*aventure yfalle*: fallen by chance
In felaweshipe, and pilgrimes were they alle,	
That toward Caunterbury wolden ryde...	*wolden ryde*: intended to ride

And towards the end of the Prologue he reaffirms the location, adding a further detail:

In Southwerk at this gentil hostelrye	
That highte the Tabard, faste by the Belle.	*highte*: called

Southwark was full of inns in the 14th century, being the chief thoroughfare to and from the city of London for the southern counties and northern Europe, as well as a favourite meeting-place for pilgrims en route to

Page opposite. The memorial plaque at the site of the Tabard Inn, Southwark.

Canterbury. In John Stow's 1598 *Survey of London* (Book 4, Chapter 1) we're told that south of London Bridge 'be many fair Inns for receipt of Travellers, by these Signs, the Spur, Christopher, Bull, Queens Head, Tabard, George, Hart, Kings Head, &c.' He doesn't mention the Bell, but he does give some extra lines to the Tabard:

> The most ancient is the Tabard, so called of the Sign, which, as we now term it, is of a Jacket or sleeveless Coat, whole before, open on both sides, with a square Collar, winged at the Shoulders: a stately Garment of old time, commonly worn of Noblemen and others, both at home and abroad in the Wars; but then (to wit, in the Wars) their Arms embroidered, or otherwise depict upon them, that every Man by his Coat of Arms might be known from others.

The Tabard was bought in 1304 with a specific purpose, as Stow recalls:

> Within this Inn was also the Lodging of the Abbot of Hide (by the City of Winchester) a fair House for him and his Train, when he came to the City to Parliament, &c.

It was, in other words, the town house of the Abbot of Hyde Abbey (Chapter 9), and by Chaucer's time it had become a popular hostelry. Chaucer gives it two lines of description:

The chambres and the stables weren wyde,	*wyde*: spacious
And wel we weren esed atte beste;	*esed*: entertained

It was indeed a spacious place. It originally contained two houses and large gardens extending south and east beyond the buildings of the present-day Guy's Hospital. One house was converted for the Abbot and his retinue; the other was turned into an inn. It was the Abbot who gave the place the name by which it's now known.

When the monasteries were dissolved in 1538, the property was sold to two brothers, Thomas and John Masters, who added extensions to the inn and turned it into a prosperous business. It was destroyed in the great Southwark fire of 16 May 1676, but rebuilt five years later, the old name giving way to the phonetically similar Talbot (according to the memorial plaque, because of a mistranscription in the title deeds). By the 19th century it had become an important coaching inn, three storeys high, but it

didn't survive the coming of the railways, and it was demolished in 1876. Today, there's no sign of it, but the name lives on in Talbot Yard, a narrow alley leading off the eastern side of busy Borough High Street.

Chaucer plays a central role in any history of the English language. The point was recognized very early on. Thomas Hoccleve, who knew Chaucer, calls him 'The first fyndere of our fair langage'. And William Caxton echoes the point in his preface to his printing of *The Canterbury Tales*, when he describes the man who 'by hys labour enbelysshyd, ornated and made faire our Englisshe'. His words express a general view of the linguistic esteem in which Chaucer was held, and the widespread reading of his work that followed from the printed editions helped to form the climate out of which standard English arose.

One of the important features of the Middle English period is the way the language developed its range of styles, reflecting the social milieu. Chaucer's characters, belonging to different classes, occupations, and regional backgrounds, come alive through his use of language in a way that had not previously been seen in English. No-one else would reflect more of a country's linguistic life until Shakespeare. And when we reflect

Talbot Yard, looking south from the gateway entrance. The memorial plaque is on the left.

The Tabard site, with its plaque and historical panels.

on Chaucer's life, we can see some of the reasons. He was not only a poet; he was also a civil servant—first as a controller of customs in the port of London, later as a clerk of the king's works—as well as a soldier, diplomat, intelligence officer, and parliamentarian. He would have known the Tabard well, and seen at first hand the streams of pilgrims, and he would certainly have known the Host, Harry Bailey, who in the poem travels with the group to Canterbury.

Bailey was a real-life character. He's mentioned several times in contemporary records, and represented Southwark in parliament twice in the 1370s. This is how Chaucer describes this 'merry man':

A semely man Our Hooste was withalle	*semely*: handsome
For to han been a marchal in an halle.	*han*: have; *marchal*: marshal
A large man he was with eyen stepe—	*eyen stepe*: bulging eyes
A fairer burgeys is ther noon in Chepe—	*burgeys*: burgess; *noon*: none;
	Chepe: Cheapside
Bold of hys speche, and wys, and wel ytaught,	*wys*: wise; *ytaught*: educated
And of manhod hym lakkede right naught.	*lakkede*: lacked

Wordsmiths and Warriors

The galleried section of The George. The White Hart Inn, in the next yard, must have looked very similar, according to Charles Dickens' description in Chapter 10 of *The Pickwick Papers*:

The yard presented none of that bustle and activity which are the usual characteristics of a large coach inn. Three or four lumbering wagons, each with a pile of goods beneath its ample canopy, about the height of the second-floor window of an ordinary house, were stowed away beneath a lofty roof which extended over one end of the yard; and another, which was probably to commence its journey that morning, was drawn out into the open space. A double tier of bedroom galleries, with old clumsy balustrades, ran round two sides of the straggling area, and a double row of bells to correspond, sheltered from the weather by a little sloping roof, hung over the door leading to the bar and coffee-room. Two or three gigs and chaise-carts were wheeled up under different little sheds and pent-houses; and the occasional heavy tread of a cart-horse, or rattling of a chain at the farther end of the yard, announced to anybody who cared about the matter, that the stable lay in that direction. When we add that a few boys in smock-frocks were lying asleep on heavy packages, wool-packs, and other articles that were scattered about on heaps of straw, we have described as fully as need be the general appearance of the yard of the White Hart Inn, High Street, Borough, on the particular morning in question.

Mine Host would be unimpressed by Talbot Yard today. It's an unprepossessing alley, gloomy on a grey day, and cluttered with the back-door detritus from nearby buildings. The building identified as the one closest to the original Tabard site is Copyprints, a business centre specializing in bookbinding, photocopying, and other printing tasks. That's rather appropriate, as Chaucer used to take his scrivener Adam to task for his poor copying skills. The location has at last been officially recognized, in the form of a blue plaque, unveiled on the wall of the present building in November 2003 by the medievalist-cum-Python Terry Jones, and now given a touch of colour with a basket of flowers. A large window panel has a detailed and atmospheric historical account of the area, and how it looked a century ago.

To find a modern Host, you have to go next door, to The George—of interest in its own right, for it is London's last remaining galleried inn. The original was destroyed in the Southwark fire, but rebuilt to the same design, and is now managed by the National Trust. In Shakespeare's time, plays would have been performed in the yard beneath the galleries. He probably drank here, for the Globe was only a few hundred yards away (Chapter 31). Charles Dickens knew it well, and it even makes a brief appearance in one of his novels. In Chapter 22 of *Little Dorrit*, Maggy suggests that it's a good place for young Tip to go to write a begging letter.

Two locations for the price of one: excellent value, for the English-language tourist. But then, unexpectedly, we discovered a third. We walked from the George Inn Yard into the alleyway on its opposite side, found ourselves in White Hart Yard, and in front of us were the offices of the Royal College of Speech and Language Therapists. As Hilary trained as a speech therapist, and I spent many years working in the associated field of clinical linguistics—indeed, that is how we met—it provided a fitting ending for our visit to the haunts of this great teller of tales. Or perhaps I should say beginning, for our next stop would be Canterbury (Chapter 21).

Getting there

Talbot Yard (postcode: SE1 1YP) is a couple of minutes' walk going south along Borough High Street from London Bridge station. It's on the left, just past the entrance to White Hart Yard and the George Inn, which is at 77 Borough High Street (London SE1 1NH). The Tabard plaque is immediately visible on the left as you enter Talbot Yard. There are car parks on nearby Southwark Street, and a certain amount of metered parking in the vicinity.

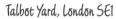

Chapter 21

Canterbury

from ancient to modern

The obvious reason for the English-language tourist to go to Canterbury is because Chaucer—or, at least, his characters—did. But Canterbury's linguistic tales go well beyond Chaucer's. In fact, I can't think of any other place in Britain which provides so many locations relevant to the whole of our period, from Old to Modern English.

Those interested in Anglo-Saxon times will pay special attention to the earliest religious settlement here, established by Augustine, the first Archbishop of Canterbury. Canterbury Christchurch Cathedral and Precinct, St Augustine's Abbey, and St Martin's Church are all now on the World Heritage list, together providing a visual record of the introduction of Christianity to Britain. St Martin's has remains of the building in which Augustine and his followers first worshipped. The present-day cathedral, begun in 1070, is on a site that Augustine chose. And the influence of the Benedictine abbey was enormous throughout the Anglo-Saxon period and beyond. Its scriptorium was a major centre of book production, and the inspiration for other centres, such as those at Jarrow and Monkwearmouth (Chapter 4).

But it was the murder in the cathedral of Archbishop Thomas Becket in 1170 that turned Canterbury into the leading place of pilgrimage in Britain, and motivated the pilgrims whose stories form the content of *The Canterbury Tales*. Their route followed the ancient Roman road, Watling Street, which ran from London through Dartford, Rochester,

Page opposite. The place to start: Canterbury Cathedral gateway.

Sittingbourne, and Faversham to Canterbury, and on to Dover. Today, the A2 covers a great deal of it, so that those wanting to walk in the footsteps of Chaucer's pilgrims have to make numerous detours.

Since the 1980s *The Canterbury Tales* have made their presence felt in the city. We called in at the visitor attraction housed in the former church of St Margaret, in St Margaret's Street, just round the corner from the High Street. The church was founded in Anglo-Saxon times, but is now home to a recreation of life in medieval England, as reflected in the tales of five of Chaucer's characters. Visitors pass through a series of rooms where they hear abridged versions of the Knight's, Miller's, Wife of Bath's, Nun's Priest's, and Pardoner's Tales, illustrated by life-size models in atmospheric settings full of sound effects. Visitors are warned in advance not to rush: it takes a leisurely hour to get around.

Page opposite. Canterbury Cathedral.

These are the must-sees of Canterbury. But there are two lesser known sites that an English-language tourist must also see. Both are near the cathedral.

Around the year 1340, Michael of Northgate, a monk of St Augustine's Abbey, wrote a prose treatise called 'Ayenbyte of Inwyt'—'Remorse of Conscience'. Today it's hardly remembered—though James Joyce used the title several times in *Ulysses*—and was never considered of great literary worth. But linguistically it's unique in Middle English, because Michael tells us everything we need to know. The author says who he is, exactly when he wrote it, and exactly where he wrote it—and affirms that the manuscript is in his own handwriting. I translate his comments from the beginning and end of the text:

A simple candle remembers Thomas Becket.

> This book is Dan Michael's of Northgate, written in English of his own hand ... and is of the book-house of Saint Austin's of Canterbury ... this book is finished on the eve of the holy apostles Simon and Jude ... in the year of our Lord's birth 1340.

That's 27th October. Additionally, in a few lines of verse at the end of his text he tells us about his local dialect: this book is written, he says, 'Mid Engliss of Kent'—in Kentish English. And indeed it is. For example, we see many words reflecting local pronunciation: an initial *z* replaces *s* and an initial *v* replaces *f*. He writes *vorzede* 'forsaid', *viftene* 'fifteen', and *vif hondred*, 'five hundred'. It's an amazing source of precise information about the English of south-east England in the 14th century. And he says he is from

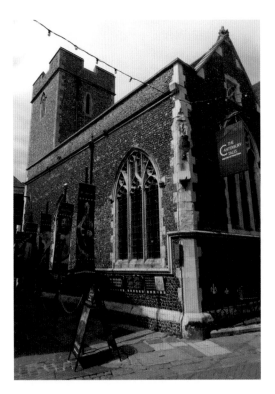 

Left. Where some of *The Canterbury Tales* are retold.

Right. The Mayflower house, with its memorial sign.

Northgate—as its name suggests, the main road into the city from the old northern gateway.

Northgate leads into a street called The Borough, and then there's a left turn into Palace Street, which winds around the western end of the cathedral. And this is where we can add an Early Modern English dimension to the city. For 59 Palace Street is the house where in 1620 one of the leading religious separatists, Robert Cushman, a Kentishman, negotiated the lease of the *Mayflower*, the ship that would carry the Pilgrim Fathers to America. The event is remembered by a large colourful sign on the wall of the building, now a café and espresso bar. For some Americans, the spot is as hallowed as the cathedral round the corner. For linguists, it's another tiny piece in the jigsaw of factors that led to American English.

Wordsmiths and Warriors

Getting there

All the locations in Canterbury are in easy walking distance from each other. The best starting place is at the cathedral (postcode: CT1 2EH). Opening times can be found at

http://www.canterbury-cathedral.org

If you face the gatehouse, you find Palace Street by following the road around to the left. Number 59 is one of the first buildings on the right. If you continue to the end of Palace Street, and bear right, The Borough leads directly into Northgate.

Back at the gatehouse, St Margaret's Street is behind you, at the other end of the short Mercery Lane. The Canterbury Tales Visitor Attraction is a little way along on the right (postcode: CT1 2TG). For opening times, see

http://www.canterburytales.org.uk

For St Augustine's Abbey, turn right at the gatehouse and go along Burgate; cross the main road (the A28), and a path leads you past St Paul's Church into Monastery Street. Turn right and follow the road left into Longport, and the walls of the abbey are ahead on your left (postcode: CT1 1PF). For opening times, see the website at

http://www.canterbury.co.uk/Canterbury-St-Augustine's-Abbey/details/?dms=13&venue=3030380

In 2012 it was closed on Mondays and Tuesdays.

There's no parking at these sites, but there's a large car park at the end of Burgate on the A28 and another directly opposite the abbey site entrance.

Chapter 22

Cursitor Street, London EC4

Chancery and standard English

It's the street names in this part of London that give the game away. And the restaurant names. Cursitor Street. Rolls Court. Chancery Lane. The Six Clerks. The Chancery. It's this last word that turns up repeatedly in histories of English, because of the way the practices of the Chancery scribes exercised an influence on the development of the standard language.

After the Norman Conquest, the first great judicial court in England was the King's Court, in which the monarch moved round the country to deal out justice. This awkward system came to an end in 1215, when provision 17 of the Magna Carta required that 'common pleas shall not follow our court, but shall be held in some fixed place'. The growth of London-based permanent offices for the civil service was an immediate consequence.

The King's Court was eventually replaced by a system of common-law courts, housed in Westminster Hall, and one of these was the Court of Chancery—so named, because it was presided over by the Lord Chancellor. Chancery Lane was once called Chaunceler Lane, and it became the record-keeping centre for government and the courts. The central building was originally an almshouse for converted Jews, but in 1377 Edward III gave it to the newly created office of Master of the Rolls [i.e. records] of Chancery, and the place became a storehouse for legal documents. In due course it was the site of the Public Record Office.

A Cursitor Street still exists, on the east side of Chancery Lane. Cursitors were the lowest level of Chancery clerks—though still commanding great professional respect, for it took a seven-year apprenticeship to become one. The name comes from a Latin word for 'messenger', but it also reflects the

Page opposite. Cursitor Street, showing The Chancery restaurant on the corner of Took's Court. It was renamed Cook's Court in Bleak House.

The eastern end of the mid-19th-century Maughan Library, today a library of King's College London, and formerly the home of the Public Record Office. The history is reflected in the name of the street: Rolls Buildings.

fact that the writs they dealt with were *de cursu* ('as a matter of course')—in other words, they were routine official matters relating to the various English counties. There were 24 cursitors, and that number remained constant until the office was abolished in the 19th century. At first they had to write out the writs themselves, but eventually the workload became so great that they had to appoint assistants. They worked from extensive premises in what is now Cursitor Street.

Another important group of people were the scriveners—scribes originally known as the Writers of the Court Letter of the City of London, who became the Worshipful Company of Scriveners in 1373. The ancestors of modern public notaries, they would witness the making of wills, charters, and other legal deeds. They needed a good knowledge of language, as

Wordsmiths and Warriors

evidenced in a revision of their ordinances in 1498. Every apprentice was to be tested by the wardens to ensure he had 'posityf gramer'—a satisfactory knowledge of grammar. The ordinance even lists some of the terms the apprentice needed in order to be 'competently erudite and lerned', such as declensions, genders, preterites, and supines. The fine for failing to observe this rule was considerable: a hundred shillings. They took grammar seriously in those days.

All these professionals, and others (such as the stationers and publishers), were intimately involved with the way the written language appeared in public. Nor must we forget the teachers of the main grammar schools in London (p. 198), for this is where the apprentices were sent if their work fell below the expected standard. So it is not surprising to see shared usages gradually emerge over the course of the 15th century. We see them chiefly in the spellings. Whereas in the 14th century there were many variants of common words, during the 15th we see a noticeable standardizing trend. Medieval spellings began to look modern: for example, *bot, wich, ony,* and *nat* became routinely *but, which, any,* and *not.* The word-endings *-li* and *-cion* (*onli, discrecion*) changed to *-ly* and *-tion.* There was still much variation, but modern standard English orthography owes a great deal of its character to the decisions made by Chancery scribes.

The legacy of the scribes lasted for centuries, and eventually earned its place in literature. It is in Cursitor Street where 'Mr Snagsby, law-stationer, pursues his lawful calling' (Charles Dickens, *Bleak House,* Chapter 10).

Getting there

The nearest underground station is Chancery Lane. Leave via exit 3, and walk towards Holborn, Chancery Lane is second on the left, and Cursitor Street is a little way down on the left (postcode: EC4A 1LL). At the end of Cursitor Street is a passage (Greystoke Place) which leads to Fetter Lane. Turn right, and Rolls Buildings and the Maughan Library are on the right (postcode: EC4A 1NL).

Chapter 23

Tothill Street, London SW1

Caxton and printing English

We know roughly where William Caxton set up his printing press in 1476, because he tells us. One of his first advertising placards has survived, and in it, in bold black lettering, Caxton instructs his hoped-for purchaser how to find his newly printed books:

> late [let] hym come to westmonster in to the almonesrye at the reed pale and he shal have them good chepe.

The 'Red Pale' was the name of Caxton's house. It stood in Little Dean Street, on the north side of the Almonry, next to Westminster Abbey and backing onto a house that was on the south side of Tothill Street. Along with the other almshouses, it was demolished in the 19th century, but accounts tell us that it was a three-storeyed building of brick, timber, and plaster.

Why did Caxton set up his press in Westminster, outside the city of London? When he was an apprentice with the Mercers' Company, he had lived in the city, so why didn't he return there? We might expect a start-up businessman to look for premises in the commercial centre. And an almonry—a place where alms were given out each day to the needy—doesn't sound like a promising location.

But for an astute businessman with an eye on patronage and aristocratic purchasers of the new product, Westminster was the obvious place to be. The royal court was nearby, and the buildings in and around the Palace of Westminster were becoming not only the seat of government but also the

Page opposite. William Caxton is said to have been buried in the cemetery now covered by the greensward in front of St Margaret's Church, Westminster.

site of the chief law courts of the land. Note that his advertisement asks people to call in to his bookshop. This would have been an easy matter for those who would have been in attendance at the many official events nearby. It would have been much more difficult if the shop had been a mile away in the city, and Caxton would have had to cope with the cost and logistics of book distribution.

Westminster Abbey precinct was a good site, containing lots of shops. Think of it as the equivalent of a modern out-of-town mall. But more important, for an up-and-coming printer, there was a goodly supply of manuscripts nearby. The abbey had an important scriptorium, which could provide texts and commissions, and the (limited) evidence suggests that Caxton was on good terms with the abbot and scribes. In his preface to *Eneydos*, he tells us 'my lorde Abbot of Westmynster ded [did] do shewe to me late certayn evydences wryton in olde Englysshe for to reduce it into our Engylysshe now usid'. And one of his earliest texts was an indulgence, presumably commissioned by the abbey, printed in 1476. Indulgences were popular documents, for they guaranteed a lessening of any punishment due to a sinner after death—as long as there was repentance (and payment). Labour-intensive to produce in handwriting, a printer could provide hundreds a day, with a space left for the name of the recipient—a boon to the hard-pressed abbey scribes.

Caxton earns his place in any English-language history for the printing tradition that he established, which fostered the emergence of a standard English in Britain. He introduced several features which would eventually help to shape the language, such as his decision to modernize the orthography, getting rid of the distinctive Old English letters, his addition of punctuation marks, and his use of spellings which had a great deal in common with those preferred by the Chancery scriveners (Chapter 22). But it takes the best part of a century before we see significant levels of standardization in printed books.

It's difficult now to imagine the situation he faced. He was a Kentish man, brought up in a dialect at some remove from that of London. He had to handle material from native and foreign sources, in manuscripts which displayed a great deal of scribal variation. He wasn't a writer, yet he had to act as an editor as well as a publisher and printer, with no-one to turn to for help. Nor was he a linguist, yet he had to cope with a rapidly changing language, and readers who were beginning to have views about what was 'good' and 'bad' English. His staff could be of little linguistic help, for they were from abroad, and they didn't know English well. Indeed, some of the language's irregular spellings come from the way they introduced foreign practices into English words—such as inserting an *h* into words like *ghost*.

Before arriving in London, Caxton had developed his abilities as a printer in northern Europe. He arrived in Westminster from Bruges, probably in the summer of 1476, bringing his assistant Wynkyn de Worde, a pile of manuscripts, and two sets of type with him. The abbey records show that he took a shop in the precincts in 1476–7 at a rent of ten shillings a year (half a modern pound). His business seems to have grown, for the records show him taking a second shop in 1483—but presumably a much smaller one, for the rent was only 2 shillings and 6 pence (an eighth of a modern pound). There is even mention of a third shop allotted to him, in 1486–8, but it seemed to have stayed empty, for no rent was paid. Doubtless there were several fluctuations in the success of the business during that first decade.

Where were these shops? The references are always somewhat vague, but they point to a location between Tothill Street and Victoria Street, about 300 yds (275 m) west of the abbey's Great West Door. This is where the Westminster Palace Hotel used to be, built in 1861, one of the most luxurious hotels in London at the time. The owners were aware of the site's history, for they had a statue of Caxton placed in the entrance hall. But the hotel eventually became offices, then was demolished. In front of the present-day building there is only an open space, marked off by bollards.

The site of the printing-house: somewhere between Tothill Street (left) and Victoria Street (right).

To find a Caxton memorial you have to cross the road to the abbey, where there's a statue on the north transept, along with the mythical Matthew of Westminster, carved by Nathaniel Hitch. Inside the abbey there's a white stone tablet on the wall just outside Poets' Corner door. The inscription reads:

1476 Near this place William Caxton set up the first printing press in England. This stone was placed here to commemorate the great assistance rendered to the Abbey Appeal Fund by the English speaking press throughout the world. 1954

We weren't allowed to photograph it, unfortunately.

Caxton was buried in the churchyard of St Margaret's, next to the abbey—now the grassed-over area between the church and Parliament Square. In the church there used to be a stained-glass window representing Caxton and his press, but this was destroyed by a bomb blast in 1940. However, a memorial tablet was placed there by the Roxburghe Club in 1882:

TO THE MEMORY
OF WILLIAM CAXTON.
WHO FIRST INTRODUCED INTO GREAT BRITAIN
THE ART OF PRINTING;
AND WHO, A.D. 1477, OR EARLIER,
EXERCISED THIS ART
IN THE ABBEY OF WESTMINSTER.
THIS TABLET
IN REMEMBRANCE OF ONE
TO WHOM
THE LITERATURE OF HIS COUNTRY
IS SO LARGELY INDEBTED,
WAS RAISED
ANNO DOMINI MDCCCXX

You never quite know where a memorial to Caxton is going to turn up. There's one in Glasgow to him and Gutenberg, sculpted by John Mossman, at the Glasgow Herald Building in Buchanan Street. There's a wonderfully meditative one above one of the pillars in the John Rylands Library in Manchester. And a statue by Paul Raphael Montford is on the side wall of the Victoria and Albert Museum in London—one of a series remembering ten craft workers of Britain, from St Dunstan to William Morris. There isn't one on the exact spot where his office was, though. Maybe one day.

Getting there

The nearest tube station to Tothill Street is Westminster. Cross the road and walk around Parliament Square to Victoria Street, keeping St Margaret's Church and Westminster Abbey on your left. As you reach the main door of the abbey, you see the junction of Victoria Street and Tothill Street immediately in front of you (postcode: SW1P 3PA).

The front entrance to St Margaret's Church is facing Tothill Street. The east door is opposite the Houses of Parliament. The memorial panel is on your immediate left as you enter the church. For opening times for the abbey and the church, see

http://www.westminster-abbey.org/visit-us/opening-times

The Victoria and Albert Museum is a five-minute walk from South Kensington underground station. It's on the main A4 route into London from the west (postcode: SW7 2RL). Go up Exhibition Road, keeping the V&A on your right, and the Caxton statue is on its upper storey a little way along, the third figure from the left.

Chapter 24

St Albans

Juliana Berners and collective nouns

There's a conspicuous absence of women in the history of the English language. We might not expect there to be many female warriors, but why so few female wordsmiths? In the early days, as several chapters in this book show, what information we can deduce about the language comes from the hands of the monks. The nuns make no contribution, until we encounter the 15th-century prioress, Juliana Berners. She can claim to be the first female lexicologist of English. If she existed.

All we have to go on is a work which was printed in St Albans, Hertfordshire, by an anonymous schoolmaster in 1486. It was called (in modern spelling) 'The book of hawking, hunting, and blazing of arms', and is generally known as *The Book of St Albans*. It's a miscellany—a compilation of treatises about outdoor pursuits, heraldry, and folklore, some of which is a translation from French. A second edition, printed in 1496 by Wynken de Worde, adds a section on fishing. The name 'Dam Julyans Barnes' appears at the head of the section on hunting in the first edition. It's spelled Bernes in the second. That's all we have to go on.

This is one of the first English printed books, and is linguistically interesting because it contains the first recorded instances of around 200 words. Several are to be found in a fascinating list of collective nouns. Collectives are nouns which express the notion of a 'group' of things, as in *a flock of sheep* and *a herd of cows*. These are the uninteresting examples. The collectives that catch the attention are those which provide an ingenious or

Page opposite. The walls of Lee Hall may reflect the dimensions of the original church at Sopwell Nunnery.

humorous description. Competitions today produce such playful creations as *an absence of waiters* or *a rash of dermatologists*.

The Book of St Albans shows how it's done. Its pages contain the first collection of its kind, with dozens of examples. Alongside *a muster of peacocks, an exalting of larks, a charm of goldfinches*, and *a watch of nightingales*, we find *a school of clerks, a doctrine of doctors, a sentence of judges*, and *a diligence of messengers*. Some are really quite naughty: *a damning of jurors, a prudence of vicars, a superfluity of nuns*, and *a nonpatience of wives*.

Where in St Albans might such a book have been compiled? Some of it was probably put together at the printer's. But if a 'Dame' was involved— the usual way of describing the superior of a nunnery—where would she have lived? The obvious candidate is Sopwell Nunnery on the outskirts of St Albans. According to legend, two local women lived here as hermits, their piety impressing the Abbot of St Albans, who around 1140 established a nunnery dedicated to St Mary. It was called Sopwell after the spring in which the women dipped their bread.

Dame Juliana could have been prioress there. The annoying thing is that the records for that period of the priory are lost. Some later writers do mention her. For example, she figures in a list of British authors compiled by Bishop John Bale in the 1540s: he says she flourished in 1460 and he assigns the whole *Book of St Albans* to her. Another reference identifies her as the daughter of Sir James Berners, who held huge estates in nearby Essex during the reign of Richard II.

Modern literary historians have been sceptical. Some argue that the Book is a compilation of older manuscripts, put together by the printer as a money-raising manual for the gentry. Some even think that the surname is a pseudonym, given that a *berner* in Middle English was an attendant in charge of a pack of hounds. But the puzzle remains: why was a female name mentioned at all? And why make her title of Dame so explicit? If someone was indeed publishing a pseudonymous work for such a masculine set of pursuits, it's unlikely that they would have chosen the name of a woman, and moreover a nun. I think she existed, and did write at least some of the Book. So we went to St Albans.

Not that there's much to see. Nothing now remains of Sopwell Priory, though its site is well remembered, half a mile south-west of the present St Albans Abbey. First impressions are misleading, however. Visitors see some splendid ruined walls—but they are not the priory. They are the remains of a mansion built around 1560 by Sir Richard Lee, one of Henry VIII's advisers, and a bailiff of the priory during the dissolution of the monasteries. He bought the site from the Crown for £13 and 6 shillings,

flattened the remains of the priory, and built a two-storey house on top, roughly following the monastic plan, with the church area becoming his Great Hall. He called it Lee Hall. It was never completed, and records suggest that it soon began to decay. Representations of the building from the 18th century show it in a very poor state. Only the ruins of one wing and parts of the hall now survive, along with some of the boundary wall and gatehouse.

Above. Lee Hall ruins from Cottonmill Lane.

Today the earlier foundation is remembered in the name of the locality: Sopwell Nunnery Green Space. The River Ver runs along the northern and eastern boundaries, with a boardwalk trail. To the east of the ruins is a country wildlife site consisting of woodland and allotments. A noticeboard lists some of the birds, insects, reptiles, and plants that can be seen at

Below. The course of the River Ver through St Albans is carved into this riverside bench.

various times of the year. Collective nouns abound. They've called this part
of the space Nunnery Allotments. Nearby roads include Nunnery Stables
and Nuns Lane. Dame Juliana would have been delighted.

Getting there

Sopwell Nunnery Green Space is on Cottonmill Lane, which is about half a mile south-east of St Albans' city centre. From the railway station it's a ten-minute walk along Prospect Road into Cottonmill Lane. Driving from the A414, turn left at the London Colney roundabout along the A1081 (London Road) signposted St Albans. At some traffic lights there's a left turn into Mile House Lane, signposted Sopwell. This takes you under a railway bridge and across a mini-roundabout; and just past Sopwell House Hotel you enter Cottonmill Lane. You know you're getting close when you pass Nuns Lane, Abbots Avenue, Priory Walk, and Monks Close: the ruins are a little way along on the right (postcode: AL1 2BY). There's limited parking on Cottonmill Lane.

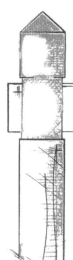

Chapter 25

Paston

a family of letters

To get to Paston, enter Norfolk and point the car in the general direction of Oslo. Norfolk roads seem to go on for ever, but eventually you will reach the North Sea. And just before you do, along the B1159 coast road that runs south of Cromer, between the small villages of Mundesley and Bacton, you go through the even smaller village of Paston.

The village lies in the heart of Norfolk's experiment to introduce Quiet Lanes in the north-east of the county—the first British county to do so. The system was introduced in 2000, and covers around a third of the roads in the area. These are country roads where motorists are asked to take special care in the presence of cyclists, walkers, and horseriders. You can't miss them, as the finger signposts all say 'Via Quiet Lanes', and there are special signs showing where they start and finish. All this I learned later. As we had never driven across this corner of the county nor seen such signs before, we weren't sure what they meant, so we spoke in a whisper as we approached Paston's church, in case a traffic warden would suddenly accuse us of talking too loudly.

The Paston name resonates immediately for anyone who has studied the English literature of the late Middle Ages, because they will have heard of the Paston Letters. This is the name given to the large collection of correspondence and associated papers written by members of a family who lived in this part of Norfolk during the 15th century, and who rose from peasantry to gentry in three generations, with connections to the junior aristocracy. The first members of the dynasty took the name of the place where they lived as their identifier (as in the 13th-century Geoffrey de Paston), and this

Page opposite. Some of the Quiet Lanes of north-east Norfolk.

eventually became a surname—a common medieval practice. The name *Paston* originally meant a settlement or estate of pasture land.

The earliest peasant about whom something is known was Clement Paston, who had a smallholding of about 100 acres at the beginning of the 15th century. He scraped together enough to send his son William to school, and the boy grew up to become a successful lawyer and—in the year of the Battle of Agincourt, 1415—a justice of the peace, later a judge. William bought a great deal of land in the area, married well, and left a valuable estate to his children. John Paston, his eldest son, also became a lawyer, as well as an MP, and was often in London. The correspondence between him and his wife, Margaret, and between her and her two eldest

THE PASTON FAMILY IN THE 15TH CENTURY

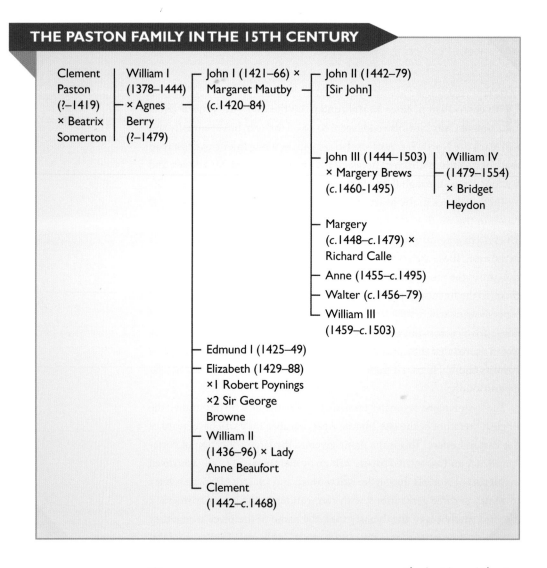

Clement Paston (?–1419) × Beatrix Somerton

William I (1378–1444) × Agnes Berry (?–1479)

John I (1421–66) × Margaret Mautby (c.1420–84)

John II (1442–79) [Sir John]

John III (1444–1503) × Margery Brews (c.1460-1495)

William IV (1479–1554) × Bridget Heydon

Margery (c.1448–c.1479) × Richard Calle

Anne (1455–c.1495)

Walter (c.1456–79)

William III (1459–c.1503)

Edmund I (1425–49)

Elizabeth (1429–88) ×1 Robert Poynings ×2 Sir George Browne

William II (1436–96) × Lady Anne Beaufort

Clement (1442–c.1468)

Wordsmiths and Warriors

sons, both called John, who were also often away on business, provide the majority of the letters.

Naming two sons by the same first name is virtually unknown today, but in medieval times it happened quite often, for it was common to name a first son after the father and a second after a grandfather. In this case, we have a 'John son of John' and a 'John grandson of John (Mautby)', the maternal grandfather. Doubtless the family had pet ways of distinguishing the two, but for editors of the letters it would prove something of a problem, solved only by calling the father 'John I', and the two sons 'John II' and 'John III' respectively.

The Paston Letters are a remarkable collection. Written between the 1420s and early 1500s, they offer invaluable insights into a turbulent period which included the Wars of the Roses, as well as major social events such as the arrival of printing in England. Not that the major political upheavals loom large in the writing. The letters for the most part deal with private matters—children, relationships, business dealings, local crime, the dangers of the plague, lawsuits, and conflicts over land with the local nobility. Reading the letters written in the middle years of the century, you would hardly know there was a civil war going on.

It is the domestic character of the letters which makes them important, for they give us one of the earliest opportunities to observe an informal level of writing in English between people who were forming a new 'middle' class of literate landed gentry. Many letters are by the women of the family—a significant development in an age when correspondence was the prerogative of upper-class men or male scribes. The sentences are long and loosely structured, plainly representing an outpouring of thoughts such as would occur had the content been spoken aloud. Punctuation is idiosyncratic, reflecting a time before the present-day conventions developed (I've modernized the spelling and punctuation in the extracts below). There are even examples of the most colloquial kind of English, such as the nonsense words we make up when we can't remember something. John II writes to John III in November 1473 and uses the equivalent of modern 'whatchamacallit':

Now bear the cup even, as what-call-you-him said to Aslake.

It's the first recorded example of such a word in English.

The men of the family were all anxious to make good (i.e. wealthy) marriages, so when John III met 17-year-old Margery Brews, there was a problem. The couple seemed to have a genuine mutual affection, and the two families approved of the match, but John III felt that Margery's father,

Sir Thomas Brews, should give her a larger dowry; Sir Thomas, on the other hand, felt the Pastons were expecting too much, for he had to keep money back for his other children. He writes: 'I would be very loath to bestow so much on one daughter that her other sisters would do worse'. The correspondence surrounding the match makes for fascinating reading, and two of the letters from Margery to John have rightly become famous. These are the letters written on Valentine's Day 1477, dictated by Margery to her secretary–scribe, Thomas Kela. It's not clear which was written first, but both express her love, and her hope that money won't get in the way of the match. She writes to her 'well-beloved Valentine' to say:

> if that you could be content with that good [money] and my poor person, I would be the merriest maiden on ground [earth]. And if you think not yourself so satisfied, or that you might have much more good [money], as I have understood by you before—good, true, and loving Valentine—that you take no such labour upon you as to come more for that matter, but let it pass, and never more to be spoken of, as I may be your true lover [friend] and beadswoman [petitioner] during my life.

It all ended well, but it took an intervention from Margaret Paston to sort things out. She arranged a house for the couple, and the marriage went ahead. It seems to have remained a love-match. A few years later, 1481, Margery writes to her husband about local affairs, and ends her letter with a lovelorn plea:

> I pray you if you tarry long at London that it will please [you] to send for me, for I think [it is] long since I lay in your arms.

The heartstrings echo down the centuries.

The Pastons lived and worked and wrote their letters in several parts of Norfolk—a plaque at 20 Elm Hill, Norwich shows one such house—but their line certainly began in this village, with Wulstan, who arrived from France soon after the Battle of Hastings. He was the cousin of William de Glanville, the founder of Bromholm Priory, a few miles away at Bacton, and he received a grant of land at Paston. As you enter the village from the north along the B road, you can't miss their presence, thanks to the surviving great barn, constructed in 1581. Behind it, there's the modern Paston Hall, on the site of the original hall built by William I. And just beyond the barn is the 14th-century parish church of St Margaret. The barn isn't open to the public, thanks to the presence of a colony of rare bats, but the church is home to a small but thriving congregation.

Wordsmiths and Warriors

The imposing monument by Nicholas Stone to Katherine Paston, who died in 1628. The inscription on the pedestal (here with spelling modernized) is by John Donne, poet and dean of St Paul's in London:

Can a man be silent and not praises find
For her that lived the praise of woman kind
Whose outward frame was lent the world to guess
What shapes our souls shall wear in happiness
Whose virtue did all ill so oversway
That her whole life was a communion day.

From the road, there appears to be no church door. You have to walk around the building to the other side to get in. This is because the course of the road was diverted in the 1440s from the south to the north side of the church, and the porch faces where the old road used to be. Inside, you find monuments to members of the family at the east end of the building, past the rood screen. Most are memorials to later generations of Pastons,

from the 17th century, but there are three tomb-chests, and the one under the main altar is thought to be that of John I. He was originally buried in Bromholm Priory, but his tomb was moved to St Margaret's when the priory was closed in the 1530s. His funeral made headlines at the time. It took three days of preparation, and during the event people drank 14 barrels of beer, 27 barrels of ale, and 15 gallons of wine, and ate a huge amount of food, including 41 pigs, 49 calves, and 1300 eggs. A sum of £20 in gold was changed into small coins for—as the writer puts it—'showering among the attendant throng'. The beautifully proportioned church, a Grade I listed building, with its ongoing programme of restoration, could do with such benefactions today.

In July 1470 Margaret Paston writes to John II, full of anxiety, begging him to come home to help look after the property, as there has been a great deal of local trouble. She reflects: 'I pray God we may be in quiet and in rest with our own from henceforth.' I thought of these words as we approached the Quiet Lanes of Paston.

The altar cloths cover a tomb chest thought to be that of John I Paston.

Getting there

Paston is on the B1159 travelling south from Cromer, and the Paston buildings can be found at NR28 9TA. There's no direct road from Norwich. The best way is to aim for North Walsham. From there you have a choice: either take the road towards Mundesley and turn right when you see the sign to Paston along Quiet Lanes; or take the road towards Bacton and turn left when you reach the B1159, signposted Paston. The Bacton route takes you past Bromholm. If you want to see the remains of the priory where John I was originally buried, turn right along the B1159 towards Walcott, and then first right into Abbey Street. The ruins are in front of you at the top of the street.

The Paston Letters are housed in the British Library, 96 Euston Road, London NW1 2DB. A collection of the letters may be found online at

http://quod.lib.umich.edu/cgi/t/text/text-idx?c=cme; idno=Paston

Page opposite. Carved pew end showing the Paston coat-of-arms. The dots above the six fleurs-de-lys represent the family wealth.

Chapter 26

Lutterworth

John Wycliffe and Bible translation

As we entered Lutterworth, in Leicestershire, from the south, we encountered a name beginning with W, but it was not John Wycliffe (1324–84). It was Frank Whittle, the inventor of the jet engine. A model of the Gloster E.28/39, Britain's first jet aeroplane, dominates the roundabout. A monument to Wycliffe does exist, but we had to wind our way through the back of the town to find it. It is a stone obelisk on a granite plinth at the corner of Bitteswell Road and George Street. And one of the marble panels gives the reason for his inclusion in this book:

>THE
>MORNING STAR
>OF THE REFORMATION
>THE FIRST TRANSLATOR
>OF THE BIBLE
>INTO THE
>ENGLISH LANGUAGE

The lettering, recording the reformer's achievements together with relevant biblical verses, has been picked out in gold. Appropriately, the national headquarters of the Gideons organization, which distributes bibles to schools and hotels, is just a few yards away.

The monument was erected in 1897, the year of Queen Victoria's diamond jubilee, next to the Wycliffe Memorial Methodist Church. The people of the town evidently felt that it was time for its most famous resident—he

Page opposite. The Wycliffe Monument in Lutterworth.

was rector of the parish church of St Mary during the last decade of his life—to receive some physical recognition. It took them 500 years, but still …

The thought of any sort of monument would have been inconceivable to his contemporaries. One of the first things a visitor to St Mary's sees inside the church is the Wycliffe Memorial, in the south aisle. It shows Wycliffe preaching to local people, while two mendicant friars behind him regard him with some suspicion. The inscription beneath says it all, though it reads somewhat uncomfortably in these more ecumenical days:

SACRED TO THE MEMORY OF / JOHN WICLIF / EARLIEST CHAMPION OF ECCLESIASTICAL REFORMATION IN ENGLAND. / HE WAS BORN IN YORKSHIRE IN THE YEAR 1324. / IN THE YEAR 1375 HE WAS PRESENTED TO THE RECTORY OF LUTTERWORTH: / WHERE HE DIED ON THE 31ST DECEMBER 1384. / AT OXFORD HE ACQUIRED NOT ONLY THE RENOWN OF A CONSUMMATE SCHOOLMAN, / BUT THE FAR MORE GLORIOUS TITLE OF THE EVANGELIC DOCTOR. / HIS WHOLE LIFE WAS ONE IMPETUOUS STRUGGLE AGAINST THE CORRUPTIONS / AND ENCROACHMENTS OF THE PAPAL COURT, / AND THE IMPOSTURES OF ITS DEVOTED AUXILIARIES, THE MENDICANT FRATERNITIES. / HIS LABOURS IN THE CAUSE OF SCRIPTURAL TRUTH WERE CROWNED BY ONE IMMORTAL ACHIEVEMENT, / HIS TRANSLATION OF THE BIBLE INTO THE ENGLISH TONGUE. / THIS MIGHTY WORK DREW ON HIM, INDEED, THE BITTER HATRED / OF ALL WHO WERE MAKING MERCHANDIZE OF THE POPULAR CREDULITY AND IGNORANCE: / BUT HE FOUND AN ABUNDANT REWARD IN THE BLESSINGS OF HIS COUNTRYMEN, OF EVERY RANK AND AGE, / TO WHOM HE UNFOLDED THE WORDS OF ETERNAL LIFE. / HIS MORTAL REMAINS WERE INTERRED NEAR THIS SPOT: BUT THEY WERE NOT ALLOWED TO REST IN PEACE / AFTER THE LAPSE OF MANY YEARS, HIS BONES WERE DRAGGED FROM THE GRAVE, AND CONSIGNED TO THE FLAMES; / AND HIS ASHES WERE CAST INTO THE WATERS OF THE ADJOINING STREAM.

That would be the River Swift.

What caused such an outcry? Wycliffe's political and religious views were highly controversial. He argued that the Church should be disendowed of its property, attacked episcopal privileges, rejected papal authority, and denied the doctrine of transubstantiation. Caught up in the reaction which

Wordsmiths and Warriors

followed the Peasants' Revolt of 1381, he was expelled as a preacher from Oxford, his writings were banned, and his manuscripts burned.

His followers—members of the order of Poor Preachers (or Lollards, as they were rudely nicknamed—the word is from Dutch, meaning 'mumblers') enthusiastically took his translation to all parts of the country. Their success can be measured by the number of manuscripts (around 200) which have survived. No English text would have reached so many people before.

Wycliffe was especially concerned that lay people should be able to read the Bible in their own language. If the people of France can have the Bible in French, he argued, why not in England? And if the Lord's Prayer can be heard in English in the York Plays, why not the whole Gospel? 'Christ and his apostles taught the people in the tongue that was most known to the people', he wrote. 'Why should not men do so now?' And so his project began.

In fact he inspired two projects. The first translation appeared around the year 1382; the second, after his death, around 1388. It's not known just how much of the earlier translation he carried out himself, and there are many differences between the two versions. But the texts contain a huge amount of innovative vocabulary. The *Oxford English Dictionary* has over 1100 entries whose first usage is recorded in one or other of the translations, such as *actor, money-changer, neckerchief, observation*, and *reprehensible*. Only about half of the first usages actually remain in Modern English—*acception*,

The Wycliffe memorial at the east end of the south aisle, by Richard Westmacott the Younger, dated 1837.

aftercoming, and *aloneness* are some of those that didn't survive—but 500+ additions to English vocabulary is still quite a contribution.

He was writing at a time when there was no standard form of English in Britain. Scribes wrote in their own dialects, and spelled words in individual ways. There were huge differences between one part of the country and another. But as the need for nationwide communication grew, and the population became more literate, a standard variety of the language did slowly evolve. It was shaped partly by the way scribes worked in the civil service (Chapter 22), partly by literary models, such as that provided by Chaucer (Chapter 20), and partly by important texts, of which none was more important than the Bible. Wycliffe's role in the story of standard English is limited, but shouldn't be ignored. It's the dialect of his area, the East Midlands, which more than any other shaped the form of this standard.

Echoes of his presence permeate St Mary's. A famous portrait hangs at the rear of the church. There are fragments of his cape on display. His font is still there, as is a table made from the sounding board of his pulpit. What is original and what is a later addition is sometimes a matter of dispute, but there's no doubting the Wycliffe door—the door through which he was carried after suffering a stroke while leading a service. (He died two days later.) And near the main communion table is the chair which is said

to have carried him out. There's no record of where in the church he was
buried, before his remains were removed. It was probably in the chancel.

And he is present outside too. On the way to the church we passed a
Wycliffe House and the Wycliffe Medical Practice, and walked along
Wycliffe Terrace. His surname is prominent on a car showroom. And just
across the main road from the church is the Wycliffe Industrial Estate. The
name of Whittle is far less in evidence. Biblical linguistics, for once, wins.

Left. Wycliffe's door.

Right. Wycliffe's chair.

Getting there

Lutterworth is well signposted from both the M6 and M1. From the M6,
leave at junction 1 and go north along the A426. This takes you into the
High Street, and Church Street is on your left, leading to St Mary's. There
is parking in sites behind the Greyhound Coaching Inn. From the M1
leave at junction 20 and follow the A4303 to the roundabout, where you
turn right and join the A426 just before the High Street. The church is a
short walk away, at the end of Church Street, where the road becomes
Church Gate (postcode: LE17 4AN). The memorial is on the corner of
Bitteswell Road (postcode: LE17 4EZ). There's a car park opposite.

Chapter 27

North Nibley

William Tyndale and the English Bible

The English language can keep you fit. We arrived at this conclusion after visiting North Nibley in South Gloucestershire. Whichever way you approach the village along the B4060, you see a tall monument on a hilltop above the trees in front of you. It's a memorial to William Tyndale (*c.*1494–1536), whose English translation of parts of the Bible in 1525 was a major influence on the language in the 16th century.

Hunts Court in North Nibley—a garden centre today—is, according to one tradition, Tyndale's birthplace. Although the King James Bible of 1611 became the most authoritative biblical text in English, it relied greatly on previous translations, all of which were influenced to a greater or lesser extent by Tyndale's. When we use such phrases as *the powers that be, suffer fools gladly, my brother's keeper, a stumbling block*, and *the signs of the times*, we're remembering Tyndale. There are over 80 such expressions which are first recorded in his translation, and which would be popularized by their continued use in King James. And over 120 words have their first known use there, such as *busybody, childishness, murmurer, ungodly*, and *zealous*.

Tyndale wanted a translation which ordinary people would understand, even 'the boy who plows the field'. It was a new translation, but it was unauthorized, and he was forced to publish it in Europe. Copies smuggled into England were seized by the authorities and publicly burned, and only two copies of this edition are known to survive today. A prohibition of 24 October 1526 gave all London citizens 30 days to hand over 'all and every one of the books containing the translation of the New Testament in the vulgar tongue'.

Page opposite. The Tyndale monument in North Nibley, looking east.

Tyndale began again, working on a new translation of the Old Testament (which he never completed) and revising the New. But opposition continued to be great. Imprisoned in Antwerp, he was executed in 1536, his last words being 'Lord, open the King of England's eyes'—a death-wish full of irony, as Myles Coverdale's translation had been published the year before, with a dedication to King Henry VIII. The irony lies in the fact that Coverdale had been Tyndale's assistant, and his translation closely followed that of his master.

It's one thing seeing a monument on a hilltop; it's another thing working out how to get up to it. The lady in the village post office advised parking in the layby next to the cemetery. The path up Nibley Knoll (660 ft/201 m) is just opposite. There are two ways up, she said: a direct way, rather steep; and an easy way, which takes a bit longer. An hour later, we reflected that this must be a local dialect use of the word 'easy'. A more apt description, for all but the really fit, would be 'knackering' vs 'very knackering'.

A decision has to be made about a hundred yards along the path. The direct route reared up on the right, a series of steps with a handrail. The 'easy' route beckoned enticingly in front of us, a gentle slope through woodland—but, as we soon discovered, a gentle slope which goes on for a quarter of a mile or so can take it out of unexercised language tourists' legs. Still, it was a peaceful walk, though with a strange acoustic. The voices of children from a nearby school playground echoed through the trees, and seemed to come from the monument above, even though the school was well below us. A local resident told me that the children call it Rapunzel's Tower.

The path wound behind the monument and up into a clearing. We were temporarily disoriented. A sign said 'footpath', pointing in two directions. We knew the monument was on our right somewhere, so went that way, but the path split into a flurry of unpromising mini-paths, with a steep scarp ahead. The correct route was to the left around the edge of the clearing, into an open field, and as we reached the brow of the hill the monument suddenly loomed up before us. A large circular inscription proudly affirms Tyndale's linguistic contribution.

The tower was much larger than I expected from a distant view. I mean larger, as well as taller. It's 111 ft (34 m) high, and wide enough to enclose a set of steps up to the top. You can get in if the door is open—and that's a point worth checking in the post office before you start the climb, otherwise you have to borrow the key (and leave a deposit). A bit late to think of doing this once you've reached the monument and found it locked.

The door was open. An honesty box asks for a few pence admission. Brain debated with legs whether we should climb to the top, and won. It's a

Wordsmiths and Warriors

very tight spiral staircase of 121 steps. The electric lighting, installed during a renovation a few years ago, helped a bit, but there were sections between the windows where it was pitch black, and we had to hang on to the handrail to ensure that this book would get written. A total of 121 steps may not seem very much, but in a narrow spiral they seem to go on for ever. The Rapunzel-hair method of ascent would have been easier.

The view from the top is very fine in all directions. The monument is on the Cotswold Way, which follows the line of the escarpment between Bath and Chipping Camden, and even on a dull day you can see the River Severn Estuary, with its two bridges, and beyond into the mountains of Wales. They say you can see the monument from as far as Bristol, but that would have to be on a very clear day and with above-average eyesight. It's difficult enough in Thornbury, 10 miles (16 km) south-west, where there's a tiny cul-de-sac called, optimistically, Tyndale View. We called by to see if a ground-level sighting was possible. Not any more: too many buildings in the way.

The hilltop position on Nibley Knoll, looking south. On a clear day, the Severn Bridge is visible in the distance to the left of the monument.

Anyone who says a climb down is easier than a climb up is lying. The spiral steps renewed their threat. We decided to go down the hill by the direct route. It was stepped, but steep, and even with the handrail it was a relief to pause on a thoughtfully placed bench halfway down. The children's voices were still echoing through the woods. *Out of the mouth of babes and sucklings* came to mind. Matthew, 21.16. William Tyndale's translation.

Leave the M5 at junction 13 and take the west exit onto the A419 which leads to the A38. This may seem like going the wrong way, for North Nibley is east of the M5, but trust us. A few miles along, turn left towards Dursley (of Harry Potter fame) along the A4135, back over the M5 (see!), go through the little village of Cam (the name is from Welsh, and means 'crooked', probably from an old river course), then right at a roundabout onto the B4060 signposted towards Wotton-under-Edge. After a while, a comforting sign points to North Nibley, and a few miles further on you see the monument in the distance. To get to the post office, turn sharp left when you reach North Nibley, and it is a few yards down on the left. The layby next to the cemetery is on the right at the top of the hill as you travel east through the village (postcode: GL11 6DS).

From the south, leave the M5 at junction 14, follow the B4509 and then the B4058 to Wotton-under-Edge and pick up the B4060 westwards from there. Watch out for the cemetery on your left as you approach the village.

Chapter 28

Chichester

William Bullokar and the first English grammar

The chief problem, when trying to track down William Bullokar, is his surname. Finding where someone was born, lived, and died, is straightforward enough if we can rely on the spelling; but names had variable spellings in the Middle Ages, and there's a particular problem when the name is unusual, as this one is. It's probably occupational in origin, to do with cattle-herding, and it turns up in a variety of forms in the 15th and 16th centuries. As well as Bullokar, we find people called Boloker, Bullaker, Bullokherd, Bolokherde, Bullockhart, and Bullocherd living in Sussex and east Hampshire. Which members belong to the same family? Which spellings belong to the same person?

Thanks to some excellent genealogical research carried out in the 1960s, we can now be reasonably certain about William Bullokar (*c.*1531–1609). One of the first spelling reformers, he devised a 40-letter phonetic alphabet for English and made a translation from Latin of *Aesop's Fables*, printed in his new spelling. But his main claim to fame, for historians of the language, is his 68-page *Pamphlet for Grammar*, published in 1586, also in his new spelling, which is the first known attempt to write an English grammar. This is how he introduces his book (I've modernized the spelling):

William Bullokar's Pamphlet for Grammar: Or rather to be said his abbreviation of his Grammar for English, extracted out of his Grammar at Large. This being sufficient for the speedy learning of how to parse

Page opposite. St Andrew, Oxmarket. The thickly rendered walls are 13th century or older, the windows being later additions.

English speech for the perfecter writing thereof, and using the best phrase therein; and the easier entrance into the secrets of grammar for other languages, and the speedier understanding of other languages, ruled or not ruled by grammar; very profitable for the English nation that desireth to learn any strange language, and very aidful to the stranger to learn English perfectly and speedily; for that English hath short rule (therefore soon learned) yet having sufficient rules therein to make the way much easier for the learning of any other language unknown before to the learner.

Unfortunately, the *Grammar at Large* hasn't survived, so all we have is this outline, heavily influenced by the grammars of Latin that were available at the time. So, for example, nouns are shown with nominative, accusative, genitive, and vocative cases, and verbs have the full range of Latinate tenses. But it is, nonetheless, an English grammar—and, surprisingly, partly written in jaunty 4-line verses.

By carefully plotting the names and dates on parish records, wills, and legal documents, we can now locate Bullokar with reasonable accuracy. We don't know where he was born, but we know he lived in Chichester, West Sussex, where he was probably educated at the Prebendal School by the cathedral. He tells his readers in the preface to his *Pamphlet* that he served in the army and studied civil law. He lived in a house at the South Gate, at the entrance to the town, where some 16th-century buildings still stand. Married at St Peter's in 1570, he must soon have moved to the parish of St Andrew, towards the north of the town, for his second child, John, is known to have been baptized there in 1574. In fact three of his four known children were baptized at St Andrew's, and one was married there. He stayed in the area for the rest of his life: his will says he belongs to that parish, and he was buried in St Andrew's cemetery.

John has his place in the history of English too. He trained abroad as a doctor, and then—somewhat like Roget (Chapter 46)—became a lexicographer, publishing in 1616 *An English Expositor: teaching the interpretation of the hardest words used in our language, with sundry explications, descriptions and discourses.* It is a development of the approach first used by Robert Cawdrey (Chapter 32), and was well received, remaining in print for over a century.

The lack of information about the Bullokar family in parish registers is probably the result of their Catholic religion. The failure of some members of the family to attend Protestant services is occasionally noted. John's

The Arts Centre gallery wing.

second son, Thomas, became a Franciscan, and in 1642 was hanged, drawn, and quartered at Tyburn for celebrating mass.

St Andrew's is now the Oxmarket Centre for the Arts. The building dates from the 13th century, with later additions, but ceased being used for church services after suffering bomb damage in 1943. It was deconsecrated in the 1950s, and left derelict until a restoration programme began in the

On the west wall of the building, next to the main entrance, is an extremely weathered early 16th-century monument to an unknown couple, kneeling with their children in adoration of the Holy Trinity.

1970s. It's now a lively exhibition centre, with four galleries providing space for hire in all areas of arts and crafts. An extension covers the site of the old graveyard.

The day I visited St Andrew's I was also due to give a talk at the university on English grammar. In my introduction I remarked on the appropriateness of the topic to the town, but it was clear from the puzzled faces of the audience that they were unaware of the allusion. The Oxmarket website mentions that they have a window memorial to the poet William Collins, who was buried there. Perhaps one day Chichester will remember another William too.

Getting there

To find St Andrew, Oxmarket, begin at the medieval Chichester Cross in the centre of the town, where North, South, East, and West Streets meet. A little way along East Street, on the left, a sign points you to the centre through a narrow walkway; or you can turn left along Little London into St Andrew's Court (postcode: PO19 1YH). There's a small car park nearby, but it serves the local shops and is often full. It's only a five-minute walk from the large car park at the top of North Street. Opening times are on the website

http://oxmarket.com/

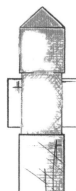

Chapter 29

Suffolk Lane and St Paul's, London EC4

Richard Mulcaster and the status of English

We're used to thinking of English as a global language today, but 400 years ago such a prospect was inconceivable. Indeed, several authors felt it necessary to defend English as having any worth at all, in the face of criticisms about its inadequacy compared with Latin. Chief among the defenders was the headteacher Richard Mulcaster (*c*.1530–1611).

Mulcaster must have been one of the best-known figures on the London scene in the second half of the 16th century. He became the first head of the new Merchant Taylors' School in 1561. He resigned in 1586, after relations with the Merchant Taylors' Company became strained (evidently there were rows over his salary). He tried to set up a school of his own, but the venture failed. Then in 1596 he became High Master of St Paul's School, where he remained until 1608. He was hugely ahead of his time. He brought music, physical education, and drama into the classroom. His pupils performed plays before the Queen. He believed in proper teacher training, recognized individual differences in children, and asserted the right of girls to have a full education. He is one of the frontrunners for the model of the pedantic schoolteacher Holofernes in *Love's Labour's Lost*. Among his famous pupils are the poet Edmund Spenser, the dramatist Thomas Kyd, and six of the translators of the King James Bible, including Lancelot Andrewes.

Linguistically, he was just as much a forward-thinker. In an age when English was considered merely a street language—good enough for plays and popular pamphlets, but little more—he argued the opposite. In his work on the principles of early education, *The Elementarie*, he claims that

Page opposite. St Paul's Cathedral.

English is 'as copious, pithie, and significative, as any other tongue in Europe'. 'Our English tongue', he says, is 'as fluent as the Latine, as courteous as the Spanish, as courtlike as the French, and as amorous as the Italian'. And it has achieved this standing because of the way it has 'beene beautified and enriched out of other good tongues'. He welcomes loan words—another heretical view for some in the 16th century.

But he was a realist. He was well aware that English was in a state of flux, and that some of its features—especially its spelling—needed stabilizing. It is, he says, 'a very necessary labor to set the writing certain, that the reading may be sure'. He rejected the radical schemes which were being proposed, in which the entire orthography would be scrapped and a new one adopted, and offers his own codification in an alphabetical list of over 8500 words with recommended spellings. It was a prescient list, as well over half of his recommended spellings are still in use today; and most of the differences are due to the fact that, when he was writing, the distinction between *u* and *v*, and between and *i* and *j*, as separate letters of the alphabet, had yet to be established.

Mulcaster would also earn his place in any book of football tourism. In an age when football was considered a game of the gutter, of 'beastly fury

A gilded St Paul peers through the trees in the North Churchyard of St Paul's Cathedral. This was where William Tyndale's New Testament was publicly burned (Chapter 27). It is also the place where many famous homilies were preached, such as those by John Donne. A virtual recreation of the original Cross and its surrounding acoustic can be found at http://virtualpaulscrossproject.blogspot.co.uk

and extreme violence' (as Sir Thomas Elyot had put it a few years before) to be 'utterly abjected of all noblemen', Mulcaster welcomed it. In his book *Positions*, on the bringing up of children, he recommends all kinds of mental, vocal, and physical exercises, including 'the Footeball play'.

Merchant Taylors' and St Paul's are still important schools today, but they have long left their original locations. St Paul's was located just north of the cathedral, but it was destroyed along with the cathedral in the Great Fire of 1666. A plaque on New Change, the road which runs along the east side of the present-day cathedral past the North Churchyard, marks where it was.

Finding the site of the original Merchant Taylors' is trickier. The school was originally in a mansion built to the south of the city centre by Sir John Pulteney in the 14th century. In Tudor times it was called the Manor of the Rose. This too went up in flames in the Great Fire. The site was somewhere between Laurence Pountney Hill—the street next to the medieval church of St Laurence Pountney (also destroyed in the fire)—and Suffolk Lane. There is a memorial plaque, but you have to look hard for it. We eventually tracked it down, thanks to the guidance of the facilities manager at the Prudential, to the portico alongside its building on Suffolk Lane. We thought this would be the most obscurely placed memorial plaque in our journey—but we were wrong (Chapter 38).

Positions wherin those primitive circumstances be examined, which are necessarie for the training up of children, either for skill in their booke, or health in their bodie.

This is the full title of his book on bringing up children. He begins it by affirming his attitude towards English:

I do write in my naturall English toungue, because though I make the learned my judges, which understand Latin, yet I meane good to the unlearned, which understand but [only] English.

And in a chapter on sports (pp. 104–5, with paragraph divisions inserted below) we see his defence of the game that has led some to call him 'the father of English football'—and also, presumably, the patron of 'trayning maisters' (i.e. referees).

the Footeball play, which could not possibly have growne to this greatnes, that it is now at, nor have bene so much used, as it is in all places, if it had not had great helpes, both to health and strength, and to me the abuse of it is a sufficient argument, that it hath a right use: which being revoked to his primative will both helpe, strength, and comfort nature: though as it is now commonly used, with thronging of a rude multitude, with bursting of shinnes, and breaking of legges, it be neither civil, neither worthy the name of any traine to health.

    Wherin any man may evidently see the use of the trayning maister. For if one stand by, which can judge of the play, and is judge over the parties, and hath authoritie to commaunde in the place, all those inconveniences have bene, I know, and wilbe I am sure very lightly redressed, nay they will never entermedle in the matter, neither shall there be complaint, where there is no cause. Some smaller number with such overlooking, sorted into sides and standings, not meeting with their bodies so boisterously to trie their strength: nor shouldring or shuffing one an other so barbarously, and using to walke after, may use footeball for as much good to the body, by the chiefe use of the legges, as the Armeball, for the same, by the use of the armes.

    And being so used, the Footeball strengtheneth and brawneth the whole body, and by provoking superfluities downeward, it dischargeth the head, and upper partes, it is good for the bowells, and to drive downe the stone and gravell from both the bladder and kidneies. It helpeth weake hammes, by much moving, beginning at a meane, and simple shankes by thickening of the flesh, no lesse then riding doth. Yet rash running and to much force oftentimes breaketh some inward conduit, and bringeth ruptures.

Football, evidently, is good for you, refreshing the parts other games cannot reach.

Site of
Merchant Taylors'
School
1561 - 1875

Left. The portico in
Suffolk Lane.

Right. The memorial plaque.

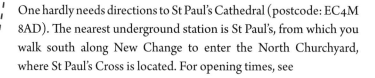

Getting there

One hardly needs directions to St Paul's Cathedral (postcode: EC4M 8AD). The nearest underground station is St Paul's, from which you walk south along New Change to enter the North Churchyard, where St Paul's Cross is located. For opening times, see

http://www.stpauls.co.uk/Visits-Events/Corporate-Events/
Venue-Hire/The-North-Churchyard

For the original Merchant Taylors' site, from St Paul's Churchyard walk east along Cannon Street, and on your right, between numbers 90 and 100, there is an alleyway leading down to Suffolk Lane. As you leave this alleyway, the Prudential portico is immediately in front of you (postcode: EC4R 0AX). Alternatively, walking east along Upper Thames Street, in the direction of London Bridge, the entrance to Suffolk Lane is on your left. You pass through some bollards and follow Suffolk Lane round to the right. The Prudential building is on your right, as is the portico with the plaque.

Chapter 30

Stratford-upon-Avon

Shakespeare and English idiom

If you approach Stratford from the east, you cross the elegant 16th-century Clopton Bridge, and immediately encounter Shakespeare in the form of the imposing Gower Memorial—by the Victorian sculptor Lord Ronald Gower. It shows Shakespeare seated in casual pose, deep in thought, holding a pen and a scroll, and surrounded by life-size statues of Prince Hal, Lady Macbeth, Falstaff, and Hamlet. The statue was moved to its present position in 1933. For some reason I can't fathom, he's turned his back on the Royal Shakespeare Theatre.

Follow the road round to the right, avoiding the town centre, and you immediately get a linguistic Shakespearean encounter: a store called 'Much Ado About Toys'. It's a reminder, if you needed one, that the language of Shakespeare gets everywhere. Type 'Much Ado About' into a search engine, and in addition to *Nothing* you will see hundreds of variants, each one expressing the notion of a dispute or argument about something. *Much Ado About Methane ... Mergers ... Mutton ... Muffins ...*

Several of Shakespeare's play titles have entered the language in this way. I've seen *As You Like It* as a heading on articles, websites, and shop names to do with cooking, catering, silverware, landscaping, and hair salons—to name just a few. And the famous quotations go the same way. If Hamlet had a pound for every time 'To be or not to be' turns up as the template for a newspaper headline, he'd be a very rich Dane. An article on photocopying in schools began: 'To copy or not to copy'. One on entrance fees for

Page opposite. The entrance to Holy Trinity Church, with news about the grave. If only ...

Above. The Gower Memorial, with Falstaff prominent, and the Royal Shakespeare Theatre behind. Lady Macbeth glowers in the distance.

Right. A typical Shakespearean encounter in Stratford: the boats are all heroines—Virgilia, Rosalind, Beatrice, Valeria, Ophelia (be especially careful when rowing in this one, I imagine), and (hidden by the fence) Ursula, Volumnia, and Juliet.

Wordsmiths and Warriors

museums: 'To pay or not to pay'. One on military intervention: 'To fight or not to fight'. One on calory control: 'To diet or not to diet'. It even turned up in *The Simpsons*: in one episode, Homer enters a bar and asks himself 'Two beers or not two beers?'

It's in the area of idiomatic and figurative speech that we most often encounter Shakespeare's permanent influence on English. The plays provide us with dozens of examples of modern everyday expressions that he created or popularized. From *The Merchant of Venice*: *bated breath, blinking idiot, green-eyed jealousy, love is blind*, and *truth will out*. From *Henry VI*: *be that as it may, knits his brows*, and *dead as a door-nail*. From *Troilus and Cressida*: *early days, good riddance*, and *fair play*. There are about a hundred in all—not as many as derive from the Bible (Chapter 35), but a goodly number nonetheless.

I'm not sure which Shakespearean idiom is the best one to be thinking of when exploring Stratford: *too much of a good thing*, perhaps (from *As You Like It*), or maybe *what the dickens* (from *The Merry Wives of Windsor*)? Certainly, I never know quite what to make of the mixture of periods presented by Shakespeare's birthplace on Henley Street. The house received a major restoration in 1858, but all they had to go on was a drawing of 1769. The facade to the right is mainly 19th century, replacing an earlier stage when brickwork was used. There's original 16th-century timber-framing,

The birthplace house on Henley Street, with the building of the Shakespeare Birthplace Trust—and the Shakespeare coat-of-arms—in the foreground.

Shakespeare's school, on the High Street.

but some of the windows are much later. The restorers have made a virtue out of necessity (*Two Gentlemen of Verona*), for the end result is both plausible and attractive, but I wonder how many of the tourists who pose for photographs in front of the building realize that what they're seeing is only an approximation to what Shakespeare would have seen.

Opposite page. Shakespeare's grave with its poetic warning (YT is an old way of abbreviating 'that'):

GOOD FREND FOR JESVS SAKE FORBEARE, / TO DIGG THE DVST ENCLOASED HEARE. / BLESTE BE YT MAN YT SPARES THES STONES, / AND CVRST BE HE YT MOVES MY BONES.

People have long wanted to investigate the grave, in the hope that the remains would yield clues about the bard, and—who knows?—perhaps yield some original manuscripts.

The bust on the wall was erected in 1623 by his widow and friends. Nearby are copies of the register entries for his baptism and burial. The adjacent graves are (to the left) his wife Anne, and (to the right) Thomas Nash, the first husband of Shakespeare's granddaughter Elizabeth.

Shakespeare began his life here, and ended it a few hundred yards away in New Place, the house he bought in 1597, and where he died in 1616. It's on the corner of Chapel Street and Chapel Lane, just opposite the imposing Guild Chapel. Only the foundations remain now. Access is from next door, Nash's House, built around 1600 but with its frontage reconstructed in the early 20th century. It's named after Thomas Nash, who married Shakespeare's granddaughter, and is a museum now, containing some excellent exhibits, including some finds from the 2011 excavations of the New Place foundations. It's likely that the later plays were written here, and so you might reflect on *such a pickle, melting into thin air*, and *keeping a good tongue in your head*, all from *The Tempest*, as you walk around.

Chapel Street morphs into Church Street, and just past the Guild Chapel, on the left, is the oldest part of King Edward VI Grammar School, which Shakespeare would have attended. It looks its age, leaning out over the street. At the end of Church Street, a left turn takes you to Holy Trinity Church, where Shakespeare is buried. Each year, around the time of Shakespeare's birthday (23 April), Stratford holds a colourful procession, attended by dignitaries from all over the world, which proceeds from the town centre and ends at the tomb. I walked in it once, and—along with everyone else—solemnly placed a sprig of rosemary on the grave. No other literary figure has an occasion to match it (with one possible exception, Chapter 40). It beggars all description (*Antony and Cleopatra*).

No visit to Stratford would be complete without a visit to the theatre, which reopened after a major refurbishment in 2011. The main house and the smaller adjoining Swan theatre have both aimed to convey something of the original Elizabethan theatre-goer's experience, with thrust stages surrounded by tiers of seats. But if you want a closer recreation of that experience, with all its liveliness and audience participation, you have to travel 100 miles south-east, to Southwark, London (Chapter 31).

Getting there

The road into Stratford from the east is the A4300. A large car park is on the left just before Clopton Bridge. From there, a footbridge allows you to cross the Avon, leading to Bancroft Gardens, where the Gower Monument is. Then walk up Bridge Street towards the town centre. Henley Street branches to the right, and a little way along on the right is the Birthplace (postcode: CV37 6QW). It includes the excellent Shakespeare Bookshop, which carries a huge selection.

If you turn left at the top of Bridge Street, you're in the High Street. New Place is a little way along on the left, in Chapel Street (postcode: CV37 6EP). It's a corner property. Keep going along the High Street, past the school building, and at the end a left turn takes you to Holy Trinity Church.

If, leaving New Place, you turn down Chapel Lane, you will find yourself in Waterside, with the theatres in front of you and Bancroft Gardens on the left. If you turn right, at certain times you can cross the river using the chain ferry. Turning right also brings you to the actors' pub, the Dirty Duck, with its many pictures of theatre personalities inside. After that, you're on your own.

Information about admission to the various Shakespeare locations can be found at

http://www.shakespeare.org.uk/home.html

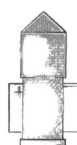

Chapter 31

Park Street, London SE1

Shakespeare and linguistic innovation

You have to let your imagination work on you, when you visit the original site of Shakespeare's Globe in London. Not when visiting the superb reconstruction of the theatre, down by the riverside. There the architects have done the job for you, to the best of their ability, given the incomplete understanding we have of how the theatre would have looked in 1599. All you have to do is just sit there and look around, and it doesn't take much imagination to feel how it might have been. You have to ignore the occasional jet on its way to Heathrow airport, of course, and some annoying helicopters. But on the whole it's a transporting experience.

To find the original Globe you have to transport yourself some 250 yds (230 m) away from the reconstruction. Turn right outside the main entrance of the theatre, and first left into Park Street, and a little way along, on the right-hand side behind some railings, you find it. This is where, as the Chorus says in the prologue to *Henry V*, you really do need to 'piece out our imperfections with your thoughts'. The imperfections, from a theatrical point of view, are the houses which cover half the site. The buildings along Anchor Terrace, and part of Southwark Bridge Road, are right on top of it. You need your imagination now.

An archaeological dig in 1989 had no choice but to concentrate on the piece of land which had no building, the former car park of a brewery, but fortunately this was an area which did contain a section of the theatre. It wasn't a huge section—a mere 140 ft × 30 ft (12 m × 9 m)—but it was enough to reveal some foundations and to provide important clues as to the theatre's original shape. After decades of speculation, the Globe had

Page opposite. From the roof of the Financial Times building, it's possible to see the curvature of the original outer theatre wall in the line of the memorial plaque, facing the rear of the buildings on Anchor Terrace.

The reconstructed Globe, as seen from the Thames embankment.

finally been found. The outline of the outer wall is now etched into the ground, and gives a clear impression of what the Chorus described as a 'wooden O'.

Anyone who visits the site must surely reflect on the plays which received their first performance there, such as *Hamlet* and *King Lear*. Linguists who visit have an additional cause for reflection: Shakespeare's role in the development of English.

It's a contribution that has sometimes been overestimated. People have talked wildly about Shakespeare 'inventing' the English language, and suchlike. The reality is less dramatic, though nonetheless significant. Certainly he coined many new words, as all his contemporaries did, and hundreds of them achieved a permanent presence in the language—words like *barefaced*, *reclusive*, and *even-handed*. He was especially adept at creating new words using prefixes and suffixes, such as *overgrowth* and *overpower*, *airless* and *noiseless*, and new compounds such as *well-behaved* and *well-respected*.

At the same time, it's now clear that many of the words which are first known from one of Shakespeare's plays or poems weren't invented by him. He was simply the first person to have written them down. And as research into the language of the period continues, it's possible that earlier users will come to light. This has already happened with *lonely*, for instance. For many years, the first recorded use of this word in the *Oxford English*

Dictionary was in a line from *Coriolanus*—a play written around 1608. But it's now been discovered in a play written in 1592 by someone else.

Still, Shakespeare's role in creating new vocabulary remains unequalled. There are currently (in 2012) over 1700 items listed in the *OED* as having him as a first recorded user. Even if research shows that this number has to be reduced by half, we're still left with a hugely impressive figure. Most people would be happy if just one of their neologisms achieved a long-term presence in the language, let alone several hundred. And then there are the idioms … but I've already told that part of the story (Chapter 30).

To my mind, Shakespeare's primary linguistic legacy lies not so much in the words he invented or popularized that became a permanent feature of the language, but in the words he created that didn't. In *Coriolanus*, a senator calls on everyone to 'unshout the noise that banished Martius'. Shakespeare could have made the senator use a different verb which would fit the metre, such as 'take back' or 'renounce'. *Unshout* has more dramatic impact. Why? Because it's impossible. You can't unshout something that's already been shouted. Making such a demand adds impact to the appeal that the senator is making.

It has to be admitted that there's precious little impact when you look through the railings at the outline on the ground at the original Globe site. All you can do is what the Chorus advises, and let the setting 'on your imaginary forces work'. However, there's a bonus just across the road, in

The original Globe site, ground-level view.

the form of the site of an even earlier theatre on Bankside, the Rose, built in 1587 and excavated in 1989. Some of Shakespeare's early plays were performed there. Indeed, it was the success of the Rose that led to the Globe being built nearby. And, unlike the Globe, the foundations of the whole area of the original theatre are visible.

Preliminary planning is essential, as the Rose is open only at certain times. And the same point applies to any visit round the corner to the reconstructed Globe, where what can be seen depends on the time of year. There's a permanent exhibition on the site, as well as tours, and the education department runs talks and other events throughout the year, but performances in the open-air theatre run only from April to October. If you want a sense of how a Shakespeare play might have been produced, taking in a performance during the play season is a must. The spirited interaction between actors and audience gives the plays a fresh presence, and the 'Globe roar' from the audience, following the jig at the end of a play, is something you never forget.

There's a great deal more to do with the Shakespearean era underneath modern London that will never be known. For contemporary Shakespearean buildings above ground, the English-language tourist has to travel 100 miles north-west, and join the crowds at Stratford (Chapter 30).

Getting there

As you approach Southwark Bridge from the south, along Southwark Bridge Road (the A300), turn left into Sumner Street and then right into Emerson Street. At the junction with Park Street you have two choices: if you go straight ahead you see the reconstructed Shakespeare's Globe on your left; if you turn right, the original Globe site is a short distance along on the right, just before Park Street goes under Southwark Bridge Road (postcode: SE1 9AS). The Rose is on the left.

Parking in this area is always a problem, though there's a little bit of meter parking on Park Street. Nearest tube stations are Waterloo and London Bridge. Many people approach the Globe via the riverside walk along the South Bank. Coming from Waterloo, the Globe is on the right just after the Millennium Bridge opposite St Paul's.

Information about events and opening times at Shakespeare's Globe is available at

http://www.shakespearesglobe.com

For the Rose, see

http://www.rosetheatre.org.uk

Chapter 32

Oakham

Robert Cawdrey and the first dictionary

It's a difficult business, tracking down Robert Cawdrey—the man who compiled the first real dictionary of the English language, a *Table Alphabeticall* of hard words, published in 1604. He wrote it while he was living in Coventry. We know this because that's the place he mentions at the end of a fulsome dedication of his book to various noble ladies. But there's no record of exactly where he lived or worked. Coventry was a tiny place in 1604—some 6000 people only—but his whereabouts within the modern inner ring road is anybody's guess.

A clue in the dedication points us in a different direction. He describes his work as something which 'long ago for the most part, was gathered by me, but lately augmented by my sonne Thomas'. And then we read that he had the noble ladies' brother as a student 'when I taught the Grammer schoole at Okeham in the County of Rutland'. Maybe the idea for a dictionary grew while he was trying to increase his pupils' English vocabulary.

Oakham is the chief town of the tiny county of Rutland. It has a castle, with a remarkable collection of commemorative horseshoes donated by visiting peers of the realm over the years. And it has a school: Oakham School, founded in 1584. That sounds promising—until we look carefully at the records. For Cawdrey never taught here. He was Master (that is, headteacher) of an earlier school, somewhere on the same site, from 1563 to 1570. That was indeed 'long ago'.

There were two manors at Oakham in those days: one in the hands of the Harrington family (the Lordshold), the other sponsored by Westminster Abbey (the Deanshold). Good schools were lacking in the area, and

Page opposite. The entrance to Oakham School.

Cawdrey's seems to have been the first. He was well connected. Among his pupils were members of the Harrington family. But it must have been a very small establishment, not enough to cope with local demand, so a new school was founded to replace it.

There's no sign of Cawdrey's school now, and we can only guess where it might have been. When Oakham School chapel was being built in the 1920s, some evidence of an earlier building was uncovered, but no serious archaeology has been carried out. Some local historians have suggested it was in the vicinity of the building now called College House (so named because the students there were being prepared for the Oxbridge colleges), but nobody is sure when this was built or even what it was originally used for. It may have been where the Westminster clergy lived.

Nonetheless it's possible to get a sense of Cawdrey's time just by walking around the centre of Oakham. In the Market Place there's a fine set of stocks, with five leg-holes (the fifth reputedly being for a regularly offending one-legged villain). In the grounds of the old school near All Saints' Church there's an old classroom, with its date of 1584 firmly inscribed on the end wall and SCHOLA LATINA GRAECA HEBRAICA carved along the side. It's an alternative possibility for the original school site. Not the warmest place to teach, said Dermot Gilvary, who was showing us around. It had been his classroom for several years when he first came to the school.

College House, Oakham School.   But nowhere closer, I thought, to Robert Cawdrey.

Wordsmiths and Warriors

The old schoolroom, with (inset) the date on the outside wall.

Cawdrey was ordained a deacon in 1565 and a priest in 1570, and the following year became rector of the Norman church of St Mary the Virgin in South Luffenham, a few miles from Oakham, at a salary of 40 shillings a year. His candidature was proposed by no less a person than William Cecil, Lord Burghley, the lord treasurer of Queen Elizabeth I. Burghley House was in Stamford, just five miles from the village. Perhaps we would find something more concrete in his old parish?

The surviving parish registers for South Luffenham date only from 1682, but St Mary's does indeed remember him. On the left as we entered the church we found a list of the rectors, with Robertus Cawdrie listed at 1571, when (according to an entry in the Lambeth Charters) he would have been 33. The variant spelling isn't unusual for surnames at the time. He's also spelled Cawdray, Cawdraye, Cawdry, Caudery, Caudry, and Cowdraie. Why so many variants? Because he is repeatedly mentioned in ecclesiastical records of the period, and surnames had no standard spelling in those days (as we also know from the variants in the spelling of Shakespeare). A new rector takes up the post unexpectedly soon, in 1588. Cawdrey was one

Light from the clerestories bathes the Norman arches in St Mary's, South Luffenham. The balloons are 21st century.

of the first nonconformists, and he regularly got himself into trouble. That explains his short period in office.

The decade following his ordination was a very uncertain time. The old (Catholic) religion and the new (Protestant) religion of England were still in contention. Only 20 years before, Catholic Queen Mary had been on the throne; now it was Protestant Queen Elizabeth. And to ensure the establishment of the new religion, post-holders had to obey the rules as laid down in the Book of Common Prayer.

Not all non-Catholics liked the way the new religion was developing. There was a nonconformist mood in the country, with Puritans the most prominent of those disapproving of some of the practices of the evolving Church of England (Chapter 35). The Puritans were tolerated, as theirs was a religious disagreement, with no political intent. They did not threaten the well-being of the throne in the way that Catholics did. But nonetheless they were under considerable pressure to conform.

Rutland was one of the areas where nonconformist views were strongly held, and it wasn't long before Cawdrey's nonconformity was noticed. Complaints were made. In 1576 he was charged with not reading the homilies and injunctions in church. A year later, the churchwardens complained to the Bishop of Peterborough that Cawdrey 'dothe not his service in due time as he ought to doo'. In 1578 he conducted the wedding of a fellow clergyman without the Bishop's permission, refused to submit himself for correction, and was suspended from his duties for three months. He

Wordsmiths and Warriors

promised to behave, but in 1586 was summoned before the Court of High Commission in London, charged with a range of offences, such as not wearing a surplice, using 'you' when he should have used 'thou', and saying in a lecture that the Book of Common Prayer was 'a vile book, fie on it'. The commissioners several times asked him to change his mind, but he repeatedly refused. Suspension from his ministry followed.

He didn't take this lying down. Claiming he had been illegally deprived of his living, he forced his way into the parish barn to get corn to feed his family. In 1587 he asked Burghley for help. A lawyer was appointed to defend him against the ecclesiastical charges. He travelled to London to defend himself on over 20 occasions, a huge outlay of time, energy, and money in those days. But it was all in vain. In 1590 he was unfrocked. A year later he wrote again to Burghley saying he was destitute, 'havinge a wife and vi smalle children at home, besides two, that are poore Schollars in Cambridge'. How much help he received we do not know. Doubtless he turned again to teaching soon after.

And English benefited, for he began to write on language. *A Treasurie or Store House of Similes* was published in 1600, and then, four years later, when he was in his sixties, the *Table Alphabeticall*. Who would have expected that such a turbulent priest would turn his hand to lexicography?

It's hard to get a sense of the importance of the *Table* when we look at it, for it is the slimmest of volumes, containing only about 2500 short entries. There had been word-lists before, and bilingual dictionaries. But no book had appeared solely on English which was not just a word-list in alphabetical order but one which gave definitions.

He explains why he did it on his title page:

A Table Alphabeticall, conteyning and teaching the true writing, and vnderstanding of hard vsuall English wordes, borrowed from the Hebrew, Greeke, Latine, or French, &c.

With the interpretation thereof by plaine English words, gathered for the benefit & helpe of Ladies, Gentlewomen, or any other unskilfull persons.

Whereby they may the more easilie and better understand many hard English wordes, which they shall heare or read in Scriptures, Sermons, or elswhere, and also be made able to use the same aptly themselues.

It isn't recorded what his aristocratic female patrons thought of this description, but there's no doubt that the book was a successful idea. Thousands of learned words had come into English in the 16th century, and people needed help. The *Table* was popular, going through four editions.

People would never have seen anything like this before—and Cawdrey knows it. In his address to the reader he gives detailed instructions about how to look words up. He couldn't assume that people would even know what alphabetical order was:

> If thou be desirous (gentle Reader) rightly and readily to understand, and to profit by this Table, and such like, then thou must learne the Alphabet, to wit, the order of the Letters as they stand, perfectly without booke, and where euery Letter standeth:

And just in case that wasn't clear, he adds an illustration:

> as (b) neere the beginning, (n) about the middest, and (t) toward the end.

And to make things even clearer, he gives two examples:

> Nowe if the word, which thou art desirous to finde, begin with (a) then looke in the beginning of this Table, but if with (v) looke towards the end. Againe, if thy word beginne with (ca) looke in the beginning of the letter (c) but if with (cu) then looke toward the end of that letter. And so of all the rest. &c.

We can imagine the light bulb going on in readers' minds. So *that's* how you find it!

Some of his definitions are very weak, by modern standards. *Barbell* is glossed simply as 'fish', *chough* as 'bird', and *citron* as 'fruit'. But others are thoughtful and precise:

> *allude*, to speake one thing that hath resemblance and respect to another.
> *circumlocution*, a speaking of that in many words, which may be said in few.
> *competitor*, hee that sueth for the same thing, or office, that another doth.
> *dialect*, the manner of speech in any language, diuers from others.

We can see here the way future dictionary definitions would evolve.

The *Table Alphabeticall* reads like the writing of any retired schoolmaster, clergyman, or civil servant. Reflecting on language is the sort of thing a professional person with a lifetime of experience and a still lively mind is likely to do. Today is no different. Several times a year I receive a draft from retirees, sometimes worked out in immense detail, of a proposed system for simplifying English spelling, or of an idea for a logical language that would avoid the problems of international communication. There are dozens of such proposals circulating nowadays. What makes Cawdrey so special is that his *Table* was a genuine first, and paved the way for more ambitious dictionary projects soon after.

Judging by the prefatory remarks in both his language books, Cawdrey never forgot his school-teaching days in Oakham, and perhaps looked back on them with a certain nostalgia. So a visit there has a certain motivation— and certainly beats driving round and round the Coventry inner ring road.

Getting there

The A606 from Melton Mowbray to Stamford runs north of Oakham, bypassing the town. Follow the signs to the town centre. If you're coming from the north, cross the railway line and turn left past the railway station into Station Road. You pass some buildings of Oakham School on your right (try not to hit crossing students, for the school is on both sides of the road, and at certain times of day it can be very busy), and then turn right into Church Street. A car park is opposite the church (postcode: LE15 6XT). Walk across the road into the park and the old schoolroom is immediately in front of you. College House is a little further along, with a pathway leading past All Saints' Church.

From the east (the Stamford Road), the B640 to the town centre leads you into the High Street, with car parking signs. On the right is Market Street (which is where the stocks are and the main entrance to Oakham School) and the next right is Church Street. All Saints is an easily visible landmark from all directions.

To get to Cawdrey's parish church, follow the A6003 south out of Oakham, turn left onto the A47, and left again onto the A6121 signposted to Stamford. A sign also points to North Luffenham, where there is a government establishment, but ignore this, for the road reaches South Luffenham first. Turn left into Back Lane, and right into Church Lane, and there's room to park by the small piece of triangular green outside St Mary's Church (postcode: LE15 8JR).

Chapter 33

Willoughby

John Smith and new Englishes

Y ou can't see the sea from Willoughby, in north Lincolnshire, but the signs of sea voyages are never far away. Whichever way you approach the village, you pass through Danish settlements, all easily identifiable by their distinctive *-by* ending. A *by*, in Old Norse, was a settlement. So, Ulceby was Ulf's *by* and Spilsby was Spilli's *by*. Skendleby was the *by* near a beautiful slope. And Willoughby was the *by* among willows.

Willoughby was where John Smith (*c.*1580–1631) was born. Captain John Smith, to distinguish him from the thousands of others with the same blacksmith-related surname. They remember him well in Willoughby. North or south, the entrance to the village proudly states: 'Birthplace of … John Smith'. Other pointers proliferate. Driving in from the north, we passed on our right, at the end of Tavern Road, a John Smith Close. A little further along, on our left, there was a Virginia Close. Near the Willoughby Arms, a Jamestown Cottage. Those are the clues, if any were needed, as to why we were there. Smith was one of the first to take the English language to America.

We'd specifically come to see the John Smith window in the 14th-century St Helena's Church. A team of builders was renovating the roof when we arrived—or rather, having lunch in their van. They'd left the radio on inside the church. The channel could not have been playing a more appropriate piece: a John Denver ballad, with its nostalgic lyrics: 'Country roads, take me home, to the place I belong: West Virginia, mountain momma; Take me home, country roads …' The refrain echoed around the walls.

Page opposite. The Danish legacy in Lincolnshire.

The welcome sign. We couldn't miss the window. It's tall, colourful, and full of biography, from his schooldays in Lincolnshire to his retirement back in England. Someone has thoughtfully photographed the baptismal register for 1580, framed it, and hung it on the wall beneath the window. Smith's entry reads: 'John the sonne of George Smyth was baptised the ix daie of Januarye'. The entry is actually listed in the year for 1579, but that's because the minister was using the Old Calendar, when the official New Year didn't begin until 25 March (Lady Day).

Smith left Willoughby around 1596 and became a soldier, fighting for the Dutch against the Spanish and for Austria against the Turks. But in 1606 he joined the expedition to the new colony in America (Chapter 55): the Virginia Company had received its charter from James I that year. They landed at the place they would call Jamestown in May 1607. Smith became a member of the first Council of Virginia, and in 1608 its governor. A year later he returned to England, becoming famous for his writings about the colony, including a general history. He is buried in the church of St Sepulchre on Holborn Viaduct in London. He has a dedicatory window there too, as well as a statue in Jamestown.

He must have begun to write his first account of the early exploration of Virginia not long after arriving there, for by 1608 his manuscript was already in the hands of a London printer. His 'True Relation', as it is often called, has the following title:

Wordsmiths and Warriors

Above. The main section of the memorial window.

Left. The baptismal register for 1579–80, with Smith's entry shown by a mark in the left margin.

A True Relation of Such Occurrences and Accidents of Note as Hath Hapned in Virginia Since the First Planting of that Colony, which is now resident in the South part thereof, till the last returne from thence.

Written by Captaine Smith one of the said Collony, to a worshipfull friend of his in England

The printer must have been a bit worried by what he read, for there is an apology:

> the Author being absent from the presse, it cannot be doubted but that some faults have escaped in the printing, especially in the names of Countries, Townes, and People, which are somewhat strange unto us.

Indeed they were. Smith's account contains many Indian place names, such as Roanoke and Appomattox, and how on earth were these to be spelled? And at one point, during a visit to the Powhatan Indians, we find a new noun:

> Arriving at Weramocomoco, their Emperour proudly lying uppon a Bedstead a foote high, upon tenne or twelves Mattes, richly hung with Manie Chaynes of great Pearles about his necke, and covered with a great Covering of Rahaughcums.

Today we spell the word *raccoons*.

That's why English-language students doff their hats to mariners like John Smith, included here as a standard-bearer for all those who were exploring the New World at the time. For in their letters home and in their early narratives we find the first evidence of what today we would call Americanisms. No-one in England would have heard the word *raccoon* before. And in Smith's later writings we find such words as *persimmon*, *moccasin*, *terrapin*, *moose*, *pow-wow*, and *wigwam*. Today, we think of them as part of standard English. In 1608 they were alien and intriguing.

John Smith helps us answer a question which is very much in the linguistic news today, as English has steadily become a global language. How long does it take for a new variety of English—a new dialect, if you will—to emerge when the language arrives in a fresh part of the world? We might think it takes decades, but when it comes to a distinctive lexicon, we see it takes only a few days. The first communicative encounters with the local people will inevitably focus on the environment. What is that fruit called? That animal? That tree? Before long, the explorers will discover the words the local people use to describe their culture—their social hierarchy, their myths and legends, their folk practices, and so on, and each domain will yield a new vocabulary. We know now that the distinctive local lexicon of a new variety of English can amount to tens of thousands of words.

As can be seen from the stories of John Trevisa and Robert Cawdrey (Chapters 16, 32), famous language personalities, known for their respectable academic output, can lead surprisingly exciting lives. None more so than John Smith—if his account is to be believed. Certainly, whether it happened or not, people evidently are desperate to believe it. For Captain Smith is the protagonist in the story of Pocahontas—a narrative that has been retold in countless children's books, and which achieved the ultimate affirmation of truth in the form of a Walt Disney animation.

The story goes that he left the fort with some other colonists to explore the area. They ran into an Indian hunting party, and he was the only survivor. He was taken to Chief Powhatan, who conducted a trial in which he was condemned to death, but his life was spared on the spontaneous intervention of Powhatan's 11-year-old daughter, Pocahontas. The story has attracted huge debate. Did it happen like that? Was it a Smithian exaggeration? Or possibly even a misinterpretation? One analysis suggests that the event was a mock ritual killing forming part of an initiation ceremony, which Smith took to be the real thing. Others think it happened just as the story says. The debate continues. But like everyone who first heard this tale as a child, I do so want it to be true. Take me home, country roads …

Getting there

Travelling south along the A16 from Louth, at the Ulceby Cross roundabout follow the A1028 signposted Skegness, then turn left onto a winding hedge-lined road signposted to Claxby and Willoughby. After you reach the village, turn left at the Willoughby Arms into Church Lane, and St Helena's is in front of you (postcode: LN13 9SU). There's room to park outside. The John Smith window is on the left as you enter the church.

From the south, on the A16 from Boston, turn right onto the A158 and then left onto the B1196 at Gunby Roundabout, signposted Willoughby. Church Lane is then on your right soon after entering the village.

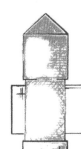

Chapter 34

East India Dock, London E14

the East India Company and global English

One of the joys of our journey in this book was the totally unexpected bonus that every now and then came our way. We would go looking for one location and find a second. Nowhere was this more so than during our visit to the East India Dock.

We went there because of the East India Company, founded by a group of merchants in 1600. As its name suggests, this was created to organize the transport of goods from India and other territories in south-east Asia, such as cotton, silk, indigo dye, opium, saltpetre, sugar, pepper, and tea. The first ship arrived in India in 1608, rights of trade were quickly established, and there was a rapid period of expansion along the east and west coasts of the country. Commercial superiority in the region led to political power, and after the Battle of Plassey in 1757 the Company became a powerful ruling force, eventually covering the whole country. Its regime ended after the Rebellion of 1857–8. The Company was dissolved, and the British government assumed control.

Substantial English-speaking communities grew up around Kolkata (Calcutta), Mumbai (Bombay), and Chennai (Madras), and an Indian variety of English was one of the consequences. Today, English is one of the official languages of India, spoken in several local varieties by several hundred million people. No other country in the world contains so many English speakers.

The vocabulary of English was considerably increased by the Indian trade. The cargo list of a fleet of five ships travelling to England in 1724 displays a new vocabulary of items, such as *alliballies, baftaes, chints, cuttannees,*

Page opposite. The East India Dock Basin, looking across at the original dock areas, as a Docklands Light Railway train passes by.

ginghams, humhums, mulmuls, and *taffaties.* Today, only a few of these terms—such as *gingham* and *taffeta*—are known outside the specialized world of textiles. But the loan words from Indian languages, illustrated by these terms, became a major strand in the history of English. And India, of course, was only one of the countries in the East Indies where the expansion of the British Empire had linguistic consequences. I've never tried to count the number of items that came into English from this period of colonial expansion, but it must be at least fifty thousand words.

So a visit to the place where all this began was a must, and that meant the East India Docks—or, at least, what is left of them. They were built on the north side of the Thames between 1803 and 1806. The easiest way of pinpointing the location today is to say that it is immediately opposite the Greenwich peninsula, home today of the O2 Arena. The area is now known as the East India Dock Basin, and is in the care of the Lee Valley Regional Park Authority. This is where the cargoes were offloaded from the ships, known as East Indiamen, before being moved by barge to warehouses in the City.

The dock entrance into the Thames is a dramatic concrete and brick barrier, refurbished in the mid-1990s, noisily spilling out overflow water. But inside is an unexpectedly peaceful wildlife sanctuary—a lake surrounded by reeds, shrubs, and trees, with panels displaying the many kinds of bird and waterfowl that can be seen in the basin. It's the beginning of the River Lee (also spelled Lea) Walkway. Only the occasional flight taking off from nearby London City airport disturbs the tranquility.

The Dock Basin gates.

Wordsmiths and Warriors

Walking around the south side of the lake, it's just possible to get a sense of the original dock structure. There are three indentations in the wall. The one nearest the Thames barrier is the original entrance lock. It was widened to 48 ft (15 m) in 1804 to allow the largest East Indiamen—up to 1500 tons—to enter.

A little further along there's a second indentation. This is the site of the Export Dock, which was where the emigration ships loaded before departure. It suffered bomb damage in World War II and was later filled in. A housing estate covers it now.

The third indentation is the site of the Import Dock. This was huge, originally covering about 60 acres (24 ha), and its walls were curved to suit the hulls of the ships. During World War II it was where floating harbours for the D-Day landings were built. This too was later filled in.

And the bonus? I had forgotten that ships went west as well as east, but I was given a dramatic reminder as we found our way from the East India Dock railway station to the riverside. We would have missed it if we had turned left outside the station, but fortunately we decided to go directly towards the river, turning left along the riverside in front of a new-build of apartments called Virginia Quay. The name didn't register for a while. But then we came face to face with the name of Captain John Smith (Chapter 33), and everything fell into place.

The Virginia settlers left from here. The event is remembered in an imposing stone monument, 'The Mariner's Astrolabe' by Wendy Taylor, commissioned in 1999 by Barratt Homes when they were building the

The Virginia Settlers memorial.

apartments. An inscription on the base tells the visitor that it replaced an earlier memorial, unveiled in 1928 on the wall of Brunswick House, which formerly stood about 100 yards to the west. And above it is the original plaque:

> FROM NEAR THIS SPOT
> DECEMBER 19. 1606
> SAILED WITH 105 "ADVENTURERS"
> THE "SUSAN CONSTANT." 100 TONS.
> CAPT. CHRISTOPHER NEWPORT,
> IN SUPREME COMMAND
> THE "GODSPEED." 40 TONS.
> CAPT. BARTHOLOMEW GOSWOLD
> THE "DISCOVERY." 20 TONS.
> CAPT. JOHN RATCLIFFE
> LANDED AT CAPE HENRY. VIRGINIA
> APRIL 26. 1607.
> ARRIVED AT JAMESTOWN. VIRGINIA
> MAY 13. 1607.
> WHERE THESE "ADVENTURERS"
> FOUNDED THE FIRST PERMANENT
> ENGLISH COLONY IN AMERICA
> UNDER THE LEADERSHIP OF THE
> INTREPID CAPT. JOHN SMITH.
> EDWARD MARIA WINGFIELD.
> PRESIDENT OF THE COUNCIL.
> THE REVEREND ROBERT HUNT.
> AND OTHERS
> AT JAMESTOWN. JULY 30. 1619. WAS
> CONVENED THE FIRST REPRESENTATIVE
> ASSEMBLY IN AMERICA.

And we know what happened there. If we had approached the Dock Basin from the other end, we would have been forewarned. The street names include Newport Avenue, Pilgrims Mews, and Jamestown Way.

The two main directions of English linguistic expansion, east and west, brought together in one place. For an English-language tourist, this is as good as it gets.

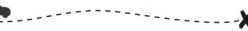

Getting there

The easiest way of reaching the East India Dock Basin is to take the Docklands Light Railway to East India Dock (make sure you take the right line, towards Beckton or Woolwich Arsenal). You get great views if you manage to sit at the front of the (driverless) train. Go straight down to the river, turn left, and you see the Virginia Quay memorial in front of you. The entrance to the dock is a little further along. You cross a small bridge to get into the basin area. If you turn left outside the station, keep to the right and you enter the basin from the other end through a small gate.

By road, the basin is at Orchard Place, Tower Hamlets (postcode: E14 9QS). Coming into London along the A13, ignore the sign left saying Royal Docks A1011 and turn left along the A1020 signposted Isle of Dogs, Canary Wharf, and Leamouth, which leads into Leamouth Road. At the roundabout, cross straight over, and the entrance to the basin is through the gate on your left. The nearest car park is some distance away, at the Excel Centre (postcode: E16 1DR).

For opening times (usually 8.30 a.m. to dusk) see the Lee Valley Regional Park Authority website:

http://www.visitleevalley.org.uk/en/content/cms/nature/nature-reserve/bow-creek/

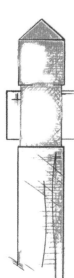

Chapter 35

Hampton Court Palace

King James and his Bible

The King James Bible has been called one of the greatest influences on the English language. Its enthusiastic supporters include Winston Churchill, Samuel Taylor Coleridge, and Charlton Heston (who read it while preparing for the role of Moses in 'The Ten Commandments'). Melvin Bragg even goes so far as to call it 'the DNA of the English language'. Visiting a KJB location is therefore obligatory for English-language tourists. But where exactly should they go?

The actual task of translation was carried out by six companies of scholars working in London, Oxford, and Cambridge, with no place standing out as the obvious one to visit. Hampton Court Palace, in Richmond-upon-Thames, Greater London, is a better option, for this is where the proposal to create the new Bible was made and agreed. It happened in 1604, in a conference that took place in King James's Privy Chamber. That, we figured, would be the closest we could get to the original setting. But we had not reckoned with the radical redesign plans of William and Mary, who, 80 years later, would choose Hampton Court as their principal residence.

The story starts in the reign of Queen Elizabeth. Although a Protestant church had been established in England in 1559, not everyone supported the way it was developing. Church government by bishops, and the ceremonies which had evolved in relation to the Book of Common Prayer, alienated those who wanted a purer form of Protestantism. The 'Puritans', as they came to be called, were kept in check during the reign of Elizabeth,

Page opposite. The entrance to Hampton Court Palace. The beasts on the bridge over the filled-in moat are recent (1950) additions.

though with many local disputes (Chapter 32), but the accession of James I offered them a fresh opportunity to argue their views. They drew up a petition, said to have contained over a thousand signatures—hence its name, the Millenary Petition—and presented it to the King, who decided to debate the issues by convening a conference.

The original plan was to hold the meeting in Whitehall in November 1603, but an outbreak of plague in London made that impossible, so there was a postponement, and it was eventually held at Hampton Court. On Thursday 10 January 1604, the relevant personalities—bishops, deans, reformers, and the Privy Council—assembled there and were told that the conference would begin in two days and consist of three all-day sessions, to be held in the Privy Chamber. The traditionalists met there on the Saturday, the reformers on the Monday, and there was a final plenary meeting on the Wednesday.

It was on the second day that the leader of the Puritan group, John Rainolds, proposed 'that there might be a new translation of the Bible, because those that were allowed in the reigns of Henry VIII and Edward VI were corrupt, and not answerable to the truth of the original'. Although the conservatives were happy with the continued use of the Bishops' Bible of 1568, the idea appealed to the King. It was a way of giving something to the Puritans, whose proposals for church reform had otherwise been entirely rejected. More important, a Bible dedicated to him would endorse

The silhouette of the Great Hall and present-day King's apartments, walking towards the palace from the maze. There was no maze at the time of the Conference.

Wordsmiths and Warriors

the notion of a national church with the monarch as head, ruling by divine right. The religious standing of his inheritance would be confirmed. James was convinced, and within a few months six teams of translators had been chosen and set to work.

The English-language tourist, then, will certainly want to visit the Privy Chamber, and we had no difficulty, on entering Hampton Court, in finding the King's apartments on the first floor of the south side of the complex. We walked up the King's Great Stair, with its brightly coloured murals of the Olympian gods covering the whole wall and spilling across the ceiling. We passed a costumed Henry VIII with courtiers. Hilary curtsied, and (despite wearing jeans) received a courteous acknowledgement. The stairs led us to some outer rooms, and there was the Privy Chamber, with its imposing red throne canopy, wall tapestries, and rock crystal chandelier. 'So this is where the Hampton Court Conference was convened', I remarked knowledgeably to the attendant. 'No', he said.

The Great Hall.

It was only then I learned that half the Tudor palace had been replaced, when William and Mary took up residence there in 1689. The state rooms dating from the time of Henry VIII were demolished, and new wings were built around Fountain Court—one for the King, one for the Queen. The King's apartments faced south over the Privy Garden, which is where we had ended up. The original Privy Chamber would have been nearer the centre of the complex. We had walked past its ghost without realizing.

Two of the intricate Tudor chimneys.

We went over to the Great Hall. At least this was the original building—though with an interior much refurbished over the centuries—and moreover was where Shakespeare and the King's Men performed some of their plays. The two entrance doors, and a minstrel's gallery above, very much reminded us of the Globe (Chapter 31). The members of the Hampton Court Conference would have no problem identifying the intricate oak hammerbeam ceiling as it is today. And much of the outside of the palace would be familiar too, especially the ornate Tudor chimneys. This is as close as an English-language tourist can get to the origins of the King James Bible.

Why is this version so lauded linguistically? Primarily because of the wealth of idiomatic expressions that it popularized—such as *fly in the ointment, thorn in the flesh, skin of my teeth*, and *how are the mighty fallen*. There are over 250 of them, by my count. No other single book or author yields so many

Harris asked me if I'd ever been in the maze at Hampton Court. He said he went in once to show somebody else the way. He had studied it up in a map, and it was so simple that it seemed foolish—hardly worth the twopence charged for admission. Harris said he thought that map must have been got up as a practical joke, because it wasn't a bit like the real thing, and only misleading. It was a country cousin that Harris took in. He said:

'We'll just go in here, so that you can say you've been, but it's very simple. It's absurd to call it a maze. You keep on taking the first turning to the right. We'll just walk round for ten minutes, and then go and get some lunch.'

They met some people soon after they had got inside, who said they had been there for three-quarters of an hour, and had had about enough of it. Harris told them they could follow him, if they liked; he was just going in, and then should turn round and come out again. They said it was very kind of him, and fell behind, and followed.

They picked up various other people who wanted to get it over, as they went along, until they had absorbed all the persons in the maze. People who had given up all hopes of ever getting either in or out, or of ever seeing their home and friends again, plucked up courage at the sight of Harris and his party, and joined the procession, blessing him. Harris said he should judge there must have been twenty people, following him, in all; and one woman with a baby, who had been there all the morning, insisted on taking his arm, for fear of losing him.

Harris kept on turning to the right, but it seemed a long way, and his cousin said he supposed it was a very big maze.

'Oh, one of the largest in Europe,' said Harris.

'Yes, it must be,' replied the cousin, 'because we've walked a good two miles already.'

Harris began to think it rather strange himself, but he held on until, at last, they passed the half of a penny bun on the ground that Harris's cousin swore he had noticed there seven minutes ago. Harris said: 'Oh, impossible!' but the woman with the baby said, 'Not at all,' as she herself had taken it from the child, and thrown it down there, just before she met Harris. She also added that she wished she never had met Harris, and expressed an opinion that he was an impostor. That made Harris mad, and he produced his map, and explained his theory.

'The map may be all right enough,' said one of the party, 'if you know whereabouts in it we are now.'

Harris didn't know, and suggested that the best thing to do would be to go back to the entrance, and begin again. For the beginning again part of it there was not much enthusiasm; but with regard to the advisability of going back to the entrance there was complete unanimity, and so they turned, and trailed after Harris again, in the opposite direction.

CONTINUED »

About ten minutes more passed, and then they found themselves in the centre.

Harris thought at first of pretending that that was what he had been aiming at; but the crowd looked dangerous, and he decided to treat it as an accident.

Anyhow, they had got something to start from then. They did know where they were, and the map was once more consulted, and the thing seemed simpler than ever, and off they started for the third time.

And three minutes later they were back in the centre again.

After that, they simply couldn't get anywhere else. Whatever way they turned brought them back to the middle. It became so regular at length, that some of the people stopped there, and waited for the others to take a walk round, and come back to them. Harris drew out his map again, after a while, but the sight of it only infuriated the mob, and they told him to go and curl his hair with it. Harris said that he couldn't help feeling that, to a certain extent, he had become unpopular.

They all got crazy at last, and sang out for the keeper, and the man came and climbed up the ladder outside, and shouted out directions to them. But all their heads were, by this time, in such a confused whirl that they were incapable of grasping anything, and so the man told them to stop where they were, and he would come to them. They huddled together, and waited; and he climbed down, and came in.

He was a young keeper, as luck would have it, and new to the business; and when he got in, he couldn't find them, and he wandered about, trying to get to them, and then he got lost. They caught sight of him, every now and then, rushing about the other side of the hedge, and he would see them, and rush to get to them, and they would wait there for about five minutes, and then he would reappear again in exactly the same spot, and ask them where they had been.

They had to wait till one of the old keepers came back from his dinner before they got out.

Harris said he thought it was a very fine maze, so far as he was a judge; and we agreed that we would try to get George to go into it, on our way back.

idioms that have stood the test of time. And the rhythmical structure of the sentences has given it a permanent rhetorical appeal.

But it's important not to exaggerate the linguistic originality of the King James Bible. When I explored its language for *Begat*, a book to celebrate the 400th anniversary of its publication, I found that the vast majority of these idioms were already present in English before the translators set to work. This was quite deliberate, on their part. As they say in their Preface, their aim was not to make a new translation, 'but to make a good one better, or out of many good ones, one principall good one'. So it isn't surprising to find that many of their linguistic choices can be found in earlier versions,

Above top. The distinctive roofscape, looking towards the Great Vine, planted in 1768 by the landscape gardener Lancelot 'Capability' Brown. The Lower Orangery, on the right, was probably designed by William Tolman c.1700.

Above bottom. The Broad Walk in the Great Fountain Garden, looking east, with its huge yew trees—not something the Conference attendees would have seen. This part of the gardens was redesigned a century later.

Wordsmiths and Warriors

and especially in the translation of William Tyndale almost a century earlier (Chapter 27). What the King James version did was put this language into the public domain in a way that had not been possible before. As I say: they popularized.

English-language tourists actually do have other interests, so a visit to the Great Vine and the Broad Walk was essential. And to the famous Hampton Court Maze. Everyone goes in thinking that they can sort it. Jerome K. Jerome recounts a famous visit in Chapter 6 of *Three Men in a Boat* (1889), when Harris enters it brimming with misplaced optimism. We entered with equal confidence, and got into similar trouble. We had to cheat our way out, using a smartphone. It adds a new nuance to *apple of his eye* (Deuteronomy, 32.10).

Ben Crystal, fortunately with us for the day, finds us the way out, thus enabling the rest of this book to be written.

Getting there

From the M3, leave at junction 1 and follow the A309 east for some six miles, which takes you directly to Hampton Court. Alternatively, follow the A309 west from Kingston-upon-Thames. From the M4, leave at junction 3 and wind south through Hounslow. From the M25 take either exit 10 on to the A307 or exit 12 on to the A308. Brown tourist signs are prominent on all approaches (postcode: KT8 9AU).

As you approach it from the west, there's a prominent car park on the left, at Hampton Court Green. Although this is a third of a mile (500 m) from Hampton Court, it's wise to use it. A small amount of parking is available within Hampton Court itself, but you'd be lucky to get in there. For opening times, see the website at

http://www.hrp.org.uk/HamptonCourtPalace/

(Make sure, in any web search, that you include the word 'Palace', otherwise you might end up at the 15th-century Hampton Court Castle in Herefordshire.)

The train to Hampton Court/East Molesey from Waterloo takes about 35 minutes. Cross the bridge, and the entrance to Hampton Court is ahead of you. During the summer you can get there by boat from Westminster, but—depending on the tides—the journey can take up to four hours.

Chapter 36

Black Notley

John Ray and English proverbs

The *Notley* part is easy to gloss: 'a clearing in a nut wood'. But why *black*? The black vs white distinction is common enough in English place names. It sometimes refers to the colour of local stone, or of the water in a river which flows over it. It can describe the stone used to build the parish church, or the tar or whitewash which covered it. It can be an allusion to the colour of the soil. In the case of Black Notley and White Notley, near Braintree in Essex, the soil explanation is the most likely, though differences in the appearance of the two parish churches can't be ruled out.

John Ray (1627–1705) was born in Black Notley, in a cottage still standing on the long Baker's Lane that runs from the village to the old London Road. His father was the village blacksmith. For most people, Ray's fame is obvious: he was a botanist, 'the father of English natural history', as it says on his blue plaque on the barn next to the cottage. He published his first catalogue of local plants in 1660 and embarked on an ambitious project to classify all living things, travelling for a decade throughout Britain and the European mainland. His eventual masterpiece, *Historia Plantarum* ('History of Plants') was published in three volumes between 1686 and 1704.

He made notes about everything he encountered—geology, fossils, mines, husbandry, local industry, archaeology, beliefs, culture ... and language. He was fascinated by unusual words, technical terms, local dialects, and proverbial expressions, and it is his *Complete Collection of English Proverbs*, first published in 1670, that warrants his inclusion in an English linguistic itinerary. It had several editions and was reprinted many times,

Page opposite. The John Ray monument echoes the spire of St Peter and St Paul.

often along with his second language book, *A Collection of English Words Not Generally Used*.

Many of the proverbs he collected are still heard today, though often with slight variations (such as *A cat may look on a king* and *Early to go to bed and early to rise, makes a man healthy, wealthy, and wise*), but it is those no longer used that I find especially fascinating, such as *Wedlock is a padlock* and *He hath got the fiddle, but not the stick* [that is, he has the books but not the learning to use them wisely]. Among his list of 'proverbial similies' we find such splendid expressions as *to blush like a black dog, as fine as fivepence, as dizzy as a goose*, and *as nice as a nun's hen*. And he provides us with a thesaurus-like paragraph of 'proverbial periphrases of one Drunk':

> He's disguised. He has got a piece of bread and cheese in his head. He has drunk more than he has bled. He has been in the sun. He has a jag or load. He has got a dish. He has got a cup too much. He is one and thirty. He is dagg'd. He has cut his leg. He is afflicted. He is top-heavy. The malt is above the water. As drunk as a wheel-barrow. He makes indentures with his legs. He's well to live. He's about to cast up his reckoning or accompts. He has made an example. He is concerned. He is as drunk as David's sow. He has stolen a manchet [loaf] out of the brewer's basket. He's raddled. He is very weary. He drank till he gave up his half-penny [i.e. vomited].

As drunk as a wheel-barrow. I love it.

His first edition evidently caught the imagination, for in later editions he includes hundreds of extra examples sent in by readers from around the

country. He is well aware that the task is not straightforward. He is worried about having included 'English phrases that are not properly proverbs', and he is very apologetic about the earthier proverbs (to do with excrement) included in the first edition which have 'given offence to sober and pious persons, as savouring too much of obscenity, being apt to suggest impure fancies to corrupt minds'. So he leaves the worst of them out—though not without expressing his regrets at losing some 'useful notions'—and abbreviates sensitive words by using only their initial letters, in order not to 'turn the stomach of the most nice'.

Above and inset. John Ray's blue plaque is on the adjacent barn.

What Ray could not have done, of course, is record his own contribution to English lexicology. The *Oxford English Dictionary* contains nearly 3000 quotations from his works, and shows him as the first recorded user in English of 356 items, including many words well known to botanists (*night-flowering, pericarpium, ramose, umbelliferous* …), a host of animal names (*brown owl, guillemot, sandpiper, windhover* …)—and not forgetting the term *botany* itself.

His friends erected a monument to him in the grounds of the nearby parish church of St Peter and St Paul, where he is buried. There's a statue of him in Braintree, and a John Ray Gallery in the town museum. And he is remembered in the John Ray Walk, which runs for 9 miles (14.5 km) along the Brain Valley between Braintree and Witham. The direction signs have a distinctive buttercup logo. *Buttercup* isn't one of Ray's coinages, though

Engraving of John Ray by his contemporary, William Elder.

butter-jags is—a dialect name for birdsfoot-trefoil. And he has several proverbs about butter, such as *What is a pound of butter among a kennel of hounds*, *No butter will stick to his bread*, and—taking a modern reader somewhat by surprise—*All is not butter that the cow shites*. That last one evidently wasn't so offensive in the 17th century, though it might turn a few stomachs today.

Wordsmiths and Warriors

A really nice heritage touch is the way images of his work—birds and plants—are shown in relief on the walls of his cottage. His image is also there, though the engraving by William Elder has more character. Nothing linguistic, however, which is a pity, for John Ray has a claim to be called 'the father of English proverbs' too.

Getting there

Take the A120 south of Braintree and leave at the King William roundabout, signposted Braintree Town Centre. However, don't go into Braintree, but turn south at the roundabout onto the London Road: it's signposted Black Notley. Pass through Great Notley and at a mini-roundabout turn left into Baker's Lane. After a mile, you'll see John Ray's Cottage on the right, just before the road bends to the right and becomes Church Road. Coming from the other direction, it's on the left just after a 'road narrows' sign (postcode: CM77 8LB).

Follow Church Road round, and the turning to St Peter and St Paul's is a little way along on the right (postcode: CM77 8LE). It's possible to park outside the church. And as it's difficult for a car to stop on Baker's Lane, it's probably easier to walk back from there to see the Cottage.

Chapter 37

Aldwincle

John Dryden and an English Academy

Aldwincle. A tiny village in the middle of Northamptonshire, between Thrapston and Oundle, population around 350. It's the birthplace of John Dryden (1631–1700), in the rectory opposite the parish church, where he was baptized. That should be an easy one to find, we thought. The parish church in such a small place will be immediately obvious.

And so it was. As we approached the village from the north, along its proudly named Main Street, we saw a church right ahead of us, St Peter's, with a fine spire. And just behind it an imposing rectory-like building. We parked in front of the church and went in. Curious, no mention of Dryden at all. The house opposite was called the Rectory, but it was a new building. The larger one must be the old rectory, we thought. We dutifully photographed, and I puzzled over how a village could ignore its most famous baby.

And then, as we drove out of the village in the other direction, along Thorpe Road, we discovered our error. For at the eastern end of Aldwincle we saw—another church. The Church of All Saints. And opposite was not just one named building, but two: Dryden House and Dryden Cottage. Our faith in human nature was restored. And in our satnav.

All Saints no longer functions as a parish church. It was made redundant in 1971, and although occasional local events still take place there, it's now in the care of the Churches Conservation Trust. The oldest part dates from the 13th century, and it had some 19th-century restoration, but it's in a sad state now, inside—as we discovered once we had tracked down a key.

Page opposite. All Saints, Aldwincle, with John Dryden's baptismal font visible behind the end pillar to the right.

A notice on the church door gave us a choice between the Manor House behind the church or Peartree Farm Tea Room. Which would you choose? No contest, really, with the prospect of tea and scones to follow.

The church is full of Dryden memories. His maternal grandfather, Henry Pickering, was rector of All Saints for 40 years, dying in 1637. His daughter Mary married Erasmus Dryden, and John was the first of their 14 children. The baptismal font is near the side door. A modern memorial plaque, with a potted life story, has been fixed to a wall. Henry's gravestone was at some point brought inside the church, to protect it from the elements. And in one corner, an unexpected sight: a bier. An original one. I have to admit that this was a word I had only ever encountered in literature, as when Ophelia sings of her dead father: 'They bore him barefaced on the bier ...' Now I saw the reality. It didn't look at all as I had imagined it. Hardly a hearse. More a cross between a wheelbarrow and a pram.

But what has a poet—and a poet laureate, moreover (in 1668)—to do with English-language tourism? Dryden was the first to take active steps towards founding an academy which he hoped would protect the language from deterioration. The idea had been around for some time. A French academy had been founded in 1635, and a number of people felt that it would be a good idea to do something similar in England. In his dedication to *The Rival Ladies* in 1664, he writes:

Only I am Sorry, that (Speaking so noble a Language as we do) we have not a more certain Measure of it, as they in *France*, where they have an Academy erected for that purpose

The bier.

The climate of his time seemed to favour the idea. Dryden was one of many who felt that the language of Shakespeare's day had several weaknesses. In a famous epilogue to the second part of his play *The Conquest of Granada*, he favourably compares the English of his own time to that of Shakespeare, Jonson, Fletcher, and others from the previous age:

> Wit's now ariv'd to a more high degree;
> Our native Language more refin'd and free;
> Our Ladies and our men now speak more wit
> In conversation, than those Poets writ.

And in an accompanying essay, he sums it up: 'the language, wit, and conversation of our age, are improved and refined above the last'. But, he felt, things needed to stay that way. The language had to be protected from decay, and its perceived improprieties dealt with. 'We are the first to have observed them; and, certainly, to observe errors is a great step to the correcting of them.' An academy, he concluded, was the obvious solution.

Several members of the newly formed Royal Society (Chapter 38) had already been discussing the matter, and in December of that year they voted that there should be 'a committee for improving the English language; and that they meet at Sir Peter Wyche's lodgings in Gray's-Inn once or twice a month'. There was plenty to talk about. An academy could sponsor a grammar and a dictionary, make collections of dialect words, produce guides to spelling reform, commission translations to act as models of excellence, and much more.

However, the end of 1664 wasn't a good time to be proposing a language project. The Great Plague arrived a few months later, and people left town in droves. The year after, there was the Great Fire of London. Language projects disappear in times of national emergency. After a few months, the meetings petered out.

But the idea didn't go away, and Dryden came back to it again in the 1680s, assisting a similar proposal by the Earl of Roscommon, Wentworth Dillon. It was another turbulent time, as the Glorious Revolution of 1688 approached. The idea again died. It was taken up a decade later by Daniel Defoe, and another decade on by Jonathan Swift. Indeed, it has surfaced at regular intervals ever since. But it has never succeeded.

It was Dr Johnson who identified the fundamental flaw in the proposal. The French academy hadn't succeeded in 'fixing' their language, he observed; and if the French were unable to do it, with their absolutist government, what chance would an academy have faced with the bolshy, democratic British temperament? 'We live in an age in which it is a kind of publick sport to refuse all respect that cannot be enforced. The edicts of an English academy would probably be read by many, only that they might be sure to disobey them.' And that was well before English became a global language, with its many national varieties. An academy to control the whole language, with its two billion speakers, is inconceivable now.

But in the 17th century it seemed like a very good idea, and as Dryden has to be given most of the credit for first trying to take the idea of an academy forward, a visit to his birthplace has good motivation. But when we closed the door on All Saints church and looked across the road, we encountered a problem. Which of the two named houses opposite was the original rectory? Dryden House or Dryden Cottage? Google Maps was showing the name of the cottage. That's misleading, as we discovered when we returned the church key to Pear Tree Farm Tea Rooms. An elderly villager at the next table gave us the answer: it's the house. There's been a great deal of renovation and extension over the years, but the old part is easily visible from the road.

Of course, Dryden isn't buried in Aldwincle. The poet laureate is in Westminster Abbey, in good poetic company. But his Northamptonshire roots are still remembered. 'He's our poet', said the lady in the tea room.

Dryden House.

Getting there

Leave the A14 at junction 12, and take the A6116 north towards Corby. A couple of miles along, there's a right turn signposted Aldwincle. As you reach the sign announcing the village, take care. The main road (Lowick Road) bears left and there's a smaller road (Lowick Lane) off to the right. If you stay on the main road, as we did, you'll enter the village at the wrong end of Main Street. You'll see the spire of St Peter's in front of you. Worth a visit, certainly, but not for English-language reasons. If it's the right time of day, Pear Tree Farm Tea Rooms, on the right just past the school, will be open, and you can ask for the key to All Saints. (Then, when you return it, stay for some excellent refreshment.) All Saints is a few hundred yards further on, on the right. There's a convenient verge to park. The key fits the small side door facing the road.

If you take the correct turn, down Lowick Lane, you will end up on Thorpe Road, the continuation of Main Street. Turn right, and All Saints is then just a few yards along on your right. And if you come at the village from the east, from the A1(M) along the A605, there's a right turn signposted Aldwincle. Just after you pass the village entrance sign, you'll see All Saints through some trees, and it will be on your left soon after. Dryden House is then on your right (postcode: NN14 3UT).

Now ...

Chapter 38

Old Broad Street, London EC2

the Royal Society and scientific English

Sometimes it is individuals who influence the development of the English language; sometimes it is groups. Or, in this case, a committee. Or, to be more precise, in the language of its time, 'an invisible colledge'.

During the 1640s, a group of scholars began discussing the new philosophy of obtaining knowledge about the natural world through observation and experiment. We would call it *science* today. Before the 17th century, that term had a much broader application, being used to refer to any branch of knowledge or trained skill. Theology was called a science. So was Law. And Grammar.

Twenty years later, all this had begun to change. On 28 November 1660 a group of 12 men met at Gresham College in London and decided to found 'a Colledge for the Promoting of Physico-Mathematicall Experimentall Learning'. They included some of the brightest brains in the land, such as Robert Boyle, John Wilkins, Robert Hooke, and Christopher Wren. The idea was to hold weekly meetings to observe and discuss experiments. In a Royal Charter of 1663 they are named as 'The Royal Society of London for Improving Natural Knowledge'. The word 'natural' was chosen to contrast with the 'supernatural' concerns of scholarship of earlier days. Their motto was *nullius in verba*—roughly, 'take nobody's word for it'.

From the outset, the Society had linguistic interests. In 1644 it set up a 'committee for improving the English language', whose members included the polymath John Evelyn and the poet John Dryden. As we've seen

Page opposite. Tower 42, Old Broad Street.

. . . where . . .   could . . .

in Chapter 37, the thought was to found an institution to look after the language—an English academy, modelled on the French one—but the meetings petered out after a few months, partly because most members of the Society were preoccupied with other things, partly because of a lack of linguistic expertise. The arrival of bubonic plague in the spring of 1665 stopped further debate, for everyone who could left London for the country.

However, a search for a scientific English continued. In 1667 Bishop Thomas Sprat wrote a *History of the Royal Society* in which he condemns the ornateness and eloquence of the pre-scientific age, what he calls its 'superfluity of talking', and argued for an approach which avoided rhetoric, metaphors, and classical vocabulary, which he thought got in the way of clear thinking. The Royal Society was going to solve this problem:

> They have therefore been most rigorous in putting in execution, the only Remedy, that can be found for this *extravagance*: and that has been, a constant Resolution, to reject all the amplifications, digressions, and swellings of style: to return back to the primitive purity, and shortness, when men deliver'd so many *things*, almost in an equal number of *words*. They have exacted from all their members, a close, naked, natural way of speaking; positive expressions; clear senses; a native easiness:

it...   be?

bringing all things as near the Mathematical plainness, as they can:
and preferring the language of Artizans, Countrymen, and Merchants,
before that, of Wits, or Scholars.

Of course, they never achieved it. Sprat's own discourse was full of the very
language he was complaining about. Under no stretch of the imagination
could it be described as 'the language of artisans, countrymen, and merchants'. But gradually, a new style of writing did emerge, and today we see
it everywhere in scientific and technical publications.

Why did they meet at Gresham College? It's named after Sir Thomas
Gresham (1519–79), a merchant and founder of the Royal Exchange, and
his large mansion in Bishopsgate was the obvious place for a meeting of
intellectuals. Gresham had directed in his will that his house should be
used as an 'Institute for Physic, Civil Law, Music, Astronomy, Geometry
and Rhetoric', and this came to pass following the death of his wife in 1596.
It quickly achieved prestige. Chief Justice Coke in 1612 called it the Third
University of England.

Gresham House survived the Great Fire of 1666, but the Royal Society moved from that building a few years later, eventually acquiring its own place in Crane Court, off the Strand. Today, its home is in Carlton House Terrace, just behind The Mall. Gresham College still exists as an educational institution, holding regular public lectures in Barnard's Inn Hall in Holborn. The original Gresham House was demolished in 1768.

So, where was it? We weren't optimistic about our chances of finding the exact site in the middle of the modern city of London, but Thomas Gresham is on the blue plaque list, with a location on Old Broad Street, so we went there. Nowhere on our journey was there a more unmissable location. Gresham House turns out to be under Tower 42, the former NatWest Tower, so called because of its 42 cantilevered floors. It's 600 ft (183 m) high, and the UK's first true skyscraper. I got vertigo just by looking up.

We walked around the base of the tower. No sign of any plaque. We walked round it again. Still no sign. So we went in, and asked the man on the front desk, who knew exactly where it was as, he informed us, he'd been working next to it for more years than he cared to remember. He pointed towards the passageway outside the building, where there was a stall selling newspapers, postcards, and lottery tickets. A Union Jack hung limply from a pole behind it. We went outside and looked at the stall, but saw no plaque. We walked across the passageway to take a closer look, and still couldn't see it. And then, on a low wall beside the stall, partly hidden by a dustpan and brush, we found it: 'In a house on this site lived Sir Thomas Gresham 1519–1579'. Unquestionably the most hidden piece of evidence in our entire linguistic journey. And, perhaps appropriately, surrounded by the clutter of artisans and merchants.

Tower 42 is there at the beginning of the BBC television series *The Hitchhiker's Guide to the Galaxy*, as part of the sequence showing the destruction of the Earth. For Douglas Adams aficionados, 42 is of course the 'answer to the ultimate question of life, the universe, and everything'. That answer is what the Royal Society searches for too.

Getting there

Tower 42 is at 25 Old Broad Street (postcode: EC2N 1HN). The nearest underground station is Liverpool Street: walk down Bishopsgate and a passageway through to Tower 42 is on your right. Alternatively, Bank station is only a few minutes' walk away: walk up Threadneedle Street and Old Broad Street is the first on your left, with Tower 42 a little way down on your right. Facing the entrance, the stall hiding the Gresham plaque is on your left.

Chapter 39

Rochdale

Tim Bobbin and local dialect

On the information panel outside St Chad's church in Rochdale, Greater Manchester, a map shows the location of all the important features in the grounds. Only two individuals are given separate mention. One is the family grave of Hamlet Nicholson, the inventor of the modern 'corkie' cricket-ball. The other is 'Tim Bobbin's Family Grave'. A short explanatory paragraph to the side is headed:

Tim Bobbin
(John Collier)
1707–1786

I've never come across another burial place where a pseudonym outranks the real name. Local dialect, for once, wins.

John Collier started out as a schoolmaster at Milnrow, a village just to the south of Rochdale, and today adjacent to junction 21 of the M62. One of nine children, he himself had nine, and to support his family he began to write. He chose as his medium the local Lancashire dialect, and in so doing produced the earliest major piece of dialect writing from this part of the country, and made himself a role model for dialect enthusiasts everywhere.

The work that made his name was published in 1746, called *A View of the Lancashire Dialect*. It took the form of a comic dialogue between two locals, Tummus and Mary, and contained a glossary of the regional words and phrases used. He signed himself 'T. Bobbin, opp'n speyker o'th' dialect' [open speaker of the dialect]. The opening exchange illustrates the style:

Page opposite. The Collier tomb at St Chad's Church.

Tum. Odds mee, Meary! whooa the dickons wou'd o thowt o'leeting o thee here so soyne this morning? Where has to bin? Theaw'rt aw on a swat, I think; for theaw looks primely.

Mea. Beleemy, Tummus, I welly lost my wynt: for I've had sitch a traunce this morning os eh neer had e'meh life ...

[Tum: My God, Mary! who the dickens would have thought of alighting on you here so soon this morning? Where have you been? You're all in a sweat, I think; for you look very well.

Mary: Believe me Tummus, I well nigh lost my wind: for I've had such a round-about journey this morning as I never had in my life ...]

It was hugely successful, especially in the north of England, going through several editions and being widely pirated.

As often happens with dialect literature, there were critics. Some people felt he was making local people look like simpletons through the use of nonstandard language. But he made a strong defence, pointing out the ancient character of the words used, and drawing parallels with the way Welsh, Silesian, and other minority languages evoked pride rather than laughter. It's a defence which, regrettably, still sometimes needs to be made today.

There were also criticisms from some who felt that his portrayal of the Lancashire dialect was not accurate. This is also a common reaction, for it's impossible to represent a regional dialect exactly without a phonetic alphabet. When Samuel Bamford made an edition of *Tummus and Meary* in 1850, he castigated Tim Bobbin for introducing too many features of a Cheshire dialect, misrepresenting pronunciations, and using words that never had any general currency. 'I have always ... been of the opinion that it is a very imperfect setting forth of the Lancashire Dialect', he says, and then presents his own version, introducing many phonetic changes, such as (in the above extract) *aw* for *I*, *mornin'* for *morning*, *wynt* for *wind*, *treawnce* for *traunce*, and *lyve* for *life*. Bobbin's original version, nonetheless, has retained its reputation.

In addition to his dialect writing, Bobbin achieved a considerable standing as an artist. He painted inn-signs, pictures for chapels, portraits of individuals and groups, oil paintings, and a large number of satirical social caricatures which led to his being called 'the Lancashire Hogarth'. A savagely critical set of engravings by Bobbin, *Human Passions Delineated*, for which he also wrote the accompanying text, was published in 1773.

Page opposite. Tim Bobbin, in a 1773 etching. His humour extended even to epitaphs. There's one attacking a vicar of Rochdale, Dr Forster, which begins:

Wordsmiths and Warriors

JOHN COLLIER,
better known by the name of
TIM BOBBIN.
Author of Lancashire Dialect, &c.

Pub. by Alex. Hogg & Cº. Jan. 1. 1808.

> Full three feet deep beneath this stone
> Lies our late Vicar Forster
> Who clipp'd his sheep to'th' very bone,
> But said no Pater Noster . . .

And he was just as scathing about himself:

> A yard beneath this heavy stone
> Lies Jack-of-all-Trades, good at none . . .

His gravestone has a rhyme on it too, written by his son, and referring to his wife, buried in the same grave:

> Here lies John and with him Mary,
> Cheek by jowl and never vary
> No wonder that they so agree
> John wants no punch and Moll no tea.

St Chad's is highly visible in Rochdale, at the top of Sparrow Hill. A flight of 122 steps lead up to it from the lower part of the town. Symmetrically laid gravestones surround the church—memorials to the innkeepers, bakers, druggists, and other townspeople of Bobbin's time. His own grave was refurbished in 1892, following a public subscription initiated by Sir Walter Scott. Iron railings make it stand out from the others.

Why did he call himself Bobbin? A bobbin is a wooden tube on which yarn is wound, so it was perhaps a natural choice, in a part of the country where spinning and weaving were major industries. In any factory picture of the period, what you see are rows and rows of bobbins. And the word had a further life outside the factory walls. A *bobbin-hat* was 'a silly fellow'; a *bobbin-gun* was 'a toy gun' made from a bobbin; a *bobbin turner* was 'a useless effeminate fellow' (all definitions from Joseph Wright's *Dialect Dictionary*). 'That's all bobbin winding', they used to say in this part of Lancashire, and maybe they still do. 'It's all rubbish.'

Broadfield Park nearby has a memorial to local dialect poets, overlooking the museum and art gallery. As we walked down to it, we passed a schoolyard full of chattering children. I could hear a broad Lancashire 'ay up' from faces which ethnically came from well beyond these shores. Dialect is alive and well up here, and certainly no longer restricted to those who have white Anglo-Saxon origins.

The monument remembers the 19th-century writers Edwin Waugh, Margaret Lahee, John Trafford Clegg, and Oliver Ormerod, as well as a

The dialect writers' memorial in Broadfield Park. The building to the left is the town hall.

Oliver Ormerod: 'Aw sed awm o Rochde felley mon un we're meterly fause theere aw'll warrunt te.' [I said I'm a Rochdale fellow man and we're tolerably false (= sharp, shrewd) there I'll warrant thee]

'Olis let o mon doo that uts reete un e's sartin shure fur to koome eawt th best ut last ov o.' [Always let a man do that it's right and he's certain sure for to come out the best at last of all]

20th-century poet, Harvey Kershaw. It has one of the most moving tributes ever made to dialect writing. In bold capitals, picked out in gold paint, we read:

> In grateful memory of our Rochdale writers of the Lancashire dialect who have preserved for our children, in verse and prose that will not die, the strength and tenderness, the gravity and humours of the folk of our day, in the tongue and talk of the people this memorial was erected A.D. 1900.

Tim Bobbin is not the only dialect poet to be remembered in Rochdale, therefore, but he's undoubtedly the most famous. If further evidence were needed, we need only ask how many other such poets have had hotels and pubs named after them? There's a Tim Bobbin Hotel in Burnley, and a pub called The Tim Bobbin in Urmston. There's even one on Clapham Common in London, today called simply The Bobbin. That's as prime (see Tummus above) as it gets.

The Tim Bobbin at Urmston, Greater Manchester.

Wordsmiths and Warriors

Getting there

Leave the M62 at junction 20, and take the A627(M) and then the A58 (the Manchester Road), following the signs into Rochdale. For St Chad's, turn right at the lights into Drake Street (A640), and a few hundred yards along turn left either into Vicar's Drive or the next street along, Church Stile. St Chad's is at the end (postcode: OL16 1QT). It's possible to park on the road nearby. The Tim Bobbin grave is to the right of the church, surrounded by railings.

You can enter Broadfield Park opposite the church, at the corner of Vicar's Drive and Sparrow Hill. Follow the path down the hill and round to the right, beneath the Broadfield Hotel, and this leads to the Dialect Writers Memorial, just in front of the entrance to the Victoria footbridge.

Chapter 40

Lichfield and London

Johnson and the dictionary

A single name invites the English-language tourist to Lichfield, Staffordshire: Samuel Johnson, whose *Dictionary of the English Language*, published in 1755, is one of the most significant achievements in the history of lexicography. The second most-quoted author in English after Shakespeare, his achievements as a creative writer, literary critic, essayist, editor, biographer, and conversationalist give him a reputation that extends well beyond the study of language. Linguists frequently quote him, for he had a great deal to say about language in general and languages in particular. 'I am always sorry when any language is lost, because languages are the pedigree of nations.'

The *Dictionary* presented the complexity of English vocabulary more fully than ever before: its two large folio volumes contained 42,773 entries in the first edition, with 140,871 definitions and 222,114 quotations illustrating the way words were used. These citations were the real innovation, and all quality dictionaries have since followed Johnson's lead. Nor did he restrict himself to 'hard words', as many previous dictionaries had done (Chapter 32), but aimed to be comprehensive. For Johnson, the 'little words' of the language, such as *do* and *make*, were just as important as the 'big words', such as *ascertainment* and *declination*. It took him five pages to explain all 124 senses of the verb *take*.

It's the precision and clarity of his definitions which has always impressed me most. When people think of Johnson's definitions, they tend to cite his more difficult or idiosyncratic examples. These are the ones which get into

Page opposite. Johnson on his plinth.

the books of quotations, such as his definition of *oats* as 'grain, which in England is given to horses, but in Scotland supports the people'. Most of his definitions aren't like this at all. And people have interpreted cases of this kind far too seriously. That one was almost certainly an in-joke, of the kind that the history of lexicography frequently displays. It would have been no more than a friendly dig at his amanuenses, five of whom were from Scotland.

Rather, to see Johnson's skill, we need to look at such instances as his elegant definition of *history*:

> A narration of events and facts delivered with dignity.

or his perceptive definition of *sorry*:

> Grieved for something past. It is generally used of slight or casual miscarriages or vexations, but sometimes of greater things. It does not imply any long continuance of grief.

His dictionary is a far more personal compilation than we are used to today, but that is part of its charm. We see his personality appearing in many entries. There is the wry observation at *lexicographer*:

> A writer of dictionaries; a harmless drudge, that busies himself in tracing the original, and detailing the signification of words.

And he makes a polite bow to his birthplace in the entry on *lich*, as well as adding a comment which was surely provided by one of his Scottish colleagues:

> A dead carcase; whence *lichwake*, the time or act of watching by the dead; *lichgate*, the gate through which the dead are carried to the grave; *Lichfield*, the field of the dead, a city in Staffordshire, so named from martyred christians. *Salve magna parens. Lichwake* is still retained in Scotland in the same sense.

Salve magna parens: Hail, great mother!

Whichever direction you come from, when you turn the corner into Market Square, in the centre of Johnson's 'great mother', you can't miss him, even on a day when the square is filled with market stalls. An imposing statue stands in front of the birthplace museum, created in 1938 by Richard Cockle Lucas, and shows Johnson in academic robes, sitting on a chair with books underneath, and clearly deep in thought. From the expression on his face, he is not having a good day.

On three sides of the plinth there are scenes from his life. The fourth side has an inscription commemorating the gift of the statue by the Chancellor of the Diocese at the time, Dr James Thomas Law, as well as a plaque added in 1984 for the 200th anniversary of Johnson's death. Look back across the square and you see another statue: Johnson's biographer, James Boswell—not facing the great man in admiration, as you might expect, but gazing in a totally different direction, towards the cathedral. It's almost as if they've had an argument, and aren't talking to each other.

Johnson spent the first 27 years of his life in the birthplace house, and often returned to it. He always felt close to Lichfield, as his 'mother' reference suggests. The museum opened to the public in 1901, and is a Grade 1 listed building now. It contains over 6500 items relating to Johnson and his period, many on permanent display in rooms recreating the environment

The birthplace museum.

in which he lived. A surprising number of personal items have survived, including his armchair, tea set, and portable writing desk. Were Johnson to visit the museum today, I think he would feel quite at home.

The walls display many prints and paintings, but the eyes of the visiting language enthusiast will very likely be drawn to the collection of manuscripts and books. There are several letters in Johnson's hand. The Wood library (named after the first chairman of the Birthplace Committee) is the museum's study area. You can make an appointment to explore the collections at your leisure (but you need to bring some photographic ID). It's on the second floor of the museum, and accessible only by stairs.

At the very top of the house is the Dictionary Room, opened in 2005 as part of the celebrations for the 250th anniversary of publication. I was president of the Johnson Society that year, as it happens, and cut the opening ribbon. I rather like the thought of the dictionary being at the top of the house, crowning Johnson's achievement in so many fields. Pride of place is devoted to a copy of the huge two-volume folio-size *Dictionary*, but there are several other items and artworks in the room. However, none of the

In the Dictionary Room, the *Dictionary* glows in the light as Johnson and a modern admirer look on.

Wordsmiths and Warriors

Dictionary was compiled here: for that, you have to visit one of Johnson's London residences.

Johnson had moved to London in 1737, along with his friend David Garrick, lodging at several addresses before renting a house at 17 Gough Square, a courtyard just north of Fleet Street. He would need the space. A team of six amanuenses would eventually help him on the dictionary project, copying out quotations and pasting them onto pages. Boswell tells us that when he moved to Gough Square, in 1748, 'he had an upper room fitted out like a counting-house for the purpose, in which he gave the copyists their several tasks'. It was evidently furnished in a very basic way, judging by the report Boswell gives of a visit to the room by Mr Burney in January 1758, after the dictionary work was over:

> After dinner, Mr. Johnson proposed to Mr. Burney to go up with him into his garret, which being accepted, he there found about five or six Greek folios, a deal writing-desk, and a chair and a half. Johnson giving to his guest the entire seat, tottered himself on one with only three legs and one arm.

Dr Johnson's house is the building at the end of the Square, next to the blue entrance sign.

The colourful Johnson portrait in stained glass, with Lichfield Cathedral in the background, in a window overlooking Gough Square.

We're fortunate that we still have the house at all. It was in a derelict state when it was purchased by member of parliament and newspaperman Cecil Harmsworth in 1911. He restored it and opened it to the public, but it was then nearly destroyed by bombing on three occasions during World War II. It's now run by the Dr Johnson's House Trust. People interested in Johnson as a whole will admire the period restoration. Lichfield is remembered in a famous stained glass portrait. English-language tourists, I imagine, will immediately climb up the tightly winding staircase from the entrance hall to the garret on the fourth floor. It's a surprisingly small space, for such a large project. At one end of the room there's a display cabinet that tells the dictionary story. At the other, a small table carries a full-size copy of one of the dictionary volumes. When we were there, two visitors were poring over it, and making notes about some of the entries. Harmless drudgery still rules!

The garret, with the stairs on the left, showing virtually its entire length.

Wordsmiths and Warriors

Getting there

You can get to Lichfield from all points of the compass. The nearest motorway junction is T5 on the M6 Toll, 2 miles (3.2 km) south of the city. You can also reach the city from junction 9 of the M42 (12 miles/19 km away) and junction 4A of the M6 (15 miles/24 km). A-class roads nearby are the A5, running west towards Telford and south-east towards Tamworth; the A38, running south to Birmingham and north-east to Derby; and the A51, running around the west and south of the city, south-west to Tamworth and north-west to Stafford.

The museum is on the corner of Breadmarket Street and Market Street (postcode: WS13 6LG). Information about opening hours is on the website:

http://www.samueljohnsonbirthplace.org.uk

Several car parks are nearby. Bird Street is the nearest, and there's a multi-storey car park in Lombard Street. The car parks are well signposted as you drive into the town centre, but be prepared to look further afield, for they're often full.

Gough Square is a short walk north from Fleet Street. Aim for the Cheshire Cheese pub at 145 Fleet Street, and turn into the nearby alleyway, Wine Office Court, then bear left, and you're there (postcode of the Johnson House: EC4A 3DE). For opening hours, see

http://www.drjohnsonshouse.org

The nearest underground station is Chancery Lane: take pedestrian exit 3 into Holborn, and walk straight ahead to Fetter Lane. Turn right, and stay on the left-hand side until you reach West Harding Street. Turn left, and at the end turn right into Pemberton Row. You then enter Gough Square from the opposite end—via a roadway that passes under the first floor of a building.

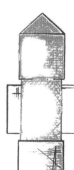

Chapter 41

Old St Pancras Church, London NW1

John Walker and pronunciation

One of the best moments, when you go searching for the English language, is when you arrive in a place expecting to find just one attraction and you find two. This happened in one of the unlikeliest settings: Pancras Road in London.

It's an easy road to find, as it's overlooked by two well-known railway stations. The Euro-bound platforms of St Pancras on the left. The King's Cross redevelopment with its huge car park on the right. Behind, the chaotic traffic of Euston Road. Ahead, the busy shops of Camden Town. Trains to the left of me; trains to the right of me. The last thing I expected, as I walked north along Pancras Road was to encounter such a peaceful backwater as Old St Pancras Church. We have to call it 'old' now, as in 1822 it was replaced by a new St Pancras on Euston Road.

It was so quiet, when I arrived, that I could have heard the softest of consonants at 50 paces. An ideal resting-place for the greatest elocutionist of the 18th century: John Walker (1732–1807). He was so well-known that people gave him his own epithet—'Elocution Walker'. They saw him as following in the footsteps of his contemporary, 'Dictionary Johnson' (Chapter 40). Such epithets are not bestowed lightly in the history of the English language.

The book which earned him his accolade had been planned as early as 1774, when he published his basic ideas in *A Pronouncing Dictionary of English*. It finally appeared, in 1791, with this lengthy title:

Page opposite. The cluster of tombstones around the Hardy Tree.

A Critical Pronouncing Dictionary and Expositor of the English Language: to which are prefixed, Principles of English Pronunciation: Rules to be Observed by the Natives of Scotland, Ireland, and London, for Avoiding their Respective Peculiarities; and Directions to Foreigners for Acquiring a Knowledge of the Use of this Dictionary. The Whole Interspersed with Observations Etymological, Critical, and Grammatical.

The book reflects the prescriptive temperament of the 18th century. It was a period of growing class distinction, with a well-off industrial middle class elbowing its way in to the established hierarchy of upper and lower classes. It was a century of politeness and manners. A new etiquette had to be learned, and advice on how to speak and write—and especially how to avoid making linguistic *faux pas* in society—played a critical part.

Today few people would take kindly to someone condemning regional accents so roundly—especially those of the Scots, the Irish, and the Cockneys (which is why they receive special mention in the title)—and asserting that everyone should aim to emulate the 'best' accent, which was to be found (of course) only among the educated speakers of London. But it suited the climate of the times, and it met a need. Walker became a household name, both in Britain and the USA.

He was somewhat taken aback by his success. He complains in the Advertisement to the Fourth Edition how the rapid sale of the third had made him take up his pen again 'at a time of life, and in a state of health, little compatible with the drudgery and attention necessary for the execution of it'. But he did it, and the book would see over a hundred subsequent editions.

He never planned it that way. He actually started out as an actor, first in a touring company and then in London, where he began as a protégé of David Garrick at the Drury Lane Theatre. But he changed direction when he was 37—probably during one of those periods of uncertainty and 'rest' that afflict all actors from time to time—and took up the lucrative career of elocutionist.

He died at an address somewhere on the Tottenham Court Road, and was buried in the graveyard of the local church, which at the time was St Pancras. This is the inscription on his tombstone:

Here lie the remains of
Mr. JOHN WALKER,
Author of the
Pronouncing Dictionary of the
English Language,
and other valuable Works on
Grammar and Elocution,
of which he was for many years
a very distinguished
Professor.
He closed a life
devoted to piety and virtue,
on the 1st August, 1807,
aged 75.

It's rare indeed for an epitaph to single out a publication, and I doubt if there are many gravestones around the world which contain the words 'the English language'. I've never seen another.

So here we have John Walker's final resting-place? Not at all, thanks to the directors of the Midland Railway, who during the 1860s wanted to

Right. The monument to John Walker, with the words: 'This memorial stone was preserved by the Baroness Burdett-Coutts June 28 1877'.

Below. Walker's name can just be made out at the top of the stone.

Wordsmiths and Warriors

extend their line into London, and found the corner of the churchyard in the way. So they bought it. The work required the removal of a huge number of skeletons and tombstones, and one of them was Walker's. His stone received special treatment, for in 1877 it was picked out from the hundreds of others by Baroness Burdett-Coutts, reputedly the wealthiest heiress in England in the mid-19th century, and a noted philanthropist. Walker must have made a great impression on her during her schooldays, 50 years earlier, to be so remembered. She had his stone mounted on a plinth in a special frame, where it can still be seen on the north side of the cemetery—though few of the words can be made out now, after a century of weathering.

Who carried out the work of exhumation? This was the unexpected bit, for it turned out to be the young Thomas Hardy, who has his own chapter in this book (Chapter 50). Hardy originally trained as an architect, and while in London during the 1860s he was working in the office of the company appointed to clear the churchyard. The head of the firm, Arthur Blomfield, gave the unpalatable task to his 25-year-old apprentice, and throughout the late autumn and early winter of 1865 Hardy found himself in St Pancras every evening supervising the exhumation. The account provided by Hardy's second wife, Florence, evokes the atmosphere of the occasion:

> There after nightfall, within a high hoarding that could not be over-looked, and by the light of flare-lamps, the exhumation went on continuously of the coffins that had been uncovered during the day, new coffins being provided for those that came apart in lifting, and for loose skeletons; and those that held together being carried to the new ground on board merely ...

His role in the project is now dramatically visible in the form of the Hardy Tree. He had over 200 of the gravestones placed around the trunk of an ash tree growing near the boundary with the railway line. Today, after 150 years of growth, the wood has expanded to enfold several of the stones, resulting in a remarkable living sculpture. The memorial is protected by a low hedge, but the stones are easily visible through pieces of railing. Its appearance changes with the seasons. When we visited, on a blustery October day, the fallen leaves from the many mature trees in the churchyard had blown into the crevices between the stones, adding flashes of brown brightness to the

O passenger, pray list and catch
Our sighs and piteous groans,
Half stifled in this jumbled patch
Of wrenched memorial stones!
We late-lamented, resting here,
Are mixed to human jam,
And each to each exclaims in fear,
'I know not which I am!'
The wicked people have annexed
The verses on the good;
A roaring drunkard sports the text
Teetotal Tommy should!
Where we are huddled none can trace,
And if our names remain,
They pave some path or p-ing place
Where we have never lain!
There's not a modest maiden elf
But dreads the final Trumpet,
Lest half of her should rise herself,
And half some local strumpet!
From restorations of Thy fane,
From smoothings of Thy sward,
From zealous Churchmen's pick and plane
Deliver us O Lord! Amen!

Passenger, incidentally, here meant 'any passer-by', though readers would probably not have missed the new railway connotation.

dull white and grey. From the roots at one side of the tree, new growth was appearing.

Hardy may well have been thinking of St Pancras when, in 1882, he wrote his poem 'The Levelled Churchyard'. It was written in Wimborne, Dorset, where the local church was also having its grounds renovated. The point which has been much debated is why in his manuscript Hardy deleted the subtitle 'W—e Minster'. Might he have wanted the poem to relate to both Wimborne and St Pancras? Certainly, the earlier event was still on his mind, for when Arthur Blomfield visited him there, Hardy records that one of the memories they shared was the moment when a coffin fell apart to reveal a skeleton and two skulls. 'Do you remember the man with two heads at St Pancras?' asked Blomfield.

Today the church is in use again, part of a Christian team ministry active in this part of London. The gardens provide an oasis of calm for local residents—and, I discovered, their dogs. I sidestepped a pair of Jack Russells furiously attacking each fallen leaf as if it were a personal enemy, and viewing me with the kind of look they reserved for unwanted intruders. The owner called them back. A distinct Cockney accent. Enough to make Walker turn in his no-longer-existing grave.

Getting there

Starting at Euston Road, the most direct walking route is up Midland Road, between St Pancras Station and the British Library. If you're coming from King's Cross Station, you turn right up Pancras Road, which temporarily becomes Goods Way. Turn left over the railway lines and then right, and Old St Pancras Church is on your right (postcode: NW1 1UL). The nearest car park is at the rear of St Pancras International station on Pancras Road, the A5202. You can only get to it from Euston Road.

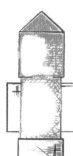

Chapter 42

York

Lindley Murray and English grammar

Is nothing sacred? Not even grammar?

We arrived in the York suburb of Holgate to see the places where the most famous grammar-book of the 19th century was written, Lindley Murray's *English Grammar*. Published in 1795, it had sold approaching two million copies by 1850, and sales kept going into the last decade of the 19th century—69 editions in all. Much of it was written in a tiny summerhouse in the grounds of his house on Holgate Road, where he lived from 1795 until his death in 1826. When the building was sold to the North Eastern Railway Company in 1901, the owner presented the summerhouse to the nearby Mount School.

It's a quaint structure, octagonal in shape, made of wood, and surrounded by stone steps on a circular base. An ogee lead roof is supported by Doric columns. Originally built in about 1774, it's now a listed building. It was at first placed against the boundary wall of the school grounds, but when new tennis courts were constructed in 1966 it was moved to its present position in a corner of the grounds, where it was later refurbished. Its white painted walls make it easily visible as soon as you enter the grounds at the back of the school, and perhaps in that lay its downfall. Thieves spotted it, and stole the lead from the roof. The lead was replaced. They did it again. It was replaced. And when we visited, the lead had disappeared for the third time. The school was hoping they'd be allowed to replace the roof with something less valuable! The latest damage was still evident when we arrived, and a temporary tarpaulin flapped dismally at us.

Page opposite. Murray's summerhouse at The Mount School. His writing desk and wheeled invalid chair are preserved in the school.

Holgate House, down the hill from the school. It was for a while a hotel (the Collingwood) and then became apartments. This is how Murray describes it in a letter to his brother (1 June 1801): 'My sitting room is pretty large, with a bow window at each end, one looking into the garden, and the other towards a fine verdant hill about two hundred yards distant.' The hill is still there, but the verdancy is long gone.

Lindley Murray was born in Swatara in Pennsylvania in 1745, became a lawyer and a merchant, then moved to England in 1785, after the Revolution, where he stayed for the rest of his life. A strong believer in Quakerism, he and his wife chose to live in York, where there was a sizeable Quaker community, and they found a house in the village of Holdgate (modern Holgate), at the time just outside the city. There he helped to establish Esther Tuke's Trinity Lane School, a boarding school for young teenage girls. This was the forerunner of the present-day Mount School, an independent day and boarding school for girls aged 11 to 18.

He wasn't a well man, and the symptoms of his illness—including a progressive weakening of limbs and voice—are now thought to have been a consequence of childhood polio. A Quaker friend wrote at the time:

> Lindley Murray has not been able to walk much more than two or three yards at a time, for about ten years past. He ... sits up the whole day, but is no more able to speak than to walk; as he can only whisper a few words at a time ...

The crippling disease crushed any hopes the Murrays had of being able to return to America. All he could do was write. He started with a spiritual memoir, and then, in 1794, received a special request from three teachers at the school who,

> having suffered great inconvenience from the want of a complete English Grammer with examples & Rules annexed, proper for this and similar Institutions ... do humbly solicit the digesting of his materials for a work so important.

Wordsmiths and Warriors

He was at first reluctant to take the job on, but then agreed, stressing that his work would not be at all original, but merely a compilation intended to improve on the grammars that were already around. He had it finished a year later. A compilation it certainly was, with long sections copied exactly from earlier grammars, such as the one written by Robert Lowth in 1762. The extensive borrowing was criticized at the time, but he defended his practice by arguing that his aim was only 'to facilitate the labours of both teachers and learners of English'.

His career took off at that point. A book of exercises followed in 1797, along with a separate book of answers and an abridged version of the grammar. An *English Reader* followed in 1799, a sequel in 1800, an introduction in 1801, and a spelling-book in 1804. According to one estimate, the combined sales of all these books eventually amounted to some 14 million copies worldwide, hugely popular in Britain and America, and frequently reprinted and translated in places as far away from England as India and Japan.

By 1900 he was being called 'the father of English grammar'. Indeed, his name became so synonymous with grammar that people would talk simply of 'Murray', without further need to specify—in much the same way that some talk of 'Fowler' today (Chapter 52). His name appeared on commercial products, such as cigar tins and matchbox holders. Oscar Wilde ends a review of a marriage handbook by describing its author as 'the Murray of matrimony and the Baedeker of bliss'. There was even a board game produced in 1857 called *A Journey to Lindley Murray*—a sort of ludo with a spinning top and coloured pieces. No modern grammarian has ever achieved such fame.

Not all the references were favourable. Critics disliked his prescriptive attitude and the mechanical exercises, and many of his rules were condemned as artificial—as has happened to prescriptive grammars ever since. The novelists in particular loved to tease their readers about the way Murray's grammatical canons were being followed so slavishly. At the beginning of *Uncle Tom's Cabin*, Harriet Beecher Stowe says of a gentleman: 'His conversation was in free and easy defiance of Murray's Grammar'. Charles Dickens, in *The Old Curiosity Shop* (Chapter 29), tells how Mrs Jarley's waxworks exhibition made a great impression on her audiences 'of a very superior description, including a great many young ladies' boarding-schools, whose favour Mrs Jarley had been at great pains to conciliate, by altering the face and costume of Mr Grimaldi as clown to represent Mr Lindley Murray as he appeared when engaged in the composition of his English Grammar'. And Murray turns up in novels by George Eliot, Mark Twain, Charlotte Brontë, and several others.

Although Murray was a grammarian, his reputation was such that he became associated with any usage issue, such as this article from *Punch* in 1854, reporting a sitting of the Court of Queen's Bench under Mr Justice Campbell dealing with cases of bad pronunciation. It was headed: LAW AND LINDLEY MURRAY. Three of the case summaries are given below.

THE QUEEN v. LORD JOHN RUSSELL.

The defendant was charged with habitually offending against HER MAJESTY's English, by making a noise sounding like 'obleege', when he was supposed to intend to say 'oblige.'

The defendant pleaded guilty, but urged that a hundred years ago his pronunciation was the fashionable one. It was derived from the French.

LORD CAMPBELL said, that in the case of JOHN KEMBLE v. the PRINCE REGENT the *dictum* had been, 'It would become your Royal mouth better to say "oblige".' The rule was clear. Had the defendant anything further to say?

The defendant said that he had once visited the Lyceum Theatre, and had heard MR. FRANK MATTHEWS say, in a burlesque called *Robin Hood*—

'With any advice about the siege,
The Field-Marshal therefore cannot obleege.'

LORD CAMPBELL said that this proved that the defendant had been warned. The object of burlesque—and he was bound to say that such object was usually attained—was to ridicule what was absurd, by pushing absurdity to the extreme. The Court did not desire to be hard upon the defendant. Would he undertake not to repeat the offence?

The defendant said that he would endeavour to conform to the customs of the day; but he believed that in Magna Charta—

He was here somewhat hastily removed from the Court.

THE QUEEN v. RICHARD CORDEN.

The defendant was charged with laying a false emphasis upon the third syllable in the word inimical, which he pronounced inimical.

The defendant said that he had not intended to give offence, and that he had heard the same pronunciation from the Treasury Bench last week.

LORD CAMPBELL said that the Treasury had better go to its 'Tyronis [i.e. beginner's] *Thesaurus*.' (*Laughter, in which nobody joined.*) The pronunciation was pedantic—why did not the defendant say severity and urbanity?

The defendant was discharged with a caution.

CONTINUED »

He became the butt of satirical articles and cartoons on both sides of the Atlantic, in such periodicals as *Punch* and *Harper's Weekly*. A widely circulated joke in the later Victorian period went like this:

> Did you hear the one about why Charles Dickens never became a spiri-tualist? At a seance, he asked to see the spirit of Lindley Murray. There came in what professed to be his spirit, and Dickens asked, 'Are you Lindley Murray?' 'Yes, I are', replied the spirit.

Now that is real fame, when you end up in the music halls.

Getting there

From the south, from the A64, turn left onto the A1237 and then the B1224 which leads straight into Holgate. From the north, the A59 leads directly into Holgate. You pass the Fox pub on the left, and Holgate House (No. 163) is immediately on your right. There's some open land opposite where it's possible to park briefly. The road then runs uphill and bends sharp right. The Mount School is on your right (postcode: YO24 4DD). Go past the school and turn right into Driffield Terrace. There's a visitor car park at the back of the school, and the summerhouse is on your left as you enter the grounds, at the far end of the tennis court. It's essential to arrange an appointment with the school.

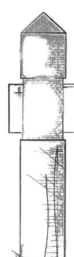

Chapter 43

Alloway

Robert Burns and Scots

Not even in Stratford-upon-Avon is there anything like this! In the centre of the exhibition area of the recently opened (2011) Robert Burns's Birthplace Museum in Alloway, Ayrshire, there is a pastiche of Leonardo's 'Last Supper'. Twelve famous personalities are ranged around the central figure. No prizes for guessing who that is. The six on his left are Gandhi, Sean Connery (as James Bond), Einstein, Nelson Mandela, Beethoven, and John Lennon. The six on his right are Elvis Presley, Marilyn Monroe, Che Guevara, William Shakespeare, Cassius Clay (Muhammad Ali), and Queen Victoria. Beethoven and Shakespeare each have a hand outstretched towards the central figure in humble acknowledgement. Elvis Presley is holding a microphone up to catch his words. In the ceiling above his head there is a halo.

The poetic achievement of Robert Burns (1759–96) is remarkable, by any standards—though what he would have made of this level of adulation is anyone's guess. But it is his linguistic achievement which attracts the English-language tourist to his birthplace. His adaptation of English to express Scottish identity built on an evolution of the language that began in the 12th century (Chapter 19). It was at the heart of a resurgence of regional literature that conferred a fresh level of national prestige upon the Scottish variety of nonstandard English. Indeed, the language became so distinctively different from varieties south of the border that it motivated a popular movement to call it a separate language, Scots.

Burns's epic poem, 'Tam o'Shanter', is partly set in Alloway. It tells the story of Tam who, after an evening's heavy drinking in an Ayr public house, sees on his way home a coven of witches and warlocks dancing at Alloway

Page opposite. A 'wee tim'rous beastie' guards the Poet's Path in Alloway.

Kirk. He stops to watch them, but they become aware of his presence, and chase him. He just manages to escape, thanks to his speedy horse which carries him across Alloway Bridge where the witches, unable to cross fresh running water, can't follow him. The bridge over the River Doon and the old church (Auld Kirk) are huge tourist attractions now.

The amount of distinctive Scots lexicon and pronunciation varies throughout the poem. Some lines are entirely standard English; some are heavily regional. The opening lines illustrate the mix:

When chapman billies[1] leave the street,   [1]peddler people
And drouthy neibors,[2] neibors, meet;   [2]thirsty neighbours
As market days are wearing late,
And folk begin to tak the gate,[3]   [3]take the road home
While we sit bousing at the nappy,[4]   [4]boozing with strong ale
An' getting fou and unco[5] happy,   [5]drunk and very
We think na on the lang[6] Scots miles,   [6]not on the long
The mosses,[7] waters, slaps[8] and stiles,   [7]marshes [8]steps
That lie between us and our hame,[9]   [9]home
Where sits our sulky, sullen dame,[10]   [10]wife
Gathering her brows like gathering storm,
Nursing her wrath to keep it warm.

The Auld Kirk, with William
Burns's tombstone.

People responded to Burns's writing because they were able to identify
with it, and appreciated its pride in a variety of English that had for centuries been obscured by the literary standards of the south. For Scottish
English, Burns opened the floodgates. Two centuries later, and some of
the most powerful and successful writing in nonstandard English would
be coming from north of the border, with authors adapting the language to
create their individual linguistic identities. We don't find uniformity, when
we look across the range of writing in Scots. Words appear in a range of
spellings—well might be spelled *weill* or *wel*, or *weel*, for example—and
there are variations in the choice of words and grammatical constructions
too. Scots has diversity, just as standard English does.

And it is prominent in the Alloway sites. As we approached the entrance
to the museum, we passed a bird-like sculpture made of dialect words and

The words in the wall at the Burns Museum. The sources are in the lines below:

'To a Mouse'
Wee, sleekit, cow'rin', tim'rous beastie,[1]   [1]small, sleek, cowering, timorous beast
O what a panic's in thy breastie![2]   [2]breast
. . .
That wee[3] bit heap o' leaves an' stibble[4]   [3]small [4]stubble
Has cost thee mony[5] a weary nibble!   [5]many
Now thou's[6] turned out, for a'[7] thy trouble,   [6]you are [7]all
But[8] house or hald,[9]   [8]without [9]holding
To thole[10] the winter's sleety dribble   [10]endure
An' cranreuch cauld! [11]   [11]hoar-frost cold

'The Lea Rig'
When o'er the hill the eastern star
Tells bughtin'[1] time is near, my jo,[2]   [1]folding [putting sheep into a fold] [2]sweetheart
And owsen frae[3] the furrow'd field   [3]oxen from
Return sae dowf[4] and weary, O.   [4]so dull

Burns Cottage.

The 'language' room in Burns Cottage.

a wall into which half-a-dozen words from 'To a Mouse' and 'The Lea Rig' have been incorporated. There are more on the walls of Burns Cottage: *ram-stam* ('thoughtless, headstrong'), *spunkie* ('will o' the wisp'), *bleth'rin* ('talking idly'), and the wonderful *crambo-jingle* ('doggerel rhymes'). In its 'language room', we felt the dialect around us, like a warm cloak.

The cottage entrance leads into the barn and byre, where there's a clever video bird's-eye view of the family going about its business, with full animal accompaniment—cocks crowing, birds singing, and cows lowing. But the English-language tourist's eye will straightaway be drawn to the next room—the spence, or parlour (originally, a place where provisions were kept, or 'dispensed'), where Robert had his lessons. Not just the eye: the ear

The Burns Monument,
Alloway.

too. As we entered the room, the voice of a teacher was solemnly informing
Master Robert (and us) that 'verbs have two numbers'. An inscription on
the wall proudly states: 'Inspired by Language and Learning'. We felt totally
at home.

Burns is not buried in Alloway—though his father's tombstone is immediately visible in the grounds of the Auld Kirk. There's a Burns Mausoleum
in St Michael's Churchyard in Dumfries. But Alloway boasts one of the largest monuments to a poet seen anywhere, set in its own gardens. And there
are plaques to him in several other Scots cities—Inverness, Edinburgh,
Montrose, Dumbarton—and statues in Melbourne, Detroit, Vancouver,
Montreal, Paris … I can't think of anyone who matches his sculpted reach.
Maybe the museum mural isn't such an exaggeration after all.

Wordsmiths and Warriors

Getting there

From Glasgow, go south along the M77 until it becomes the A77, and after you pass Ayr there's a right turn to Alloway. It's well marked with tourist signs: Burns Cottage and the Birthplace Museum. The road into Alloway is called Murdoch's Lone. The Museum is at the end on the left (postcode: KA7 4PQ). To get to the birthplace, you turn right at the T-junction, and Burns Cottage is a few hundred yards along on the left. There are car parks at both places. Some people drive from one to the other, but it's better to leave the car at one of the locations and stroll along the landscaped path which joins them, Poet's Walk, with its series of weather-vane silhouettes telling the story of Tam o'Shanter. A not so wee tim'rous beastie, sculpted by Kenny Hunter, is guardian of the Walk. For opening times, see the website at

http://www.burnsmuseum.org.uk

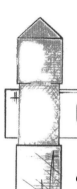

Chapter 44

Peebles and Edinburgh

the Chambers brothers and
encyclopedic English

There's an old music-hall joke which goes like this:

A: I say, I say, I say, I can speak French.
B: I didn't know you could speak French. Let me hear you speak French.
A: Paris, Marseilles, Bordeaux . . .

I didn't say it was a good joke—but it illustrates a good point: the difference between encyclopedia and dictionary. Clearly, knowing the names of people and places is very different from knowing how to talk about people and places. And yet, there are overlaps. Getting names right requires knowledge of spelling and pronunciation. We have to know how to exploit names grammatically in a sentence (as when we say, in front of a painting, 'That's a Renoir'). And we have to be prepared for extensions in meaning (as when we say 'Downing Street has spoken'). American dictionaries typically include proper names in their lists—and some British ones do too, these days.

Encyclopedias and dictionaries are bedfellows in another way, as can be seen when they are placed together under 'general reference' in many a bookstore. They are part of a language's *institutions*—the major works which try to find order in the multifarious ways in which a language is used. They are part of the codification of language—along with thesauruses, grammars, pronunciation manuals, and style guides. There are several places in England where people have codified aspects of English (Chapters 37, 41, 42, 46, 52); but for the English of encyclopedias, and the link

Page opposite. William Chambers' statue, by John Rhind, in Chambers Street, Edinburgh. Chambers was Lord Provost of Edinburgh between 1865 and 1869.

between encyclopedias and dictionaries, the best place to go is Scotland. To be precise: to Peebles, where William and Robert Chambers were born at the beginning of the 19th century (1800 and 1802 respectively).

It's another 'rags to riches' story, and—having reflected on the stories of Joseph Wright (Chapter 51) and others—it makes me think that there's something about language which motivates people from poor families and with little formal education to achieve such heights. Perhaps it's to do with the way spoken language puts everyone on a level playing field. It costs nothing to listen to the accents and dialects of one's social milieu, and one doesn't need a degree to become a fluent and aware speaker or to develop a fascination with the way language works. But it does take an event of some kind to trigger the process. And in the case of the Chambers brothers, it starts in the attic of their house at 18 Biggiesknowe in Peebles—the oldest street in the town, running alongside Eddleston Water, a tributary of the Tweed.

Riverside view of the white-walled Chambers house in Peebles, built in 1796 by the brothers' grandfather, and today a listed building and private house. In William Chambers' Memoir, it's described as 'a modern-slated house ... a neat, small mansion, fronting to the Eddleston Water. . . . a ground-floor full of looms, and a garret full of webs and weft.' The front entrance, with a memorial plaque, is now on Biggiesknowe.

Wordsmiths and Warriors

Their father had bought a copy of the fourth edition of *Encyclopædia Britannica* from a Peebles bookseller, but—as Robert recounts in the *Memoir* written by his brother (p. 56):

> It was a cumbrous article in a small house; so, after the first interest in its contents had subsided, it had been put in a chest (which it filled), and laid up in an attic beside the cotton wefts and the meal ark. Roaming about there one day, in that morning of intellectual curiosity, I lighted upon the stored book, and from that time for weeks all my spare time was spent beside the chest. It was a new world to me. I felt a profound thankfulness that such a convenient collection of human knowledge existed, and that here it was spread out like a well-plenished table before me. What the gift of a whole toy-shop would have been to most children, this book was to me. I plunged into it. I roamed through it like a bee. I hardly could be patient enough to read any one article, while so many others remained to be looked into.

The reference to cotton wefts is to the hand-loom weaving business their father ran from their house. A meal ark was a wooden storage bin.

The arrival of power looms, along with some unwise financial decisions, led to the closure of the business, and in 1813 forced a move to Edinburgh, where the family fell on hard times. William had no chance of further education, and found work as a bookseller's apprentice. Robert did complete his school years, but the cost of a university education was well beyond him. So, at the age of 16, he set up as a bookseller, renting a single-roomed premises in Leith Walk, with space outside for a stall, and was joined there by William when his apprenticeship was completed. William, needing to

William's first shop, with a space for a stall in front, was on Leith Walk, opposite Balfour Street (at the time called Pilrig Avenue)—somewhere on the left of this picture, looking north. He adds a grammatical dimension to the description of Leith Walk: 'a broad kind of Boulevard stretching a mile in length to the seaport':

'The oddest thing about the Walk . . . was an air of pretension singularly inconsistent with the reality. The sign-boards offered a study of the definite article—The Comb Manufactory, The Chair Manufactory, The Marble Work, and so forth, appearing on the fronts of buildings of the most trumpery character.'

An internet shop now stands roughly where William's shop was.

In William Chambers' *Memoir* (pp. 189–91) we read of a Mr Moffat, who worked at the Excise Office in Edinburgh:

I was one day in my room at the office. It was a busy day with me. I had to sign several papers brought to me by Grubb. After that was over, when I was just sitting down to the newspaper, a message was brought, requiring my presence at the Board. I could not imagine why I was sent for. Surely, thinks I, it cannot be on account of going out a few minutes daily for necessary refreshments. However, there was no time to consider. So off I went to the Board-room, trusting to put as good a face on the matter as possible. Well, to be sure, there were the whole of the Commissioners—a very full meeting that day—seated around the table covered with green cloth, each of them with fresh pens and sheets of paper before him, as if about to take down a deposition. I am going to be pulled up, thinks I. Things certainly looked very bad. My feelings were a little calmed when the chairman—a polite man, exceedingly so—requested me, in a softened and pleasant tone of voice, to take a chair near him. Well, I sat down accordingly, making a bow to the Board. The chairman then addressed me:

'Mr Moffat, the Commissioners have had a great difficulty under their consideration. It is a thing of no small importance, for it concerns the interest of the Department. Some of the Commissioners incline to one view of the matter, and some to another. In short, not to keep you in suspense, that which puzzles the Board is the pronunciation of a word—a very important word; not, indeed, that I am puzzled, for my mind is clear upon the subject. To settle the matter definitely, we appeal to you. Knowing your scholarly acquirements, and more particularly your acquaintance with the drama and the correct elocution of the stage, we have agreed to abide by your decision.'

Here, of course, I again bowed.

'Yes,' continued the chairman, 'we put ourselves into your hands. To be perfectly fair, I will not utter the word, but write it down, letter by letter, thus: —

R-e-v-e-n-u-e,

and leave you to determine how it should be pronounced.'

I felt honored. I had for years studied the word. I had made up my mind about it. Bowing once more to the Board, and turning towards the chairman, I said:

CONTINUED »

> 'Sir, I feel the importance of the occasion. That word is certainly a very important word. It is a word in which the whole nation has a very great interest. Knowing especially its value to the Department, I have for years made it my study, and will state the opinion at which I have arrived. The common or vulgar pronunciation of the word is Rev'enue; but that is decidedly incorrect. The true pronunciation, which I hold by, is that of John Kemble—namely, Reven'ue—a heavy emphasis to be laid on the n.'
>
> Instantly there was a shout of applause from various members of the Board, and the chairman, who was vastly pleased, said to me most emphatically: 'Thank you, Mr Moffat; you and I must eat mutton together!'

occupy himself during the many hours when the weather was too bad to display books outside, and no customers were in the shop, bought a cheap letterpress machine, and taught himself to be a printer. He chose as his first venture (1819) a pocket edition of the songs of Robert Burns. It took him months to prepare: he personally printed and bound 750 copies—for which, he tells us, he had to pull the handle of his press down some 20,000 times. But it was worth it, for it was a success, and the Chambers name began to be known.

It led to a business partnership: Robert would act as chief writer and editor; William as printer, publisher, and occasional writer. In 1821 their first collaboration appeared: the *Kaleidoscope, or Edinburgh Literary Amusement*, just 16 pages, once a fortnight, price three pence. It wasn't easy, maintaining the output—the brothers worked 16 hours a day—and the venture folded after just a few months. But other books on Edinburgh and Scotland were having more success. And then in 1832 they began to publish a weekly newspaper, *Chambers's Edinburgh Journal*, with the masthead quaintly (to modern eyes) telling the readership that it was 'conducted by William and Robert Chambers'. It was a remarkable miscellany, with long and short articles covering current affairs, science, geography, religion, poetry, literary extracts, and more. They wrote many of the articles themselves. Opening the issue for 9 January 1841 at random, I see an article on railway accidents, another on Lord Clive, and another on a cure for squinting.

It was the era of the 'cheap-literature' movement. William wrote in his *Memoir*:

> I resolved to take advantage of the evidently growing taste for cheap literature, and lead it, as far as was within my power, in a proper direction.

He would do this, he says, by keeping the stylistic level plain, making sure it was not 'too technical and too abstruse for the mass of operatives'. It was an explicitly educational motive. Literature, he observes, has hitherto been for the privileged few, and he wants to put good writing into the hands of everyone:

> Every Saturday, when the poorest labourer in the country draws his humble earnings, he shall have it in his power to purchase with an insignificant portion of even that humble sum, a mean of healthful, useful, and agreeable mental instruction.

William and Robert got it right. Literacy was rapidly growing. Estimates vary, but the likely growth of literacy in Britain during the 19th century was from around half the population to over 90 per cent. And the numbers were growing too—from around 10 million in 1801 to nearly 40 million in 1901. The price of three halfpence made the *Journal* widely accessible. It sold 50,000 copies within a few days, and circulation soon grew to 80,000.

One popular project followed another. *Chambers's Information for the People* appeared in 1833, followed two years later by *Chambers's Educational Course*—including a book written by Robert on the history of English language and literature. The scale of the enterprises grew. In 1844 they made a compilation of English literature that they called a *Cyclopaedia*—a term first used by an earlier Chambers, Ephraim (no relation to William and Robert), who had published *Cyclopaedia: Or, an Universal Dictionary of Arts and Sciences* in 1728. That work had impressed Dr Johnson, who told Boswell that he had partly based his style upon that used by Chambers. It also influenced the French encyclopedist Diderot, who had been asked by a French publisher to make a translation. Then the wheel turns full circle, for we end up in Scotland again. Diderot's *Encyclopédie* so impressed a small group in Edinburgh, known as the Society of Gentlemen, that they set to work on a project which they subtitled 'A Dictionary of Arts and Sciences, compiled upon a New Plan', published in 1768. We know it today by its main title, *Encyclopædia Britannica*. The geographical origins of this great work can still be seen. Look carefully at the colophon on the front cover and title page, and you see a Scottish thistle.

The *Cyclopedia* was another success, so the Chambers brothers went for the big one. Between 1859 and 1868 they produced the first *Chambers's Encyclopaedia: a Dictionary of Universal Knowledge for the People*, written by a hundred contributors. It was issued in 520 parts at the same three-halfpence price, eventually producing a 10-volume compilation costing 90 shillings (= £4.50). After a slow start it became a huge success, selling 50,000 sets in Britain alone. A new edition followed in 1874. There was a second revision in 1888–92, with over a thousand contributors, including William Gladstone. The third edition (1923–7) had articles by Shaw, Chesterton, and Daniel Jones. Chambers' Encyclopedia (the extra *s* was eventually dropped) became a household name. The publishing house of

One of the unpredictable encounters that arise when a place is personally visited. A little further along Leith Walk, we saw what was probably the most unusual collocation of names encountered in this book (though see Chapter 43 for a close competitor).

W & R Chambers grew to be an established part of the Edinburgh scene and a flagship of Scottish publishing.

What the Chambers brothers did was blend the two institutions, dictionary and encyclopedia, in a novel way. In their *Journal* in 1874 they write: 'an encyclopedia ought to be nothing more than a comprehensive dictionary, handy in dimensions, easily purchased, and conveniently accommodated in a library'. Over a century later, I found myself making the same argument, as editor of a family of encyclopedias in a joint-venture project for W & R Chambers and Cambridge University Press. The production was entirely in the hands of Chambers, so we would frequently find ourselves in its Edinburgh office at 43–5 Annandale Street, where there was a fine stained-glass window memorial of the Chambers' house in Peebles. In the end, the project was published by Cambridge alone, as *The Cambridge Encyclopedia*, in 1990. Chambers had been taken over—the first in a series of takeovers which led to the firm finally closing its Edinburgh premises in 2009. Only William's statue remains, in the street named after him.

We felt a traveller's connection with William as we walked along Chambers Street. One of his publications was a *Gazetteer of Scotland*.

> To impart a sufficient degree of freshness, I made several pedestrian journeys to different parts of the country, gathering here and there particulars which I thought would be of value.... My object was to see as many places as possible, and fix their situation and appearance in my mind.

With photography and a car, the task is so much easier today. But we have had to do a fair amount of walking, to complete this book, and the point about freshness is as valid as it ever was. Derivative accounts of places are all well and good, but you never know what is going to surprise you when you make a personal visit.

Getting there

Peebles is due south of Edinburgh, on the A703 where it joins the A72. Travelling west along the A72, Biggiesknowe is on the left just before the bridge over Eddleston Water, but there's no left turn here from the A72. From the east, just before the High Street turn right into Northgate and immediate left into Bridegate, and Biggiesknowe is on the left (postcode: EH45 8HS). There's a convenient car park down the hill just opposite Biggiesknowe. From the A72, No. 18 is a little way along Biggiesknowe on the right. The back of the house can be seen from the riverside walk, across the bridge and down some steps.

For Chambers Street, walk up North Bridge (the A7), above Waverley Station, passing the Royal Mile, until it becomes South Bridge, and Chambers Street is on your right. The Chambers statue faces the National Museum (postcode: EH1 1JF).

For Leith Walk, turn left at the Waverley Station end of Princes Street, and walk down Leith Street past the shopping centre and the Roman Catholic Cathedral. After two roundabouts you enter Leith Walk (the A900), and Balfour Street is a third of a mile along on the left (postcode: EH6 5DG). You pass Annandale Street on the way. Turn left at the youth hostel if you want to see the former publishing house, which is now a community centre (postcode: EH7 4AZ).

Chapter 45

Grasmere

William Wordsworth and poetic language

There aren't many literary authors in this book. That's deliberate. The book isn't about the places associated with those who used English brilliantly in their novels, poems, and plays: that's a different story, and one which has already been addressed, not least by Margaret Drabble in her *Writer's Britain* (1979). It's a book about the places associated with those whose activities significantly influenced the development of the language or who played a major role in studying it or reflecting upon it. William Wordsworth falls clearly into the latter category. So we went to Grasmere.

And were immediately distracted by the Good Bag Company, whose shop on the main street was on the way to St Oswald's cemetery, where the Wordsworths are buried. It sells environmentally friendly jute shopping bags with appealing slogans. English-language tourists can't fail to notice the exclamation marks waving at them as they pass by, or the playfully warm typography. 'mums are good!!!' 'Knitting is ... GOOD!!!' 'DOGS ARE ... GOOD' (with each O replaced by a paw mark). 'CHOCOLATE is ... Soooo GOOD!!!' We went in, and bought 'BOOKS are ... Good!!!'

Dove Cottage, where Wordsworth and his sister lived between 1799 and 1808, is just outside the town, on the main road between Kendal and Keswick. It had previously been a small inn, The Dove and Olive Bough, and in 'The Waggoner' Wordsworth expresses some sympathy for the travellers for whom the inn is no longer a welcoming port of call:

Page opposite. The Rock of Names.

The Wordsworth graves in St Oswald's cemetery. The one on the left says simply: William Wordsworth 1850, Mary Wordsworth 1859. The neighbouring graves are those of his sister, brother, and children. The grave behind, with the carved cross and rose stone, is that of Hartley Coleridge, the eldest son of Samuel Taylor Coleridge. Eight of the yew trees in the grounds were planted by William.

At the bottom of the brow,
Where once the Dove and Olive Bough
Offered a greeting of good ale
To all who entered Grasmere Vale;
And called on him who must depart
To leave it with a jovial heart;
There, where the Dove and Olive Bough
Once hung, a poet harbours now,
A simple water-drinking Bard.

It was in Dove Cottage, as it later came to be called, that he wrote the long Preface to the second edition of the poems he and Coleridge included under the title of *Lyrical Ballads*, and which has since come to be seen as the linguistic clarion-call of the Romantic movement in English literature.

Opposite top. Dove Cottage.

Opposite bottom. Looking south towards Grasmere.

The principal object, then, proposed in these Poems, was to choose incidents and situations from common life, and to relate or describe them throughout, as far as was possible, in a selection of language really used by men, and, at the same time, to throw over them a certain colouring of imagination, whereby ordinary things should be presented to the mind in an unusual aspect.

It was a firm rejection of the preceding poetic age.

By 'real language' Wordsworth had in mind a kind of writing which would avoid the elaborate syntax and elegant diction employed by the 'Augustan' poets, such as Pope and Dryden, and capture the direct simplicity of expression he saw in Chaucer. As he says in another part of his Preface:

> There will also be found in these volumes little of what is usually called poetic diction; as much pains has been taken to avoid it as is ordinarily taken to produce it; this has been done for the reason already alleged, to bring my language near to the language of men.

We hear the colloquial rhythms, for example, in the third canto of 'The Waggoner', where Benjamin the waggoner encounters a superstitious sailor who is petrified when he hears an owl screeching:

> 'Yon owl!—pray God that all be well!
> 'Tis worse than any funeral bell;
> As sure as I've the gift of sight,
> We shall be meeting ghosts to-night!'
> —Said Benjamin, 'This whip shall lay
> A thousand, if they cross our way
> I know that Wanton's noisy station,
> I know him and his occupation;
> The jolly bird hath learned his cheer
> Upon the banks of Windermere;
> Where a tribe of them make merry,
> Mocking the Man that keeps the ferry;
> Hallooing from an open throat,
> Like travellers shouting for a boat.'

The writing does indeed convey the illusion of everyday speech, even though the poetic medium inevitably distances the language from what would have been real early 19th-century conversation. And it is in his Preface that Wordsworth provides us with his linguistic rationale that has become one of the classic statements in the study of English literary style. It was all worked out in Dove Cottage.

We walked up the garden slope behind the house, and at the top, in a niche in the hillside, we found the fascinating Rock of Names, containing fragments of a rock on which Wordsworth and his friends once carved their initials in large seriffed capitals: W.W. (William Wordsworth), M.H. (Mary

Page opposite. A detail from the Rock.

Wordsmiths and Warriors

Light is the strain, but not unjust
To Thee, and thy memorial-trust
That once seemed only to express
Love that was love in idleness;
Tokens, as year hath followed year,
How changed, alas, in character!
For they were graven on thy smooth breast
By hands of those my soul loved best;
Meek women, men as true and brave
As ever went to a hopeful grave:
Their hands and mine, when side by side
With kindred zeal and mutual pride,
We worked until the Initials took
Shapes that defied a scornful look.——
Long as for us a genial feeling
Survives, or one in need of healing,
The power, dear Rock, around thee cast,
Thy monumental power, shall last
For me and mine! O thought of pain,
That would impair it or profane!
Take all in kindness then, as said
With a staid heart but playful head;
And fail not Thou, loved Rock! to keep
Thy charge when we are laid asleep.

The lines are found in the manuscript of the third canto of 'The Waggoner' (1805), but omitted from the published version. The carving of the letters is likely to have been in 1800, when John Wordsworth lived with his brother and sister at Grasmere, though the memorial plaque by the lake at Thirlmere says it was 1801–2. The poem could have been written at any time in the first few years of the decade.

Hutchinson, later his wife), D.W. (Dorothy Wordsworth, his sister), S.T.C. (Samuel Taylor Coleridge), J.W. (John Wordsworth, one of his brothers), and S.H. (Sarah Hutchinson, Mary's sister). Some of the original letters can still be made out—but it's remarkable that any were preserved at all.

The rock was located on the roadside at the southern end of Thirlmere lake. It was a place where Wordsworth, Coleridge, and their friends often met, as it was roughly halfway between Grasmere and Keswick (where Coleridge lived). The carving event is even recorded in a poem (see panel). But when the lake was turned into a reservoir for Manchester in the early

1890s, the rock had to be moved, and it broke up in the process. The conservationist and co-founder of the National Trust, Canon Hardwicke Rawnsley, managed to preserve the crucial pieces and formed them into a cairn at the side of the road at Thirlmere. Then, in 1984, it was moved to behind Dove Cottage, the pieces incorporated into a model of the original rock, with missing letters re-carved. So, although much 'impaired and profaned', the rock has indeed managed to 'keep its charge'.

The rock spoke to us more than the house did. Inscriptions are goood.

Getting there

Leave the M6 at junction 46, and follow the signs for Kendal, Windermere, and Ambleside (postcode: LA22 9SQ). As you approach Grasmere from the south, Dove Cottage is on the right, just before the turning into the village. There is car parking outside. For opening times and other details, see the website at

http://www.wordsworth.org.uk

To visit St Oswald's Church (and the Good Bag shop!), you have to drive into Grasmere village along Stock Lane and over the bridge into Church Stile. Turn left into Red Bank for a car park, next to Grasmere Garden Village.

Chapter 46

West Malvern

Roget and the thesaurus

An edition of Roget's *Thesaurus* must be on millions of household shelves; but I doubt whether many of the owners could say the first name of the author. He is simply 'Roget'. Even the word 'thesaurus' is redundant. We only have to say 'I looked it up in Roget', and everyone knows what we mean. This is special. Few writers on the English language are known by their surname only.

Most of the names on the old gravestones of St James's Church in West Malvern, Worcestershire, are worn away. A few have been retouched. Roget's is very visible. Unlike the old crosses and stumpy headstones, spread unevenly over the tree-lined hillside at unpredictable angles, his grave is marked by a prominent rectangular slab, which glistens even on a dull day. The name is there, in neat capitals: Peter Mark Roget, MD FRS, died at West Malvern, 12 Sept 1869 aged 90. His daughter, Catherine Mary, who looked after him in his final years, is there too.

He didn't live in West Malvern. It was an annual holiday visit, and it coincided with an intense heatwave which gave him severe and fatal heat-stroke. His home was London—from 1808 at 30 Bernard Street (just off Russell Square), and later at 18 Upper Bedford Place (now Bedford Way), in the heart of Bloomsbury. The point was noted by J. M. Barrie, who pays him special homage at the beginning of Act 1 in the play version of *Peter Pan* (1904):

Page opposite. The entrance to St James's Church, West Malvern, with welcoming feet.

St James's Church
cemetery, with Roget's grave
prominent.

The night nursery of the Darling family, which is the scene of our opening Act, is at the top of a rather depressed street in Bloomsbury. We have
a right to place it where we will, and the reason Bloomsbury is chosen
is that Mr. Roget once lived there. So did we in days when his *Thesaurus*
was our only companion in London; and we whom he has helped to
wend our way through life have always wanted to pay him a little com-
pliment. The Darlings therefore lived in Bloomsbury.

And Roget is there in spirit throughout. At one point, after an angry Mr
Darling chains up Nana the dog, Barrie adds a stage comment:

Let us hope that he then retires to his study, looks up the word 'temper' in his *Thesaurus*, and under the influence of those benign pages
becomes a better man.

And at another, he even shows some sympathy towards Captain Hook:

Wordsmiths and Warriors

The man is not wholly evil—he has a *Thesaurus* in his cabin.

Roget's gravestone.

What made the book so popular? It was a first—a new kind of thesaurus.

A thesaurus is different from a dictionary. When we use a dictionary, we know a word and want to look up its meaning. When we use a thesaurus, it is the opposite: we know a meaning, and want to look up a word. The thesaurus provides us with words and phrases that are similar in meaning (synonyms), so that we can choose the best one for our purposes. What expressions are there in English to express the notion of 'dead'? This is the entry in an edition from the 1960s (omitting cross-references):

> dead, deceased, no more; passed over, passed away, released, departed, gone; long gone, dead and gone, dead and buried, in the grave, six feet under, buried; born dead, stillborn; lifeless, breathless, still; extinct, inanimate, exanimate, bereft of life; stone dead, cold, stiff; dead as mutton, dead as a doornail, dead as a herring, dead as nits; departed this life, out of this world, called to one's eternal rest, gathered to one's fathers, in Abraham's bosom, numbered with the dead; launched into eternity, behind the veil, on the other side, beyond the grave, beyond mortal ken;

gone to Elysium, gone to the happy hunting-grounds; defunct, late, lamented, regretted, sainted; martyred, slaughtered, massacred, killed.

Monty Python saw the comic potential of such lists in its famous 'dead parrot' sketch.

There had been books of synonyms before Roget, listed alphabetically, like a dictionary. What Roget did was to group these thematically, and organize his themes into a hierarchy that covered all areas of meaning. The synonyms for 'dead' are part of an entry on 'death', which is next to an entry on 'life', and these are part of a larger section called 'vitality' (as distinct from 'sensation'), which in turn is part of an even larger section called 'organic matter' (as distinct from 'inorganic matter' and 'matter in general'), and this is part of a still larger section called 'matter' (as distinct from 'space', 'intellect', 'volition', 'affections', and 'abstract relations'). Nobody had tried to combine synonyms and topics in this way before.

Why do it? The full title gives the answer: 'Thesaurus of English Words and Phrases Classified and Arranged so as to Facilitate the Expression of Ideas and Assist in Literary Composition'. People, quite simply, found it invaluable. The book sold a thousand copies a year, after its publication in 1852. By the time Roget died it had been reprinted over 30 times. It has never been out of print, and there have been hundreds of editions, revisions, and adaptations, the earliest ones by his son and grandson. The original book contained only 15,000 words; today it has over a quarter of a million.

It took him the best part of 50 years to complete. He says in his preface that he had been collecting and classifying words from as early as 1805, for his own personal use—'to supply my own deficiencies … in literary composition'—but he did not publish his collection until he was 73. Why so late? Although he had often thought of publication, he continues in his preface, 'a sense of the magnitude of the task, amidst a multitude of other avocations, deterred me from the attempt'. However, retirement from his duties as secretary of the Royal Society finally gave him the leisure to work on the project. He spent some four years preparing it, doing very little else, and continued to revise it incessantly, even when ill during those final days in Malvern.

The letters after his name on the tombstone indicate his avocations— the MD for medicine, and the FRS (Fellow of the Royal Society) reflecting his work in several scientific fields. There is no mention of his lexicography. But his obituary in *The Lancet* (25 September 1869) anticipates what we now know: 'the work which has given a lasting and widespread repute to his name is his admirable Thesaurus'.

Getting there

If you approach along the A449 from Worcester, you join the B4232, a narrow winding road up the eastern slope of the Malvern Hills, past Great Malvern. You glimpse increasingly fine views across Worcestershire through the trees and houses. St James's eventually appears on the right (postcode: WR14 4BB). There's parking on the road. Someone has painted pairs of yellow feet on the ground at the entrance to the churchyard (46.1). Don't follow them—unless you want to visit the church itself—but walk past the church to the far end of the cemetery. Roget's grave is on the right, at the top of the slope.

Chapter 47

Bath

Isaac Pitman and English shorthand

On the north wall of Bath Abbey, surrounded by a dozen ornate memorials, is a simple grey plaque with a blue insignia. An eight-spoked wheel in the insignia has a special significance. Its curves and radial lines provided Isaac Pitman (1813–97) with the inspiration for his system of shorthand, or 'phonography', as he called it, which had a remarkable popular following in the second half of the 19th century and into the 20th. The full title page of his most successful work, published in 1840, sums it all up:

> A Manual of Phonography or Writing by Sound: a Natural Method of Writing all Languages by one Alphabet, composed of Signs that represent the Sounds of the Human Voice, adapted also to the English Language as a complete system of Short Hand, briefer than any other system, and by which a speaker can be followed verbatim, without the use of any arbitrary marks, beyond the Letters of the Alphabet.

That's the description from the fifth edition in 1841. By the end of the century it had gone through 12 editions and sold a million copies. The follow-up *Phonographic Instructor*, with its practical exercises, did even better: two million by the end of the century. And in the Education Code of 1890, shorthand was included as an optional subject in the school curriculum.

Linguists are sometimes described as 'sad', because of their obsessive attention to points of linguistic detail. If so, no-one was sadder than Pitman. He was a voracious reader as a child, and as a consequence picked up a wide vocabulary—which he was unsure how to pronounce. Accordingly, when

Page opposite. The distinctive Georgian architecture of Royal Crescent, Bath. Pitman lived in number 17, which is just left of the large bush in the middle of the Crescent. The house has now been turned into flats.

The memorial plaque in Bath Abbey. The text reads:

IN MEMORY OF
SIR ISAAC PITMAN KT
1813–1897
INVENTOR OF PITMAN'S
SHORTHAND

His aims were steadfast, his mind original, his work prodigious, the achievement world-wide. His life was ordered in service to God and duty to man.

he was 17, he read through the whole of Walker's *Pronouncing Dictionary* (Chapter 41), and corrected some two thousand words he was mispronouncing. And to make sure he hadn't missed anything, he read it through again. That's sad, in the best sense.

Soon after, he began to study shorthand, and first started to teach his new method when working as a teacher in a school at Wotton-under-Edge in Gloucestershire. His elder brother Jacob was living in nearby North Nibley—another location visited in this book (Chapter 27). Isaac's approach gave a sign to each consonant, devising shapes which related sets of consonants, and introducing abbreviations for consonant clusters. His first publication, *Stenographic Sound-Hand*, appeared in 1837, when he was 24. It immediately caught on. A decade later he was sending out hundreds of booklets a month, travelling all over the country, and receiving 10,000 phonographic letters a year.

It was a full-time occupation, and as the popularity grew, he found he had to leave teaching and devote himself to promoting his invention. He called his house the Phonographic Institution—later, the Phonetic Institute. In fact there were five Phonetic Institutes in all. Finding premises of sufficient size and comfort proved a problem, and he regularly found himself having to move around Bath. His account of one location, published in *The Phonetic Journal* (12 April 1873) is a horror story:

> The Phonetic Institute is a single spacious room on the third floor above the ground floor of a large building formerly used as a brewery in Parsonage Lane, Bath, and is reached by a dreary staircase of fifty steps. It is exposed to the extremes of heat and cold, being under the roof, and the walls only six inches thick.... Close to the street entrance

is a slaughter-house, and underneath and round about the building are the necessary appliances for keeping, killing, and cutting up sheep and cows for a large butcher's business. A more unsavoury entrance to business premises, I think, does not exist in the city. Although the refuse from the slaughtered animals is usually removed every three or four days, it is sometimes allowed to accumulate for a longer period, and the smell thence arising is extremely offensive [he had been a vegetarian for over 30 years]. I have occasionally been driven from my desk by its pungency … The dampness of this office has several times been the cause of loss in the damage of books by mildew. The roof is repaired almost every year, yet a violent storm or snow-fall always sends the water through the ceiling.

And a fortnight later, he adds (26 April 1873):

The present phonetic printing office is literally a rat's hole. . . . rats of an enormous size find a congenial home. They scamper across the floor in the evening, when the sound of busy hands and feet has died away. We have seen and heard them scores of times when, in former years, we worked on till bed-time in the quiet evening hours, after the general closing of the office; and many a time the workmen have found their paste eaten by these voracious creatures, when it has been carelessly left within their reach. One of them made his bed in the waste-paper box one night, and having overslept himself, was in a dreadful state of perturbation when, on waking, he found the large and comfortable

A letter from Isaac Pitman to publisher Samuel Bagster, 14 November 1837. It reads as follows:

I have sent 200 Stenographies for present sale, and the rest, to make up 1500, will follow by wagon in about a week. I think I shall want 1500 for myself. Please let me know in a month or two how they sell. I must beg pardon for the manner of sewing in this 200. The next will be dark coloured thread, and done properly. Also the labels will be more nearly in the centre. The stitching was done by the elder boys in my school, who have learned the system. They are quite delighted to spend two or three days in this sort of half play. Since this first essay we have had a lesson on the subject from a stationer.

'rat's hole' in the possession of many tenants of another species. Having endured for above an hour the torture of feeling certain he was caught at last, he screwed up his rat-courage to the sticking place, took a desperate leap out of the rustling paper, scared the boys who were at work, and scampered away from his bed-room to his other home.

Fortunately the later Institute locations were infinitely better.

Pitman was one of several famous robust Victorian linguists who were prepared to work in appalling conditions in support of a language cause (see also Chapter 48). Actually there were two causes: shorthand and spelling reform. His belief was that by learning shorthand, with its unremitting concentration on regular sound-spelling correspondences, people would develop a frame of mind in which they would become increasingly dissatisfied with conventional spelling, and gradually a new climate of opinion in favour of reform would grow. This second hope was never fulfilled, though activism for spelling reform has never gone away (Chapter 53).

The development of shorthand, and the proposals for spelling reform, didn't take place in a calm atmosphere, as might befit a gentleman's club. The arguments for and against different systems (several others had been proposed in addition to Pitman's) were heated, personal, and lengthy. There were anonymous accusations of lying, and forged letters to the press. The emotional level of the outpouring would bear comparison with any present-day activism.

> Every public man, whether he be in the whirl of politics, or the republic of letters, knows that shadows of abuse will be poured on the unhappy syllables of his name, and if his heart be in his work, he, of all men, will regret the storm the least. In the change of the vowel-scale of Phonography ... and in the case of every minor improvement ... my name has been roundly abused, both in print and correspondence. I do not complain. It is the well-known privilege of every Englishman to grumble at, and curse in his own fashion, perhaps with a mild 'Bother it!' anyone that puts him out of his way. But the scattering of such firebrands, arrows, and death, as charges of 'broken faith', and insinuations of insanity, are more serious matters than mere grumbling and hard words, such as obstinacy, fickleness, and ingratitude—charges which are to be estimated according to the mental state and capacity, and the interests, of the utterer.

He goes on to refer to his critic's remarks as slanderous, perverted, egotistical, and incapable, commenting: 'Quackery is not confined to vendors of

A contemporary photograph of the fourth Phonetic Institute, with the name in Pitman's reformed spelling. The location, Kingston Buildings, is next to Bath Abbey.

patent medicines'. And the source of this row? An argument over the best way of writing the shorthand shapes for initial and final *l* and *r*.

Pitman, in his last lecture on Phonography, given in the Town Hall of his birthplace, Trowbridge, in 1892, observed that when he looked back over his career, he often thought of the words of Scripture, 'What hath God wrought!' There is an irony even here for, only 15 years before, Thomas Alvar Edison had devised the phonograph, the first machine that could both record and reproduce sound, and the first words he recorded on that device were 'What God hath wrought!' The phonograph, of course, was

In 1862 a vivid character sketch of Pitman was published in a popular periodical, Weldon's Register:

If we were asked to name the most diligent and hard-working man we know, it would be Isaac Pitman. It is a treat to visit his printing office in Bath. Printing offices are usually very dirty and untidy places; but Mr Pitman's office, save for its furniture, might be a lady's drawing-room ...

In a large room sits Mr Pitman himself, writing an article, reading a proof, or answering a letter. His correspondence is immense; letters and papers flow in upon him from every part of the world. He attends to it all himself. Those who write to him in ordinary handwriting he answers in long-hand phonetic spelling, but the mass of his correspondence is in Phonography; and the speed and ease with which he writes enables him to get through an amount of work which would else seem fabulous. ...

Mr Pitman carries into his printing office the régime of the schoolmaster; he is a strict disciplinarian. No talking is allowed, beyond necessary questions and orders, and the quiet is unbroken except by the click of the types, or the packing of parcels for the carrier or the post. ...

Pitman is tall ... spare and muscular, with bright eyes, a keen face, and rapid motions ... his habits are regular, and almost ascetic. He goes to bed early, and rises early summer and winter, and may almost invariably be found posted at his desk by six in the morning. Except for the progress of his work, he seems to have no care in the world. He sees no company; he seldom dines from home, or pays visits, and, first in his office in the morning, he is last to leave it at night. He delights in walking exercise, and scampers over miles of country with the same ease that his pen goes over paper. ...

He is very abstemious: wine, beer, or spirits of any kind never pass his lips: nor fish, flesh, nor fowl. For years he has been a strict vegetarian; and, but for a cold now and then, he has enjoyed perfect health. ... He preaches twice each Sunday in a little chapel, at Twerton, a village a short way from Bath. ... He has no love for money, save for its uses in promoting his ends. His personal wants are few and simple, and every penny beyond what is required for them is devoted to the phonetic propaganda. ...

He has a governing and despotic temper. In all things he takes his own way. ... Alternately, he is accused of fickleness and obstinacy: of fickleness, because when he sees, or fancies he sees, a possible improvement [to his phonography], he will pull down any amount of building to make room for it; and of obstinacy, because what he thinks right he does, whatever be the outcry.

the great-grand-daddy of the dictaphone—a device which, more than any other, was to knock the bottom out of the secretarial shorthand market.

Shorthand will probably always have a role to play in society, as there will always be situations where people wish to make rapid notes about what is being said, and where electrical voice recording is impracticable or undesirable. It's all very well capturing everything that someone says on a smartphone, but listening again to the recording requires our real time, whereas shorthand notes allow points to be succinctly summarized as we listen. And shorthand isn't dependent on the lifetime of a battery. I taught myself Pitman's Shorthand when I was a teenager, and found it extremely easy to learn, aesthetically elegant, and very useful when taking notes in university lectures. I never built up much of a speed, though. And with quality speech-to-text software on the horizon, I don't suppose I ever shall.

Isaac Pitman in 1868, aged 55.

Getting there

Royal Crescent is in the very centre of Bath (postcode: BA1 2LT). From the A4 (Upper Bristol Road), turn into Marlborough Lane, and Royal Crescent is at the top on the right. It overlooks Royal Victoria Park, which is a short walk from Queen Square along Royal Avenue.

There is little to see of the original five Phonetic Institutes. The first one was at 5 Nelson Place, today called Nelson Place West, near the river just south of the Upper Bristol Road. The building is still there (postcode: BA1 2BA). The second was just round the corner, at 1 Albion Place on the Upper Bath Road (postcode: BA1 3AD). The third [the rat-hole] was somewhere along Parsonage Lane, off Cheap Street, near the Theatre Royal (postcode: BA1 1ER). The fourth was in 6 and 7 Kingston Buildings, Abbey Churchyard, on your left along Orange Grove as you approach the Abbey (postcode: BA1 1LT). The fifth was on the site of the buildings of the former Bath Press, on your left as you travel west along the Lower Bristol Road (postcode: BA2 3BL). The site is now up for redevelopment. The proposal includes a heritage museum which I hope will include some Pitmania.

Chapter 48

Oxford

James Murray and the *Oxford English Dictionary*

If there is an academic 'rags-to-riches' story to match that of Joseph Wright (Chapter 51), it must be that of James Murray, the founding editor of the *Oxford English Dictionary*. First published in its complete form in 1928, it consisted of 414,800 defined word forms and 1,861,200 quotations used to illustrate their senses. There had never been such a dictionary before. Dr Johnson's *Dictionary* (Chapter 40), which Murray's project was intended to replace, was a tenth of its size.

Today, the *OED*, as it is usually called, continues to grow. By the time of the second edition in 1989, the number of word forms defined had grown to 615,100 and the number of quotations to 2,436,600. Some 10,000 more entries were added in the 1990s. An ongoing revision towards a third edition began in 2000, and new entries are published online every three months.

It's amazing that the first edition was completed at all. K. M. Elisabeth Murray published a biography of her grandfather, *Caught in the Web of Words* (1977), in which she tells the history of the uphill battle Murray had to face to keep the project going as it grew and grew. Nobody had anticipated the amount of work it would involve. The original scheme proposed a dictionary of four volumes and 6400 pages, to be completed in 10 years. In the event, it took 70 years, from the date of approval of the project, 10 volumes, and 15,490 pages. The publishers, anxious to recoup their investment, and initially uncertain of the importance of the enterprise, kept pressing Murray for cuts in scale and method. There were

Page opposite. James Murray's personal post-box outside his house at 78 Banbury Road, Oxford.

personality clashes and changes of policy to deal with. Murray resisted any attempts to interfere with the editorial standards which he felt would guarantee the ultimate quality of the dictionary. He was often near to resignation. No businessman, he routinely underestimated the costs involved, and found it hard to make ends meet. It eventually took a toll on his health.

Murray was born in 1837 in Denholm, near Hawick in southern Scotland, the son of a village tailor. His story has striking parallels with that of Joseph Wright, with whom he formed a strong friendship in his later years. He left school at 14, but continued to educate himself, using—like Wright—Cassell's *Popular Educator*. He became a teacher, then a bank clerk in London, developed his philological interests, especially in English dialects, and got to know all the leading philologists and phoneticians of the time. He contributed talks to the prestigious Philological Society, in 1869 became a member of its Council, and gained editorial experience by editing material for the Early English Text Society. He accumulated a wide general knowledge—something essential for a lexicographer who, though concerned with words, has to be aware of the realities behind them if definitions are to be accurate.

It was in April 1878, while working as a teacher at Mill Hill School in north London, that he was invited to Oxford to meet the Delegates of the University Press, and a year later he was appointed editor of what was at first called the New English Dictionary—'new', because it would replace the 'old' dictionary of Johnson. The big question was: where should the work be carried out? The project needed a sufficiently large space to house the huge amount of paperwork which would quickly accumulate, as well as the assistants who would be required.

The answer was to construct special premises, which he called his 'scriptorium'. In fact he built two scriptoria. The first was in the grounds of Mill Hill School, and consisted of a corrugated-iron shed. A fire destroyed the original building in 1902, but five years later the school built a second 'Murray Scriptorium', which today houses some of the school's IT provision. They call it 'The Script'.

With such a massive project to supervise, it was soon apparent that Murray could not manage to keep a teaching job while compiling a dictionary. Part-time lexicography is a contradiction in terms. But leaving the school meant that a new scriptorium would have to be constructed. He found a house at 78 Banbury Road, recently built on St John's College land, and lived there from 1885. Elisabeth Murray describes it in this way:

The Murray home was one of the many villas which sprang up in North Oxford in the 1880s and '90s, roomy, brick-built and high gables, standing back from the road with a space in front for a flower bed, two beech trees and large old elm, while at the rear there was a walled garden on the site of an old orchard.

He called it Sunnyside.

The area both at the front and the back was large enough to erect a scriptorium, but there were complications. The college refused permission for anything to be built at the front of the house, but agreed to it being at

A faded photograph of the scriptorium—the low-lying shed on the right—at the rear of Sunnyside, taken in the late 1880s.

the back—as long as his neighbour had no objections. Unfortunately, the neighbour did have one. This part of Oxford at the time wasn't built up: fields lay beyond, and the neighbour was worried about losing his view. So the scriptorium had to be sunk about three feet into the ground, and this caused problems. His granddaughter recalls (p. 242):

> the Scriptorium was always somewhat damp. It was also ill ventilated. In summer it was stuffy, in winter dank and cold.... There was a stove to warm it in winter, but owing to fear of fire it was always extinguished at night and in cold weather James wore a thick overcoat and sometimes sat with his feet in a box to keep them from the draught.

It wasn't enough to prevent regular colds, and even pneumonia.

The Sunnyside scriptorium was much larger than its Mill Hill predecessor, with more storage space for the thousands of slips that were coming in from his small army of contributors. There was room for several assistants—including his children, who were brought in to sort slips for a few pence a week. The volume of post was so great that the Post Office installed a special post-box outside his house to cope with it. Accuracy of address wasn't important. 'Mr Murray, Oxford' would reach him.

He repeatedly made predictions about dates for the completion of the dictionary, but these always proved to be too optimistic. In 1880 he had hoped that the work would be finished by 1900. In 1897 he thought it would be 1908. In 1912 he told a colleague that he was halfway through letter T, and anticipated completion by 1916. He wrote in a letter that year: 'If I live to then I shall be 80, and it will also be my Golden Wedding; let us hope that the Grand Conjunction of all these cycles will really take place'. Unfortunately, it didn't. Colds and a prostate problem sapped his energy, and he died following pleurisy in July 1915. It took another 13 years to complete the first edition.

There is no scriptorium to be seen now at the house on Banbury Road. It was pulled down many years ago. All we have are a few photographs showing Murray and his team at work. It's estimated that he himself edited some 7200 pages of the first edition—just under half of the whole. And yet he was always self-deprecating about his achievement. At the beginning of her biography, Elisabeth Murray reports his strong views about the 'hateful' genre: 'I am a nobody—if you have anything to say about the Dictionary, there it is at your will—but treat me as a solar myth, or an echo, or an irrational quantity, or ignore me altogether'. That is simply not possible.

Murray and colleagues in the scriptorium in the early 1900s.

Alice's Shop in St Aldates.

LEWIS CARROLL AND LANGUAGE QUOTATION

As you approach Oxford town centre from the south, along the Abingdon Road, you'll pass the gardens of Christ Church College on your right. Look left, and there is Alice's Shop.

This is Lewis Carroll's Alice. It's here because Charles Lutwidge Dodgson was a lecturer in mathematics at Christ Church, and Alice Liddell, the inspiration for *Alice's Adventures in Wonderland* and *Through the Looking-Glass*, was the daughter of the College Dean. By all accounts the origin of the story lies in a river trip Dodgson made with Alice and her two sisters one day at Oxford in 1862.

The Alice stories are full of wordplay—as indeed is Dodgson's pseudonym. *Lutwidge* is *Ludovicus* in Latin, which is *Lewis* in English; and *Charles* is *Carolus* in Latin, which has an equivalent in *Carroll*. His interest in language is seen not only in the wordplay he puts into the mouths of his characters, but in his word games, such as doublets, and in the puns, anagrams, and acrostics scattered throughout his writing.

CONTINUED »

Wordsmiths and Warriors

The shop sold sweets in Alice's day. Today it's a gift shop selling Alice memorabilia. In Chapter 5 of *Through the Looking-Glass* it's managed by a sheep—hence the sign name of *The Old Sheep Shop*. Alice has trouble exploring it, because things keep moving and disappearing, but eventually she is able to buy an egg. This is an event of huge significance for language enthusiasts, because in the following chapter the egg turns into Humpty Dumpty, whose observations about words and meanings, along with his word creations (*un-birthday*), his idiosyncratic definitions (*impenetrability*), and his explanation of the coinages in 'Jabberwocky' (*brillig*, *slithy*, *toves* . . .) have endeared him to linguists ever since. He is probably the most quoted individual in English-language study.

Getting there

Banbury Road (A4165) is one of the two main roads leading north out of Oxford. From the city centre, go along St Giles and follow the road round to the right, signposted Ring Road Headington and Summertown. This is Banbury Road. A few hundred yards along, you pass Bardwell Road on the right, and Murray's house is just opposite St Margaret's Road on the left (postcode: OX2 6JT). You can't miss it because of the red pillar box outside.

The scriptorium is at Mill Hill School, which is on The Ridgeway in Mill Hill Village. It's on the B552, and the school postcode is NW7 1QS.

The Abingdon Road is the A4144. Alice's Shop is at 83 St Aldates (postcode: OX1 1RA). As you cross the river from the south, aim for the city centre, and just past Speedwell Street, opposite the gardens of Christ Church, is the shop. It's about a 15-minute walk from the railway station.

Chapter 49

Winterborne Came

William Barnes and speech-craft

The strangest thing about Winterborne Came must be its name. Not the first part, which is straightforward: a 'winter burn' is a seasonal stream, drying up in the summer. There are two Winterborne Rivers in Dorset, and this is the southern one, giving its name to several settlements along its banks as it winds towards the River Frome. The spelling has varied over the centuries. Today, two of the villages have *ou*—Winterbourne Abbas and Steepleton; the others are just plain *o*, including Winterborne Came. But why *Came*?

The manor was owned by the abbey of St Stephen of Caen, in Normandy—one of the properties re-assigned to French overlords following the 1066 invasion—and the name of the town or the lord was used to mark the ownership, and to distinguish one place from another. This happened quite often with place names in those days—Burton Hastings, Burton Fleming, Burton Overy … Newton Abbot, Newton Ferrers, Newton Tracy … We can imagine the Anglo-Saxon folk of Dorsetshire having trouble pronouncing *Caen*, with its unfamiliar nasal vowel—and even more trouble spelling it. It's recorded as *Caam* in 1280, and *Cam* in 1288. *Came* is the spelling from the 15th century, and stayed long after the abbey ownership ceased.

French names would not have appealed to William Barnes (1801–86), who became rector of the parish of St Peter at Winterborne Came in 1862. He was a Dorsetshire teacher turned minister who wrote over 800 poems

Page opposite. The William Barnes memorial at Winterborne Came.

about his native county, becoming famous as 'the Dorset Poet'. But he was also a keen amateur philologist, writing a grammar of Old English, exploring the Germanic origins of the language, and strongly advocating the replacement of all foreign loan words in English by words with Anglo-Saxon roots.

In his *fore-say* (preface) to his *Outline of English Speech-craft* (grammar), he describes his book as a small contribution 'towards the upholding of our strong old Anglo-Saxon speech'. 'English youth', he says, 'will want an outline of the Greek and Latin tongues ere he can well understand his own speech'. So grammatical terms are all translated into their Anglo-Saxon equivalents. We find *speech-lore* (philology) and *book-lore* (literature), *thing-word* (noun) and *mark-word* (adjective), *twin-words* (synonyms) and *wordlings* (particles). In general vocabulary, he recommends *year-day* (anniversary) and *folkdom* (democracy), *afterkin* (posterity) and *spyglass* (telescope), *onquicken* (accelerate) and *bendsome* (flexible). *Unfrienden* (alienate) anticipates modern social networking. His *Outline* contains several hundred words processed in this way.

His Anglo-Saxonisms had little permanent impact on the language as a whole. Only a handful of his coinages, such as *push-wainling* (perambulator), made it into the *Oxford English Dictionary*, and they are only of historical interest now. But his return to the Anglo-Saxon roots of English, and his enthusiasm for a style that avoids Classical and Romance words, influenced several later writers, such as George Orwell. His dialect poetry is a record of a rapidly disappearing rural culture, at times bright and light-hearted, at times deeply nostalgic and moving. It was greatly praised by Hardy, Hopkins, and Tennyson, among others, and continues to be appreciated today.

Barnes remained at St Peter's until his death, and is buried in the churchyard there. The church is a redundant building now, in the care of the

St Peter's Church. Barnes's monument is to the left of the tower.

Left. The original inscription . . .

Right. . . . and its replacement.

Churches Conservation Trust. It doesn't look its age: the nave, the earliest part, dates from the 14th century. His family erected a Celtic cross over the grave, which makes it easy for an English-language tourist to spot, as it's the tallest stone in the cemetery, in a corner next to the church tower. The original inscription on the base of the Celtic cross is badly weathered, but it has been reproduced in a plaque on the grave itself.

EVENÉN IN THE VILLAGE

From *Poems of Rural Life in the Dorset Dialect* (1844)

Now the light o' the west is a-turn'd to gloom,
An' the men be at hwome vrom ground;
An' the bells be a-zendén all down the Coombe
From tower, their mwoansome sound.
An' the wind is still,
An' the house-dogs do bark,
An' the rooks be a-vled to the elems high an' dark,
An' the water do roar at mill.
An' the flickerén light drough the window-peäne
Vrom the candle's dull fleäme do shoot,
An' young Jemmy the smith is a-gone down leäne,
A-playën his shrill-vaiced flute.
An' the miller's man,
Do zit down at his ease
On the seat that is under the cluster o' trees,
Wi' his pipe an' his cider can.

The surrounding parkland, with its fields, trees, horses, and even the broken fence, is a perfect setting for someone who was so profoundly at one with the Dorsetshire countryside. But I have no doubt that William Barnes would have preferred an Old English *minding* to a Latin *memorial*.

Getting there

Follow the road that curls south around the town of Dorchester and take the A352 south-east towards Wareham. After a few hundred yards, behind some trees on the left, you pass the Old Came Rectory where Barnes lived, and a few hundred yards further on there's an unmarked road on the right. It's easy to sail past it, as I discovered. The postcode (DT2 8NT) throws in the towel at this point. If you reach Whitcombe, you've gone too far.

The unmarked road bends to the left between fields. A sign says Private, No Through Road (unpromising), then Bridleway and Church only (promising). The road turns into a track between trees, leading up to the front of the old manor, Came House. This is the point where you might feel you've gone horribly wrong, for there's no sight of a church, but look within the bushes on the right and you'll see the half-hidden sign: 'To the Church'. A path runs alongside the high wall of the manor kitchen garden, and suddenly, round a corner, until then hidden by the trees, appears the tiny church and cemetery.

Chapter 50

Higher Bockhampton

Thomas Hardy and Wessex dialect

They're very aware of Thomas Hardy in Dorset. The cottage where he was born in 1840 is in Higher Bockhampton, and the house where he later lived, Max Gate, is down the road in Dorchester. Apart from his time studying in London (Chapter 41), Hardy lived at the cottage until he was 34. Today, a stone monument erected by 'a few of his American admirers' in 1931 marks the place, and the inscription tells us that this is where he wrote *Under the Greenwood Tree* and *Far from the Madding Crowd*. The heathland near the cottage was the inspiration for Egdon Heath, which functions almost as a character in *The Return of the Native*.

A warning. Don't confuse the monument by Hardy's Cottage with the much grander Hardy Monument to the south-west of Dorchester at Black Down, overlooking the English Channel. The latter is Vice-Admiral Sir Thomas Hardy, flag-captain of HMS *Victory* at Trafalgar (and immortalized through the dying Nelson's request, 'Kiss me, Hardy'), who was born nearby.

The writer Hardy deserves his place in this book for his creation of one of the most memorable literary dialects in English, reflecting his imaginary world of Wessex. It's a dialect that finds its origins in a local world that extended well beyond Dorset. He did not share the purist enthusiasm of William Barnes (Chapter 49), who kept a school near to Hardy's office, even though he often asked Barnes for dialect advice. But the vocabulary and turn of phrase used by his characters gives his novels a regional identity

Page opposite. The lane from the wood leading down to Hardy's cottage in Higher Bockhampton.

Thomas Hardy (1840–1928).

that few other writers have matched, as these examples in *Far from the Madding Crowd* illustrate:

Hardy's birthplace cottage.

> take up the God-forgive-me (a two-handled tall mug)
> a lammocken vagabond (slouching)
> a nesh young thing (delicate)
> you draw-latching rogue (dawdling)
> a morsel of scroff (wood fragments)
> a thirtover place (ill-tempered)
> you stun-poll (blockhead)

It's all part of a style which Virginia Woolf described as 'the charm of a muddy country road, or of a plain field of roots in winter'.

The country divided Hardy after his death. It was his wish to be buried in Stinsford, and that's where you will see a gravestone, in St Michael's churchyard, but it contains only his heart. His ashes are buried in Poets' Corner in Westminster Abbey, London. A little scammish [untidy], as Grandfer Cantle (in *The Return of the Native*) would say.

DOMICILIUM

The panel outside the small thatched cottage, built by his great-grandfather in 1801, displays a poem, 'Domicilium', written by Hardy when he was 18, and clearly showing the influence of Wordsworth. There can be few better descriptions of a property, and it has little changed today. The wild scene he describes is fictionalized in his writing as Egdon Heath.

It faces west, and round the back and sides
High beeches, bending, hang a veil of boughs,
And sweep against the roof. Wild honeysucks
Climb on the walls, and seem to sprout a wish
(If we may fancy wish of trees and plants)
To overtop the apple trees hard-by.

Red roses, lilacs, variegated box
Are there in plenty, and such hardy flowers
As flourish best untrained. Adjoining these
Are herbs and esculents; and farther still
A field; then cottages with trees, and last
The distant hills and sky.

Behind, the scene is wilder. Heath and furze
Are everything that seems to grow and thrive
Upon the uneven ground. A stunted thorn
Stands here and there, indeed; and from a pit
An oak uprises, Springing from a seed
Dropped by some bird a hundred years ago.

In days bygone—
Long gone—my father's mother, who is now
Blest with the blest, would take me out to walk.
At such a time I once inquired of her
How looked the spot when first she settled here.
The answer I remember. 'Fifty years
Have passed since then, my child, and change has marked
The face of all things. Yonder garden-plots
And orchards were uncultivated slopes
O'ergrown with bramble bushes, furze and thorn:
That road a narrow path shut in by ferns,
Which, almost trees, obscured the passers-by.

Our house stood quite alone, and those tall firs
And beeches were not planted. Snakes and efts
Swarmed in the summer days, and nightly bats
Would fly about our bedrooms. Heathcroppers
Lived on the hills, and were our only friends;
So wild it was when we first settled here.'

PIDDLE AND PUDDLE

The individuality of the Dorchester area is seen in the place names, which Hardy adapted in his novels. Weymouth becomes Budmouth, Cerne Abbas becomes Abbot's Cernel, Dorchester becomes Casterbridge. To the north of Hardy's cottage is Puddletown, and as you drive north along the B3143 you pass through Piddlehinton and Piddletrenthide. There is a Little Puddle Farm. It's all because of the River Piddle, which rises to the north of Dorchester then flows east down to the sea at Wareham. On its way it names a cluster of villages—Tolpuddle, Turnerspuddle, Affpuddle, Briantspuddle. Hardy used the name too: Piddletrenthide and Piddlehinton became Upper Longpuddle and Lower Longpuddle in his Wessex.

Today, names with *piddle* tend to get onto lists of 'rude place names in Britain'. But the origins are innocent. The Dorset river is recorded as *Pidelen* in Anglo-Saxon times, a version of a river name found also in northern Europe, where the word meant low-lying land or marshland. The variants usually relate to the people who lived nearby: in the above cases, Tola, Turner, Æffa, and Brianus, respectively. Piddletrenthide was an area of thirty hides (French *trente*) on the river. Piddlehinton was a religious household on the river.

Why are some villages spelled with *i* and some with *u*? All the names had an *i* originally. Was it embarrassment over *piddle*? The timing is right. The use of this word as a euphemism for *piss* arose in English during the 18th century. There's no truth in the story that the villages were renamed to avoid embarrassing the young Princess Victoria, when she came to Dorset in 1833, because her visit was to other parts of the county. But 19th-century prudery may well have been a factor. The towns are all spelled with an *i* in John Cary's map for the *New British Atlas* in 1805, but by 1848, when *Pigot's Atlas* was published, the ones downstream of Dorchester are shown with a *u*. Local pronunciation of the *i* vowel would have been close to the sound of *u*, motivating the more familiar word. The atlases vary over the next few years until they settle down with the modern spellings. And when in 1956 Dorset County Council tried to change the name back to *i*, the people objected; so embarrassment turns out to be a factor after all.

THOMAS HARDY O.M.
WAS BORN IN THE ADJACENT
COTTAGE 2ND JUNE 1840.
AND IN IT WROTE
"UNDER THE GREENWOOD TREE"
AND
"FAR FROM THE MADDING CROWD."

THIS MONUMENT ERECTED TO
HIS MEMORY BY A FEW OF
HIS AMERICAN ADMIRERS
1931

The birthplace monument.

Getting there

Travelling north along the A35 towards Poole, you turn right through Stinsford and the village is a mile or so ahead. The car park is a little way from the cottage, and gives you a choice of routes, by a lane or through woodland (Thorncombe Wood). If you take the woodland route, there's a steepish start and then the path bears left and flattens out. Innumerable squirrels will protest at your arrival. It takes a little longer than you expect, but follow the signs and eventually you come across the fencing at the rear of the cottage garden, Hardy's slate-roofed green shed, and a path down the side of the building. The route via the lane isn't much quicker, and ends at the stone monument.

For opening times at the cottage (postcode: DT2 8QJ), see the National Trust website

http://www.nationaltrust.org.uk//hardy-country

This also gives details for Max Gate, Allington Avenue, Dorchester (postcode: DT1 2AA), where Hardy lived for over 40 years until his death in 1928. The house name comes from Mack's Gate—the name of an old turnpike barrier and toll house which stood opposite. Hardy would have found that etymology jonnick [satisfactory] enough.

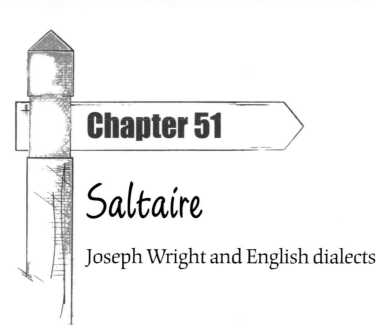

Chapter 51

Saltaire

Joseph Wright and English dialects

There can't be another linguistic story to match this one: an illiterate quarry-boy and mill-worker becomes a professor of comparative philology at Oxford University. In later life Joseph Wright (1855–1930) had to get used to dramatic newspaper headlines—such as 'From Donkey-boy to Professor'—whenever he carried out a public engagement.

His masterwork was the six-volume *English Dialect Dictionary*, published between 1898 and 1905. Nobody did more to lay the foundation for the study of English dialects, and his dictionary is an impressively detailed account of the regional vocabulary of Britain at that time. It claims to be 'so far as is possible, the complete vocabulary of all dialect words which are still in use or are known to have been in use at any time during the last two hundred years in England, Ireland, Scotland, and Wales'. That is quite a claim, but the entries certainly support it.

His entry on *dog*, for example, takes up over six columns of small print, and shows 150 usage variations from over 60 parts of the British Isles, all supported by quotations. Do you know *one dog, one bull* (i.e. 'fair play!') recorded in Shropshire? Or *dog in a blanket* (i.e. 'jam roly-poly pudding') heard in Derbyshire and Wiltshire? Or *as thick as dogs' heads* (i.e. very intimate) from Scotland? The quotations tell us where Wright found them. They may still be used today.

His story begins in Thackley, a village north-east of Bradford in West Yorkshire. He was born in one of the tiny single-roomed cottages belonging to Park Hill Farm. It's long since been demolished. A famous photograph of Wright in 1928 shows him sitting on a pile of stones nearby.

Page opposite. Salts Mill, Saltaire.

When he was six, he got a job driving a donkey-cart, carrying tools belonging to the men working in a stone-quarry at Woodend in nearby Shipley. The job, from 7 in the morning till 5 at night, involved taking the tools to the nearest blacksmith's to be sharpened, and then bringing them back. It earned him 18 (old) pence a week (= 7.5 new pence), and he got an extra penny bonus from each quarryman.

A year later, his mother took him to a cotton mill—at the time, the largest one in Europe—which had been built by the philanthropic manufacturer Sir Titus Salt in 1853. Salt had created a model village for his workers which (being on the River Aire) he called Saltaire. Joseph was under the legal age, but he was a sturdy lad, so he was taken on half-time as a doffer in the spinning department. A doffer, according to his dictionary, was 'a boy or girl employed in a factory to remove the full bobbins from the throstle-frame and replace them by empty ones'—no menial task, as there were 144 spindles on each frame, and over 16,000 on all the machines in the vast (637 ft/194 m long) spinning shed. He worked from 6 until 12.30 each morning, which meant an early start, as the mill was two miles from his home.

Wordsmiths and Warriors

He worked in Room 13 in the 'Old End' of the mill–or 't' slave 'oil' ('the slave hole') as it was called by the workers, because there were few opportunities for rest. In Elizabeth Wright's biography of her husband, there's an old photograph of the mill on which Wright has initialled the location where he worked. You can still see the place today: from the far end, it's behind the eighteenth window-space on the third floor, just before the tower buttress. The mill hasn't changed much on the outside since the 1860s.

The other half of Wright's day was spent in a school which the enlightened Titus Salt provided for the children. It was the only school Wright ever attended, and—as he reflected later—it didn't teach him a great deal. He later wrote in *John o' London's Weekly* (15 May 1926): 'When I left school, I knew very little more than when I first went. I knew the alphabet, and had a smattering of elementary arithmetic, and I could recite, parrot-like, various Scriptural passages, and a few highly moral bits of verse; that was almost precisely the extent of my educational equipment after three or four years of schooling. Reading and writing, for me, were as remote as any of the sciences.' But, as he also liked to recall, the mill gave him a strong sense of local dialect and its variations, for the men came from all around the area.

He left Saltaire when he was 13 and worked at a mill in Shipley, graduating to the more specialized work of wool-sorting, and stayed there for seven years. It was here, during his dinner-hour, that he taught himself to read and write, using just two books: the Bible and Bunyan's *Pilgrim's Progress*. Although naturally left-handed, a fellow-worker pressed him to write with his right, and his ensuing ambidextrousness at the blackboard impressed everyone when he eventually became a lecturer. His education progressed with a weekly purchase of Cassell's *Popular Educator*, which became, as he put it, his 'constant companion'. Two or three evenings each week he went to a local night-school, where he began to learn French and German. By the time he was 20, he had taught himself Latin and learned shorthand, receiving a certificate signed by Isaac Pitman himself (Chapter 47).

He might have stayed a wool-sorter indefinitely, but in 1876 the mill had a temporary closure, so he used this as an opportunity to move on. Through his mill-work, along with some income from running a small night-school of his own, he had saved £40—enough to pay for a term at a university. He chose Heidelberg, in Germany. On his return, he found work in Windhill as a schoolteacher, but his language interests motivated a return to Heidelberg in 1882, and there he began his studies as a philologist, eventually gaining a doctorate. He joined the university in Oxford in 1888, and leased a house at 6 Norham Road. A string of publications followed, including a grammar of his local dialect of Windhill, which appeared in 1893, and then the big dictionary, which he financed himself.

Salts Mill (no apostrophe) is a UNESCO World Heritage Site today, and is well signposted. It's open virtually every day of the year, and admission is free. The way in to the old mill is past its tall chimney, set a little apart from the main building and towering above it like an Italian campanile. Just before you get to the entrance is an early music shop, full of recorders, viols, and other instruments of the past, some of a considerable size. Plenty of space in a former mill for such a grand display of stock, I thought. But I wasn't at all prepared for the scale of the space that followed.

The ground floor of the mill has been turned into a huge art gallery, called 'The 1853', after the year of the mill's opening. It's almost the length of a football pitch. Above, a redbrick ceiling. On the walls, a sparkling array of work by Bradford-born David Hockney. At one end, his enormous painting of the mill, showing its golden sandstone gleaming in bright orange on a fine Yorkshire day. Against a side wall the bright red cubist pillar-box made to his design, with its angular canopy and chair-like base—a work of art now, but used as a real post-box at Salts Mill for just a month, following its creation in 1992.

It was a weekday, but the mill was busy with a mix of shoppers, tourists, and local families having a day out. And it was the same on the second floor, where there's a restaurant and a vast (that space again), well-stocked bookshop. Another gallery on the third floor, with a new Hockney exhibition showing while I was there. And everywhere, a colourful diversity of arts and crafts for sale. When you include all the offices and shops, over 1000 people work on the site now. It's an amazing refurbishment, by any standards. No wonder it achieved its world heritage status.

As we left, we walked through the children's book section. There was a small decorated table, where children could sit and read, and an old-fashioned school desk. A little boy, around seven years old, was sitting at the desk poring over a book, his father leaning over him and helping him with the difficult words. It would have made the former donkey-lad proud.

Getting there

From the south, turn off the M62 onto the M606, and follow the signs around Bradford, along the A650 in the direction of Keighley. Go through Shipley, and turn right at the roundabout onto the A657 and you immediately see the green sign heralding Saltaire as a World Heritage Site. This road takes you past the railway station on your left. If you've come by train, there's just a short walk from here down some steps to Salts Mill, but in a car you have to go quite a way further, turning left just past the Shipley Pride pub into Victoria Street. A sign points you towards Salts Mill, and as you cross the railway line you see a mill straight ahead with a tall chimney, but this isn't it. Turn left at the roundabout onto Salts Mill Road, and follow it round. There's another mill and tall chimney on your left, but that isn't it either. The chimney to aim for is the one straight ahead of you. The car park is at the end of Salt Mills Road, but beware if you use GPS to find it. If you input the official Salts Mill postcode, you'll end up at the wrong side of the building, where there's no access; you need to input BD18 3TT. It's the kind of error you make only once. We'll know next time.

The Salts Mill website gives details of opening times:

http://www.saltsmill.org.uk/

If you want to visit Ellar Carr Road, go straight through Saltaire village on the A657, past Victoria Street, and after a mile or so you reach Thackley. You pass the primary school on your right, then turn left into Park Road, and a little way down on the right is a lane that leads on to Ellen Carr Road. Park Hill House is on the corner, behind a high wall and trees, and Joseph Wright's cottage was just by the entrance to the lane (postcode: BD10 0TD).

Chapter 52

Hinton St George

Henry Fowler and English usage

Before computers arrived, the last thing a lexicographer wanted to do was move house. Apart from the usual cares that afflicted ordinary mortals, such as ensuring that crockery remains unbroken, there was the overriding question of how to handle the slips. The slips! These are the small rectangular sheets of paper on which dictionary entries would be written—particular examples of the usage of a word, taken from a source such as a newspaper or a book. Today, it's all done online, but in Henry Fowler's day everything was on paper. A typical dictionary project would collect tens of thousands of slips, all alphabetically organized and sorted into sets of neat bundles. Tell that to the removal men.

Henry Fowler moved to Hinton St George in Somerset early in 1925, and lived there until he died in 1933. The move, he thought, took a year out of his compilation schedule. And what a schedule it was! He had been involved in dictionary preparation for the Clarendon Press in Oxford for years, along with his brother Frank; and when Frank died in 1918 he carried on alone. His first year in Hinton saw the publication in 1926 of *The Dictionary of Modern English Usage*—the book that would eventually turn his surname into nouns and adjectives. People would look points of usage up 'in Fowler', and talk about attitudes to language which were 'Fowlerian', 'Fowlerish', and 'Fowleresque'.

I've edited an edition of his *Dictionary*, and while I don't share the prescriptive attitude which was a characteristic of his age, I can't but be impressed by his attention to linguistic detail. He was decades ahead of his time in the way he collected and cited examples of usage for a book of this type. He gives the

Page opposite. Henry Fowler's house in Hinton St George.

impression of having extracted citations from virtually every available quality newspaper during his compiling years, and he was able to use material from the growing files of the *Oxford English Dictionary* (Chapter 48). He presents his opinions on points of usage with a determination that appealed to his readers, eager for advice about correctness in a strongly class-conscious age. At the same time, he has no truck with what he calls 'superstitions', and fiercely condemns those who are overly pedantic by insisting that prepositions should never go at the ends of sentences, or that sentences should never begin with *and*, or that infinitives should never be split.

Several entries display an ironic tone, a dry sense of humour, and an imaginative turn of phrase. Three examples: the mock-suffering analogy in his entry on *not*, the gardening metaphor in the middle of *compound prepositions*, and the daring allusion at the beginning of *nor*:

> *Not only* out of its place is like a tintack loose on the floor; it might have been most serviceable somewhere else, & is capable of giving acute and undeserved pain where it is.
>
> … they are almost the worst element in modern English, stuffing up the newspaper columns with a compost of nouny abstractions.
>
> *nor* is a word that should come into our minds as we repeat the General Confession. Most of us in our time have left undone those things which we ought to have done (i.e. failed to put in *nor* when it was wanted) & done those things which we ought not to have done (i.e. thrust it in when there was no room for it).

Why did Fowler go to Hinton? He his wife Jessie had been living in Guernsey after the War, but they were forced to move because the lease on their house would not be renewed. Jessie's deteriorating health (it turned out to be breast cancer), made it desirable to be nearer her doctors in London. The West Country beckoned. There were memories of childhood holidays. Brothers Arthur and Charles both lived in Dorset. And Jessie's mother was born in Crewkerne, just a few miles from Hinton. 'If west, there best' Fowler wrote in a Christmas verse in 1924.

Hinton was a delight—'this very exquisite village of old stone & thatch'. They found an early 19th-century detached house, with a hipped Welsh slate roof and a brick chimney stack, just across the road from the parish church. This is how his biographer Jenny McMorris describes it in *The Warden of English* (p. 177):

> The house itself, although much smaller than Moulin de Haut [in Guernsey], was just right for the elderly couple and the garden was

also more manageable, a small piece in front with a larger walled plot behind the house where they could sit out and eat in summer. Here there were neighbours in thatched cottages on each side and the Fowlers seem to have made friends very quickly. For his morning swim Henry was allowed to use two pools set deep among trees in the garden of a handsome house just along the lane. For running he could at first use the park attached to the great house in the village, but after access to this was closed he ran on the roads …

They called the house Sunnyside—an echo of the name James Murray had given to his house in Oxford (Chapter 48).

The *Dictionary* was an immediate and continuing success, selling 60,000 copies in its first year. Some writers might have called it a day at that point, but not Fowler. He carried on with the *Shorter Oxford English Dictionary* (eventually published in 1933), and prepared the second edition of the *Concise* (1929). He was well aware of the pressures. He wrote in a letter to the publisher in 1927: 'a new edition is a teasing business unless you have a private Einstein to provide you with a time–space continuum'.

There were plans to compile a further *Dictionary of Modern English*, but the project was never completed. To take on a ten-year project at the age of 72, he commented, would be 'flying in the face of the actuaries'. He began work on it nonetheless, despite losing an eye, suffering a broken rib, and looking after his wife, Jessie, who finally succumbed to her cancer in 1930. This was a huge blow. We get a sense of their relationship in the poetry he wrote to her, published a year later as *Rhymes of Darby to Joan*. He had the church bells of St George repaired in her memory. The gesture is recorded on a memorial tablet in the tower.

Fowler carried on working with a collaborator who eventually moved into the house next door. Hinton was hosting a veritable lexicographic cottage-industry. But by 1932 his health was declining. He suffered bouts of giddiness, and the sight in his other eye was failing. The following year, an influenza infection led to pneumonia, and he died at home on Boxing Day.

Fowler is one of a tiny group of English-language writers whose residence is commemorated by a blue plaque. The one on his Hinton house reads:

> LIVED HERE
> H. W. FOWLER
> LEXICOGRAPHER
> 1925–1933

He would have appreciated the unusual word order.

Getting there

Travelling west along the A303, turn left at the roundabout signposted Ilminster town centre, Seavington St Michael, and Lopen, and follow the road through Lopen. Just after you leave the village, watch out for a right turn; there's a small signpost pointing to Hinton Saint George. When you get to the village, turn right into the High Street, which bears right into Church Street, and you'll find Fowler's house at the end on the right, just opposite the road leading up to the parish church of St George. You can't mistake it, as there are white railings along the front and a blue plaque on the wall. The postcode is TA17 8SP. It's no longer called Sunnyside.

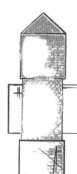

Chapter 53

Ayot St Lawrence

George Bernard Shaw and spelling reform

There's an award that doesn't yet exist. I think of it as an ELF—a prize for English Language Fanaticism—in the best sense of that word. To qualify for this, you have to do more than just say you're interested in English, or have a concern about English. You have to demonstrate its central role in your life, by working with it, spending time on it, and giving money to it. It should be evident in everything you do. And no 20th-century author, to my mind, deserves this award more than George Bernard Shaw.

It would take a whole book to describe the full range of Shaw's linguistic interests. There are frequent observations about language in the Prefaces to his plays. We see regional accents carefully portrayed in the way his characters talk. He learned Pitman's shorthand (Chapter 47), and routinely wrote in it. His work displays a distinctive orthography, with the apostrophe omitted from contracted forms, as in *dont*. He was a supporter of the Simplified Spelling Society, founded in 1908. He learned about phonetics from the academics of his time, especially Daniel Jones (Chapter 56). He was a member of the BBC's Advisory Committee on Spoken English, set up in 1926, and in 1931 became its chairman.

He was a great language commentator. When Hilary and I were compiling our book of language quotations, *Words on Words* (2000), we found Shaw far outnumbering any other 20th-century author. Sometimes it's him talking:

England and America are two countries divided by a common language. (Attributed, in *Reader's Digest*, 1942)

Page opposite. The revolving writing shed at Shaw's House, Ayot St Lawrence.

Effectiveness of assertion is the alpha and omega of style. (Preface to *Man and Superman*)

The English have no respect for their language … They spell it so abominably that no man can teach himself what it sounds like. (Preface to *Pygmalion*)

Sometimes it's his characters:

Reading is a dangerous amusement (Lord Summerhays, in *Misalliance*)

You can spot an Irishman or a Yorkshireman by his brogue. I can place any man within six miles. I can place him within two miles in London. Sometimes within two streets. (Professor Higgins, in *Pygmalion*)

I dont want to talk grammar. I want to talk like a lady. (Eliza, in *Pygmalion*)

It's *Pygmalion*, of course, which made Shaw's use of language front-page news. On 11 April 1914, the *Daily Sketch* ran the headline:

TO-NIGHT'S 'PYGMALION', IN WHICH MRS. PATRICK CAMPBELL IS EXPECTED TO CAUSE THE GREATEST THEATRICAL SENSATION FOR YEARS

In the character of Eliza Doolittle, she was to speak the line 'not bloody likely'. The paper went on:

Mr. Shaw Introduces a Forbidden Word.
WILL 'MRS PAT' SPEAK IT?
Has The Censor Stepped In, Or Will The Phrase Spread?

The censor did not step in. Indeed, in the report from the Lord Chamberlain's Office, he goes so far as to say that 'The Play is entirely without offence'. So the phrase was used. It's reported that the audience gave a gasp of surprise, and then roared with laughter. A linguistic milestone had been passed. And soon after, a new phrase entered the language: 'not pygmalion likely'!

The play eventually won Shaw an Oscar for best screenplay, when it was filmed in 1938. It was his second great accolade. He already had a Nobel Prize (for Literature), given in 1926. That makes him unique—the only person to have received both of these awards. You can see them side by side in a display cabinet in the Museum Room at his large house in Ayot

St Lawrence, Hertfordshire. (Ayot's an unusual name. The first part comes from a personal name in Old English, *Æga*; the second part from *geat*, for a gap or pass. The 'Ay' rhymes with 'hay' and the 'ot' with 'not'.)

The house was built in 1902 for the local rector, but he found it too large to maintain. Shaw and his wife discovered it on a house-hunting trip in 1906, and he remained there until his death in 1950, aged 94. Although it was called the New Rectory, as Shaw's fame (and eccentricity) grew, the villagers started calling it Shaw's Corner, and that is its name today. It's in the care of the National Trust now—something Shaw planned himself. He intended his home to become a literary shrine, and within six months of his death it was opened to the public.

The preservation of the detail of his life is extraordinary, by any standards. The bedroom remains as it was the day he died—the clothes in the wardrobe open to view, his shoes by the bed, Shakespeare and the Bible by the window. The study has his desk, complete with typewriter (a Remington Noiseless Portable) and a range of writer's paraphernalia – pens, a hole-punch, blank cablegram forms . . . a bottle of glue and a brush, for pasting press clippings and drafts of his writing. A pair of his spectacles rests on a writing pad. He has, it appears, just left the room for a few minutes.

Shaw's writing desk.

One of the most interesting features of Shaw's Corner is the hut at the bottom of the back garden. It was built on a frame that allowed it to turn on its axis, so that Shaw could change the view or follow the sunlight. Hugely protective of his privacy, he worked there most days, so that when unwanted visitors arrived at the door of the main house, they could honestly be told he was 'out'—'visiting the capital', even (for the hut was nicknamed 'London').

But for the English-language tourist, the most interesting piece of memorabilia is the framed plaster plaque above the fireplace in the Museum Room. It shows the word 'Schorr'—his surname in a reformed spelling—made for the title-sequence in the film *Caesar and Cleopatra* (1945). And it is in relation to spelling reform that most of his linguistic energy was directed. And what energy! His opinions were always forceful, but it's unusual, to say the least, to find such strong language as we read in his preface to R. A. Wilson's *The Miraculous Birth of Language* in 1948. Reform English spelling or war? Shaw was in no doubt.

> Take the words *though* and *should* and *enough*: containing eighteen letters. Heaven knows how many hundred thousand times I have had to

Wordsmiths and Warriors

Above left. Shaw at the door of his writing shed. He writes in his *Rhyming Picture Guide to Ayot St Lawrence*, 'In shattering sunlight here's the shelter / Where I write dramas helter skelter'. He took all the photographs in this booklet himself—another of his many interests.

Above right. Shaw at work. The hut had an electricity supply for a heater, so Shaw was able to work there in all weathers.

Left. The shed as it is today.

Another bearded writer peers in.

write these constantly recurring words. With a new English alphabet replacing the old Semitic one with its added Latin vowels I should be able to spell t-h-o-u-g-h with two letters, s-h-o-u-l-d with three, and e-n-o-u-g-h with four: nine letters instead of eighteen: a saving of a hundred per cent of my time and my typist's time and the printer's time, to say nothing of the saving in paper and wear and tear of machinery. . . .

If the introduction of an English alphabet for the English language costs a civil war, or even, as the introduction of summer time did, a world war, I shall not grudge it. The waste of war is negligible in comparison to the daily waste of trying to communicate with one another in English through an alphabet with sixteen letters missing. That must be remedied, come what may.

In the late 1940s, two of the leading proponents of reform, Daniel Jones and James Pitman (the grandson of Isaac), visited Shaw at his house to try to persuade him to leave part of his estate to fund the kind of reform being advocated by the Simplified Spelling Society. They failed. Shaw had very definite ideas about the kind of reform that was needed. Tinkering with the existing system, as other spelling reformers did, wasn't enough. Only a radical change to a completely new alphabet would do. So in his will he appointed the Public Trustee to seek and publish a Proposed British Alphabet of not less than 42 letters. The will was contested, but after lengthy legal arguments a small part of the legacy was used to fund a competition for a new phonetic alphabet. It was won by Kingsley Read, and called Shavian. It remains a glorious idiosyncrasy in the history of English orthography.

Getting there

Travelling north along the A1(M), leave at junction 4 and follow the B653 north towards Wheathampstead. There's a right turn signposted Ayot St Lawrence (Codicote Road), and some way along a National Trust sign points you left to Shaw's Corner along Bride Hall Lane. Turn left at the next National Trust sign (Bibbs Hall Lane), and the house is a hundred yards along on the left (postcode: AL6 9BX). There's a small car parking area.

It's slightly more complicated from the north along the A1(M). Leave at junction 6 and turn right towards Welwyn. Follow the A1000 north and turn left onto the B656, signposted Welwyn and Codicote. Leave the B656 by turning sharp left onto Fulling Mill Lane at a roundabout signposted Ayot St Lawrence. Follow the road to the left (Kimpton Road) until it meets Codicote Road, where you turn left towards Ayot St Lawrence. Just after the left turn to Ayot St Peter, turn right into Hill Farm Lane, which leads to Ayot St Lawrence and Bibbs Hall Lane. Let the satnav do the work!

From the M1, leave at junction 10 and follow the signs towards Wheathampstead.

For opening hours, see the website at

http://www.nationaltrust.org.uk/shaws-corner/

Chapter 54

Laugharne

Dylan Thomas and Welsh English

The English heard and seen in Wales has, over the centuries, evolved into a recognizable regional variety, shaped partly by Welsh, and characterized by distinctive sounds, rhythms, words, and grammar. Many Welsh writers could illustrate this evolution; but for me, having to choose one to represent English in Wales, it has to be Dylan Thomas (1914–53). So we went to Laugharne, in Carmarthenshire, where he lived and worked for the last few years of his life.

The first thing that is likely to strike the English-language tourist is the spelling of the place; but awareness of its Welsh name provides the explanation. In fact there are two names in the oldest records: *Talacharn* and *Abercoran*—Welsh *tal* 'end', *aber* 'river mouth', and *Corran*, or *Charn*, the name of the stream that flows through the town into the estuary of the River Taf. *Talacharn*, a written version of *tal y charn*, meant 'ending-place of the Corran'. In Welsh, the penultimate syllable of a word is the one that usually carries the main stress; so over time the first syllable of *Talacharn* weakened and eventually disappeared, leaving the name as *Lacharn*. Then the spelling altered. In this part of little England beyond Wales (Chapter 18), many place names were Anglicized during the Middle Ages. The Welsh velar 'ch' sound was given the nearest English spelling, *gh*, which was used in Middle English for the same sound in such words as *daughter* and *brought*. Finally, the pronunciation changed. Just as the *gh* sound eventually disappeared from those words, so it did in Laugharne. The modern pronunciation, 'larn', is the result.

Page opposite. Dylan Thomas's 'house on stilts' at Laugharne (as he calls it in 'Poem on his birthday').

I chose Dylan Thomas because he has lived with me longer than anyone else I can remember in English literature. He was already a poetic name to be reckoned with when I was growing up in Holyhead in the 1940s, and I remember hearing his 'Child's Christmas in Wales' and other tales on the radio. I loved his short stories more than the poems, and his 'play for voices' *Under Milk Wood* most of all. I've since performed it several times, and directed it once. When I started doing 'evenings of readings', he was always there, in poetry or prose. So even though his recorded literary voice, with its sonorous chanting tone, couldn't by any stretch of the imagination be considered a typical Welsh accent, there is more than enough local colour in his work for him to represent the voice of English in Wales.

A local linguistic identity is more than just sounds and grammar. The language expresses a culture too, especially in the settings, characters, and atmosphere it reflects. Thomas's writing is full of local place names, for example, and he milks the resonances of the Welsh phonetic forms, as in the morning hymn of the Reverend Eli Jenkins in *Under Milk Wood*, with its listing of river names: 'Claerwen, Cleddau, Dulais, Daw, / Eli, Gwili, Ogwr, Nedd ...' Although Dylan didn't speak Welsh, he was well aware of the way Welsh words and phrases form part of the English of Wales. *Ach y fi*, shouts Jack Black the cobbler, as he chases naughty couples out of the woods. *Eisteddfodau*, murmurs the dreaming Reverend in his sleep— using the Welsh plural *au* ending (rhymes with *I*), not *eisteddfods*. And Welsh culture is sometimes so much part of the story that a non-Welsh reader would need glosses, as when the Second Voice describes Jenkins:

> He intricately rhymes, to the music of crwth and pibgorn, all night long
> in his druid's seedy nightie in a beer-tent black with parchs.

This is lexically as distinctive as any other global variety of English. (A *parch* is a minister.) Echoes of Welsh grammar are regularly heard. Lines such as *There's a husband for you, there's wives for you, there's a lovely morning*, and *there's glamour!*, all from *Under Milk Wood*, show the direct influence of a Welsh construction.

Laugharne itself is present in the poems, especially in 'Poem in October', but it is given its fullest treatment in a piece for radio that he called, simply, 'Laugharne':

> this timeless, mild, beguiling island of a town with its seven public-
> houses, one chapel in action, one church, one factory, two billiard tables,

one St Bernard (without brandy), one policeman, three rivers, a visiting sea . . .

And the town now has taken him to heart. There is a Dylan Thomas Walk, and some of the buildings that he frequented in his time have been refurbished—notably his favourite drinking-hole, Brown's Hotel, which actually reopened on the day (13 July 2012) I was writing this chapter, in good time for the 2014 hundredth birth anniversary. You never quite know when a Thomasian echo is going to greet you, as you walk around. Along King Street there is a Manchester House (the name of Mog Edwards' emporium), and around the corner there is a Rose Cottage (another *Under Milk Wood* character, Mae Rose Cottage).

But the main target of a visitor will be the Boathouse, where Dylan lived from 1949 until his death. This isn't the only location in Laugharne which claims him. He first visited the town in 1934, and later stayed with his wife Caitlin in the Georgian house next to the castle, as well as living in 'Eros' in Gosport Street and in 'Sea View' near the Castle. But it's the Boathouse which stands supreme, for it was here that he wrote most of his late poetry and began *Under Milk Wood*, with the town of Llaregyb (it has to be read backwards to get the joke, remembering that *y* in Welsh is pronounced with

The Boathouse on the Laugharne headland, with Thomas's writing shed just above it to the left. The estuary shallows are where the boats in the opening description of Llaregyb 'tilt and ride'.

the same vowel as the one in unstressed *the* in English) in part modelled on Laugharne.

Or, to be precise, he began it in the Boathouse garage—a tiny shed on the cliff path above the house. This is the first thing you come to as you follow the signs to the Boathouse—and the encounter has evidently confused many visitors, who must have stopped at this point and thought they had reached their goal, for the panel outside tells you firmly: 'This is not the Boathouse'. But it's a significant place nonetheless, for it was in this 'word-splashed hut', as Dylan once called it, that the writing got done.

What is it about small sheds that attracts writers so much? This was the third time we'd peered into a writer's tiny workplace, away from his main residence (Shaw, Murray)—probably more than three, if we count the various cells in which the monks wrote. Certainly, in this case the reasons are fairly clear: first and foremost, the view across the vast estuary of the Taf and Towy rivers is truly inspirational—the Gower Peninsula in the distance, the wooded Sir John's Hill ahead (the subject of another poem, 'Over Sir John's hill'), and the long curving shoreline below. The Boathouse brochure mentions the other reasons: 'a safe distance from his family and conveniently placed to slip away to the town and the pub'.

The Boathouse is a few steps further along the cliff path. To get to it you have to descend a flight of steps, for it is right at the water's edge. You enter the house through the garden and you're on the first floor. The house is largely as it was when Dylan lived in it, with the bedrooms on the top floor turned into a display area full of photographs, books, letters, and other

Page opposite. The shed has been restored, but is largely as it was when Dylan Thomas used it. The table and chairs belonged to the family. The crumpled papers on the floor are discarded drafts.

Wordsmiths and Warriors

The 'heron-priested shore' described in 'Poem on his birthday'. St John's Hill is far right.

As we walked towards the shed, a lone 'fishing holy stalking heron' did indeed appear to greet us.

Wordsmiths and Warriors

things from his time there. An old wireless. A record-player. His chanting tones reverberate around the room from a recording of his poems. And there is the often-reproduced original photograph of him as a young man, signed by him to the writer Pamela Hansford Johnson. A copy went into space with other artefacts in Voyager 2. If aliens do arrive one day, having followed this up, they'll probably be speaking Welsh English.

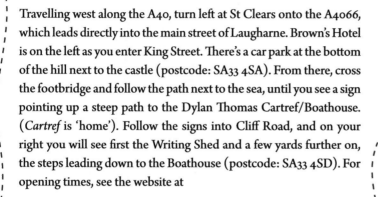

Getting there

Travelling west along the A40, turn left at St Clears onto the A4066, which leads directly into the main street of Laugharne. Brown's Hotel is on the left as you enter King Street. There's a car park at the bottom of the hill next to the castle (postcode: SA33 4SA). From there, cross the footbridge and follow the path next to the sea, until you see a sign pointing up a steep path to the Dylan Thomas Cartref/Boathouse. (*Cartref* is 'home'). Follow the signs into Cliff Road, and on your right you will see first the Writing Shed and a few yards further on, the steps leading down to the Boathouse (postcode: SA33 4SD). For opening times, see the website at

http://www.dylanthomasboathouse.com/

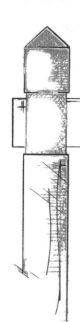

Chapter 55

Tilbury

the *Empire Windrush* and new dialects

There's always a risk, when telling the story of the English language, that older periods of history attract all the attention, so that significant events in living memory come to be ignored. This can't happen when visiting Tilbury, Essex, for that is where the MV *Empire Windrush* arrived in 1948. It's a moment that has achieved mythic status in British cultural history, and it had major consequences for the language too. Our tourist journey in this book stays within the shores of Britain, and doesn't take in the places around the globe where the language has evolved into many distinctive varieties. Tilbury is an opportunity to redress the balance, for it acts as a symbol of the new wave of English dialects that emerged in Britain during the second half of the 20th century.

The *Windrush* was at the end of a long voyage, beginning in Australia. It had called at Kingston, Jamaica, where it had picked up an unexpectedly large number of would-be immigrants to Britain. An advertisement had appeared in a Jamaican newspaper offering a cheap passage to anyone wanting to make good the labour shortfall in post-war Britain. It proved a popular offer. The group that arrived in Tilbury was the first large group of West Indian immigrants after World War II. Many more would follow.

Commentators now talk about the 'Windrush generation', and that is how it is remembered. For the fiftieth anniversary of the event, a part of Brixton was renamed Windrush Square. For the sixtieth, a Thurrock Heritage plaque was unveiled at the London Cruise Terminal in Tilbury.

Page opposite. The Empire Windrush arrived outside Tilbury on 21 June 1948, and dropped anchor somewhere here, outside Tilbury Fort. The passengers disembarked the next day.

The ship itself no longer exists: in 1954 it sank in the Mediterranean Sea after an engine-room fire.

Page opposite. The *Empire Windrush* finally docks.

The statistics are important, in view of the way the event has become charged with cultural significance. Many online sources give the impression that the ship was carrying only people from Jamaica—492 of them is the usual figure cited—whereas in fact the passenger log shows that there were 1027 passengers on board, from a wide range of countries. Just over half (537) gave their last permanent residence as being in Jamaica, but there were many also from Trinidad and Bermuda, and some from other Caribbean territories. The log also shows that there were 76 'aliens and stowaways'—a figure that included 66 Poles.

A BBC newsreel from the time shows interviews with some of the passengers. They all look forward to finding work, or joining (in some cases rejoining) the armed forces. Not all are planning to be in London, or even England. The most famous of the interviewees was Lord Kitchener, the 'king of calypso', who was asked to perform in front of the camera, and rather self-consciously improvised with 'London is the place for me; London this lovely city; You can go to France or America; India, Asia or Australia; But you must come back to London City'.

Although there were already thousands of immigrants in Britain—including many from the Caribbean (the West Indian cricketer Learie Constantine, for example, moved to Britain in 1929)—the surge in immigration that became a major feature of the second half of the 20th century has come to be symbolized by this moment, captured pictorially by the newsreels and press. There was little talk of a 'multiracial' or 'multicultural' Britain before the 1950s. A couple of decades later, and the linguistic consequences were beginning to be observed in a new generation of Anglo-Caribbean writers, as well as on the streets in the form of British versions of the creole dialects that the immigrants brought with them.

When the children of these families went to school, many had difficulty when their creole-influenced English was penalized by an educational system unused to coping with nonstandard grammar. Today, there's a real pride in Anglo-Caribbean linguistic identity. English classes in schools now routinely study the work of such poets as John Agard and Benjamin Zephaniah, and analyse their distinctive rhythms, lexicon, and grammar. And in the streets of many British cities we can hear mixed varieties, in which Caribbean, Indian, African, and other dialects of ex-colonial English blend with home-grown ones such as Cockney, Scouse, and Geordie.

Tilbury

A container ship disturbs the fish.

Tilbury Fort is probably the best place to imagine the arrival of the *Empire Windrush*. The Thames is still very wide at this point, and huge container ships come and go. The immigrants would certainly have seen the fort, as the ship manoeuvred its way to the landing stage a little upriver. We walked along the sea wall outside the fort, passing clusters of fishermen, their radios and CD players providing a multidialectal musical counterpoint to their gloomy observations about fishlessness. Rap competed with reggae for our attention, and—it being a Sunday afternoon—with the Estuary English of a football commentator.

At least we were on the same estuary, I thought, as we entered the fort to get a better view of Tilbury docks. We went in through the Water Gate, with its impressive monumental face commemorating King Charles II. The fort was built in his reign, following a crisis in 1667 when a Dutch fleet sailed unchecked up the Thames, burning part of the English fleet at Chatham. It replaced a much smaller fort that had been built over a century earlier by Henry VIII. The new one was massive, with a brick curtain wall

Wordsmiths and Warriors

and parapet on top of a high earth rampart, and a complex arrangement of bastions. We clambered up the rampart and got an excellent view of the estuary from the top.

The River Thames at Tilbury Docks, looking upriver

Looking east, it was possible to see the hill at West Tilbury where Queen Elizabeth I, anticipating the arrival of the Spanish Armada in 1588, made her famous speech to her army: 'I know I have the body of a weak and feeble woman; but I have the heart and stomach of a king, and of a king of England too.' Looking west, through the fort walls, across the broad inner moat, Tilbury docks and cranes filled the horizon. To the south, there was only the wide estuary, with the Kent shoreline in the distance, and the North Sea beyond. We had left our car outside the pub called The World's End. It felt like it.

The road away from the fort is called Fort Road. Then there's Ferry Road. Apt, if unoriginal. But leaving Tilbury along Feenan Highway is a totally different matter. It felt like entering an astonishing artistic world. Raphael, Gainsborough, Elgar, and Sullivan name roads to the west. Dickens, Burns,

Looking towards Tilbury docks from the parapet of the fort.

Cowper, and Milton name roads to the east. We turned off to explore. A few minutes' browsing eastwards brought an encounter with Shakespeare Avenue, Chaucer Close, Coleridge Road, Shaw Crescent, Dryden Place, and Tennyson Walk. It was like driving through an English literature degree.

But there were no names reflecting literary Britain of the second half of the 20th century. That, however, was something imagination could fix. On our way back to the M25, with the *Windrush* very much in mind, we imagined ourselves passing Agard Avenue, Dabydeen Drive, Brathwaite Boulevard, Walcott Walk, and Zephaniah Crescent. And Johnson Way, of course—but Kwesi, not Samuel.

Getting there

From the M25, leave at junction 30 onto the A13, and take the next exit at the sign saying Tilbury & Docks A1089 (the Dock Approach Road). At the roundabout, an English Heritage brown sign points you towards Tilbury Fort (Ferry Road). Turn left just before the London International Cruise Terminal onto Fort Road. Bear right at a mini-roundabout, and The World's End pub is immediately ahead (postcode: RM18 7NR). You can park there, or continue round the corner and park outside Tilbury Fort.

The BBC newsreel can be seen at

http://www.youtube.com/watch?v=auaaPrEdn8Y

Chapter 56

University College London, WC1

Daniel Jones and English phonetics

I remember my first ever visit to the Phonetics Department at University College London (UCL). I was an undergraduate in the English Department, and had decided to take phonetics as one of my courses, but had no idea where the phoneticians were based. 'Somewhere over there', said my English tutor, pointing vaguely. I went in search of them, and eventually found them by climbing up an unpromising iron staircase and through a back entrance into one of the Victorian houses that form the western terrace of Gordon Square. A gloomy corridor. A steep staircase up to pokey offices. So many university rooms are like this! Unattractive. Unassuming. But, when you enter them, you find occupants who blow open your mind.

Or, in this case, my mouth and ears. I took to phonetics straightaway—as, much later, did Hilary, who studied there as part of her speech therapy course. Phonetics is, as Professor Henry Higgins says in George Bernard Shaw's *Pygmalion* (aka *My Fair Lady*), 'the science of speech'—or, slightly more precisely, the science of the making, transmission, and reception of speech sounds. As a real-life Henry—Oxford philologist Henry Sweet—once said, it is 'the indispensable foundation' of all work on spoken language. And it was in this unprepossessing place on Gordon Square that the subject chiefly developed in Britain.

The prime mover was Daniel Jones (1881–1967), the first professor of phonetics at a British university, and the pre-eminent British phonetician for over 60 years. He's one of the few people linguists often refer to just by initials: DJ. He gave his first series of lectures at UCL in 1907, and within

Page opposite. The Gower Street view of University College London.

The front (top) and rear
(bottom) views of
21 Gordon Square.

Wordsmiths and Warriors

Daniel Jones in his UCL office, during the 1950s. The language on the board is a transcription of Finnish.

a decade had formed a department, including a small phonetics laboratory. He was appointed professor in 1921. The phoneticians were originally housed in cramped offices in the main college building, but in 1922 they moved to Arts Annexe 1, at 21 Gordon Square, and there they stayed—apart from the disruption caused by World War II—for the next 75 years. (Since 2008 they've been housed elsewhere, as part of a reorganized Division of Psychology and Language Sciences.)

The new premises were curious. The front door was permanently locked, to deter unwelcome visitors (especially those who thought that phonetics was, as Shaw portrayed it, all about achieving a posh accent). You had to get into the place, as I did, through the back door. Once inside, you had the choice of descending down a dark staircase into the kitchen area of the original house, which housed the phonetics laboratory, or ascending equally dark stairs to the first floor, where Jones had his office. Other lecturers occupied the higher floors. My two tutors in phonetics, A. C. Gimson and J. D. O'Connor, were on those floors. I came into the business in the 1960s, and had only a small contact with Jones, receiving from him a genteel letter of thanks for reviewing a birthday volume of essays in his honour. But I was lucky to get the kind of individual tuition from my tutors that Jones had initiated decades before. Phonetics is that kind of subject. To become really proficient, you need one-to-one.

It's difficult to overstate the importance of that department. Its phonetics lab was, for a long time, the only one in Britain. Many of DJ's students became heads of other phonetics departments. His books became standard works, both in the theory of phonetics and in its application to such fields as language teaching and speech therapy. Although phonetics deals with all languages—and Jones worked on many—his leading publications have an English theme: *The Pronunciation of English, An Outline of English Phonetics,* and the *English Pronouncing Dictionary*. This last—the *EPD*, as it's often called—was the first pronouncing dictionary since John Walker's (Chapter 41).

DJ always lived in or near London. His birthplace—12 Norfolk Crescent, near Edgware Road—has long been demolished and replaced. So has his house in Marsham Way, Gerrards Cross, where he lived from 1934. We called by to see if there was any sign of it. Flats and offices now. The pavement looks the same, though.

I know this because, in the biography of DJ by Beverley Collins and Inger Mees, there's a photograph of him in 1965 standing on the pavement outside his house. They called their book *The Real Professor Higgins*. The back story is that, for many years, people thought that Shaw's model for Higgins was Henry Sweet, whose post at Oxford was officially in phonetics. But Shaw says quite plainly in the Preface to *Pygmalion* that 'Higgins is not a portrait of Sweet'. If it's anyone, it has to be Jones. I've already written this up, in my *By Hook or By Crook*, but as the Sweet myth is still widespread it's worth repeating the points here.

Jones helped Shaw in several ways. He gave him advice on phonetic detail, corresponded with him several times, and invited him into his department. The technology that we see in *My Fair Lady* is close to what would have been Jones's lab. After the play was completed, Shaw offered Jones an unlimited supply of complimentary tickets to see it.

Where did the name of Higgins come from? By all accounts, it was borrowed from a shop sign. One of Jones's students tells the story that Shaw was on a bus going through South London, wondering what name he should give his character, and saw the shop of 'Jones and Higgins'—at the time the largest and most prestigious department store in the area, in Rye Lane, Peckham. The student recalled Jones saying: 'he could not call me Jones, so he called me Higgins'. Jones and Higgins closed down in 1980, but the distinctive building is still there.

Why couldn't Shaw call his character Jones? It would have been very risky to portray a living character as a fictional one. Flattering as the idea might seem at first, we can immediately imagine the real-life source being unflattered by aspects of Higgins's character. The plot contained taboo language. Higgins, moreover—to put it in modern terms—has an affair with one of his students. Not the best set of associations for a career academic.

Moreover, the play wasn't doing phonetics many favours. True, it brought the word *phonetics* to the attention of millions who might not otherwise have heard of it, but—as Jones himself remarked—'In *Pygmalion* phonetics is represented as providing a key to social advancement', and he adds, drily, 'a function which it may be hoped it will not be called upon to perform indefinitely'. His dryness it seems was replaced by fury, when he saw the play on the first night. This was not how he wanted phonetics to be seen.

In *The Real Professor Higgins*, Jones's biographers conclude that he wanted to distance himself from the character and the play, and that Shaw agreed. Shaw then went further, writing a preface which made no reference to Jones but hinted at a portrayal of the now-deceased Sweet. The ruse was successful. Nobody publicly associated Jones with Higgins, and Sweet remained the link in the public mind.

In Shaw's view, phonetics was a seriously underrated subject, and he concludes: 'if the play makes the public aware that there are such people as phoneticians and that they are among the most important people in England at present, it will serve his turn.' Phoneticians among the most important people in England? When non-phoneticians say so, it makes you think, maybe they are. And Shaw is not alone in his opinion. The novelist Anthony Burgess states just as firmly, in the epilogue to his language memoir, *A Mouthful of Air*: 'Phonetics, phonetics, and again phonetics. There cannot be too much phonetics.'

Getting there

The imposing portico of University College (postcode: WC1E 6BT) can't be missed on the left as you travel south along Gower Street. (Film buffs will recognize it as the location for the teaching hospital in *Doctor in the House*.) The nearest tube station is Euston Square, immediately opposite the northern end of Gower Street. But to get to Gordon Square, you need to turn left outside the underground station and walk towards Euston Station. At the traffic lights, turn right into Gordon Street, and the Square is at the end. No. 21 Gordon Square is on the right. If you go into UCL through the Gordon Street entrance, and follow the walkway around to the left, you'll see the back stairs into where the Phonetics Department used to be.

If you continue past this point and go under an arch, you will find yourself approaching Foster Court (Chapter 57).

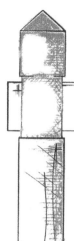

Chapter 57

University College London, WC1

the Survey of English Usage

It's another unassuming place. Two first-floor windows set against Victorian brickwork along the side entrance to University College London, in the heart of Bloomsbury. The buildings on each side are tall, and that side of the passageway doesn't get much sun. A plaque on the wall tells you that this part of the college is Foster Court, after the first provost of the College, Sir Gregory Foster. It has been the home of the English Department for decades. And what an English Department it has been! UCL (as it's usually called now) was the first university in England to offer English as a degree subject. It was probably the first in the world.

As so often with British universities, it's what goes on behind the windows that is the exciting thing. And Foster Court is the location of what, to my mind, is the most important development in the study of English grammar in the 20th century: the Survey of English Usage. It was founded by Professor Randolph Quirk in 1959. I worked on it myself for a year in the early 1960s, and have stayed in touch with it ever since. Usage here means chiefly grammar. And when the Survey began, it was grammar which desperately needed some life-blood.

There's a remarkable passage in a 1921 report from the Board of Education in Britain. Talking about the English curriculum in schools, it says:

> [it is] impossible at the present juncture to teach English grammar in the schools for the simple reason that no-one knows exactly what it is.

Page opposite. The Torrington Street entrance to University College, showing Foster Court on the right. The offices of the Survey are on the first floor, the last two before the building in the middle distance that juts out on the right.

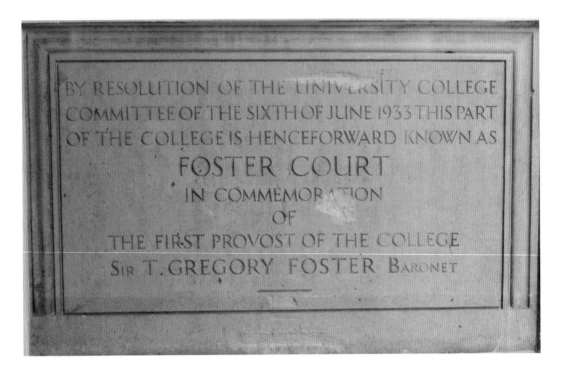

Grammar had been getting a bad press for some time. Teachers were becoming increasingly doubtful about the value of the old-style traditional grammar, associated with such writers as Lindley Murray (Chapter 42), which had dominated teaching in the 19th century. They found it complex and unrewarding. They didn't like the use of a battery of terms (such as *nominative* and *accusative*) which suited Latin grammar but not English. They didn't like the rigid and complicated system of parsing. They didn't like the way the prescriptive approach presented so much personal taste, and focused on idiosyncrasies instead of on the broad picture. They didn't like the use of concocted examples rather than real usage.

On the other hand, what was to be put in its place? Hardly any academic research was taking place into grammar in the early decades of the century in Britain. And the academic work which *was* being done—the historical study of the language, or *philology*—was considered to be irrelevant to children whose primary need was literacy. Philology was particularly repugnant to teachers of English literature, who found it a dry and dusty subject. And literature teachers in any case were naturally reluctant to give up some of their precious teaching time to the study of a subject whose value hadn't yet been demonstrated.

Where was help to come from? There were no academic specialists to advise; and the teachers themselves lacked experience. Grammar hadn't been compulsory in primary schools since 1890, and the secondary schools

Grammar is on screen in the Survey office of today. Modern digital technology sits alongside the old tape recorders, seen being well used in the archive photograph.

were doing little more than recycling old material, which sometimes dated back to Murray. Fresh initiatives were lacking. The subject was still being taught, but without any life. In Britain, it had disappeared from most schools by the end of the 1960s, and for the next 40 years the vast majority of children received an education which included no awareness of grammar at all. 'What's a preposition?', I recall one undergraduate asking me in the 1970s. It summarized the age.

Despite the lack of teaching, people continued to worry about grammar. Writers such as Henry Fowler (Chapter 52) had kept issues of usage before the minds of the public. But the kind of English that was being discussed was a very limited segment of the language as a whole. It was written English—and a rather formal written English, at that. Spoken usage was being ignored. And yet it is speech that takes up most of our language-using lives.

It was time to redress the balance, and this is what the Survey did. Walk into the office in the 1960s, and the first thing you'd notice would be the tape recorders and the headphones. People were listening, listening, listening. Samples from radio broadcasts, speeches, sermons, commentaries, everyday conversations, and a great deal more were being carefully transcribed and analysed. Written texts were being analysed too. The aim was to obtain a comprehensive and realistic picture of the way the entire grammar of the language was being used. A million words of data, in the first instance.

And not just in Britain. In the 1980s, the Survey initiated an international project involving samples from all over the English-speaking world. Another collection of data focused on the way English grammar was changing. New technology offered fresh perspectives. Software facilitated the task of grammatical analysis, and fast search techniques made it easy to home in on points of interest. Educational applications followed. And in 2011 there was an interactive grammar app for the iPhone. Whatever your point of interest in English grammar, information on it now is available at your fingertips.

The Survey did for grammar what dictionaries did for vocabulary. It provided a description which could be used as a reference point. If we want to know the way a word is used, we look it up in a dictionary. If we want to know the way a grammatical construction is used—*really* used—we can, thanks to the publications produced by the Survey, look it up in a grammar. That's the linguistic legacy of the building with the unpromising facade in Foster Court. And in its creative use of the latest technology, it shows the way the English language will be studied in the future.

Getting there

For getting to UCL, see the end of Chapter 56. For the Survey premises, walk down Gower Street, past the main UCL entrance, and turn left at the traffic lights into Torrington Place. The side entrance to the College is immediately on the left. Walk through the big gates into the College, and the entrance to Foster Court is a little way down on the right.

Information about the Survey can be found at

http://www.ucl.ac.uk/english-usage/index.htm

REGIONAL GROUPING

This page, and the maps at the front and rear of the book, show the geographical distribution of the places visited in this book, along with their postcodes. The numbers preceding a location refer to chapters.

England

EAST ANGLIA

Norfolk
2 Caistor St Edmund, NR14 8QN
2 Norwich, NR1 3JU
25 Paston, NR28 9TA

Suffolk
3 Undley Common, IP27 9BZ

EAST MIDLANDS

Cambridgeshire
11 Ely, CB7 4DL

Leicestershire
26 Lutterworth, LE17 4AN

Lincolnshire
14 Bourne, PE10 9UQ
33 Willoughby, LN13 9SU

Northamptonshire
12 Peterborough, PE1 1XS
37 Aldwincle, NN14 3UT

Rutland
32 Oakham, LE15 6XT
32 North Luffenham, LE15 8JR

NORTH-EAST

Northumberland
4 Jarrow, NE32 3DY
4 Durham, NE1 3EH
5 Lindisfarne, TD15 2RX

Yorkshire, North
42 York, YO24 4DD

Yorkshire, West
51 Saltaire, BD18 3TT
51 Thackley, BT10 0TD

NORTH-WEST

Cheshire
16 Chester, VH1 2HU

Cumbria
45 Grasmere, LA22 9SQ

Greater Manchester
39 Rochdale, OL16 1QT

SOUTH-CENTRAL

Hampshire
9 Winchester, SO23 7DQ

Oxfordshire
48 Banbury Road, Oxford,
 OX2 6JT
48 St Aldate's, Oxford, OX1 1RA

Wiltshire
7 Stourton, BA12 6QD
7 Edington, BA13 4SP

SOUTH-EAST

Essex
8 Maldon, CM9 5JQ
36 Black Notley, CM77 8LB
55 Tilbury, RM18 7NR

Hertfordshire
24 St Albans, AL1 2BY
53 Ayot St Lawrence, AL6 9BX

Kent
1 Pegwell Bay, CT12 5HY
1 Reculver, CT6 6SU
1 Sarre, CT7 0JY
1 St Nicholas at Wade, CT7 0PW
21 Canterbury, CT1 2EH

Sussex, East
13 Battle, TN33 0AD
13 Normans Bay, BN24 6PS

Sussex, West
28 Chichester, PO19 1YH

SOUTH-WEST

Cornwall
16 Trevessa, TR8 5AN

Dorset
10 Cerne Abbas, DT2 7JQ
49 Winterborne Came, DT2 8NT
50 Higher Bockhampton,
 DT2 8QJ
50 Dorchester, DT1 2AA

Somerset
47 Bath, BA1 2LT
52 Hinton St George, TA17 8SP

WEST MIDLANDS

Gloucestershire
16 Berkeley, GL13 9PJ
27 North Nibley, GL11 6DS

Staffordshire
40 Lichfield, WS13 6LG

Warwickshire
30 Stratford-upon-Avon,
 CV37 6EP

Worcestershire
15 Areley Kings, DY13 0AR
46 West Malvern, WR14 4BB

LONDON

East
34 East India Dock, E14 9QS

East-Central
22 Cursitor Street, EC4A 1LL
29 Suffolk Lane, EC4R 0AX
29 St Paul's Cathedral, EC4M 8AD

38 Old Broad Street, EC2N 1HN

40 Gough Square, EC4A 3DE

Greater

35 Hampton Court Palace,
KT8 9AU

North-West

41 Old St Pancras Church,
NW1 1UL

South-East

20 Talbot Yard, SE1 1YP

31 Park Street, SE1 9AS

South-West

23 Tothill Street, SW1P 3PA

23 Victoria and Albert Museum,
SW7 2RL

West-Central

56, **57** University College,
WC1E 6BT

Scotland

AYRSHIRE

43 Alloway, KA7 4PQ

DUMFRIES AND GALLOWAY

6 Ruthwell, DG1 4NP

EDINBURGH

19 Castle, EH1 2NG

44 Chambers Street, EH1 1JF

44 Leith Walk, EH6 5DG

FIFE

19 Dunfermline, KY12 7PE

SCOTTISH BORDERS

44 Peebles, EH45 8HS

Wales

CARMARTHENSHIRE

18, **54** Laugharne SA33 4SA

DENBIGHSHIRE

17 Rhuddlan, LL18 5AD

PEMBROKESHIRE

18 Manorbier, SA70 7SY

SOURCES AND ACKNOWLEDGEMENTS

The photographs in this book were taken by us, apart from the following cases, which we here acknowledge.

Ch.2   Urn N59: J. N. L. Myres and Barbara Green, *The Anglo-Saxon Cemeteries of Caistor-by-Norwich and Markshall Norfolk*, 1973): The Society of Antiquaries of London.
        The Caistor astragalus: Norwich Castle Museum and Art Gallery.
Ch.3   The Undley bracteate: The Trustees of the British Museum.
Ch.5   Lindisfarne Gospels: The British Library Board: Cotton Nero D.IV, f.90.
Ch.6   Ruthwell Cross transcription: Bruce Dickins and Alan Ross, *The Dream of the Rood* (Methuen, 1934).
Ch.10   Ælfric's Colloquy: The British Library Board: Cotton Tiberius A.iii, f.60v.
Ch.36   John Ray: National Portrait Gallery, London.
Ch.39   Tim Bobbin: The Bridgeman Art Library Ltd.
Ch.47   Isaac Pitman letter, Pitman portrait, Phonetic Institute: Alfred Baker, *The Life of Sir Isaac Pitman* (London: Pitman & Sons, 1913), pp. 42, 178, 196.
Ch.48   Murray's scriptorium, external and internal: K. M. Elisabeth Murray, *Caught in the Web of Words* (Oxford: Oxford University Press, 1977), pp. 241, 299.
Ch.49   William Barnes: National Portrait Gallery, London.
Ch.50   Thomas Hardy: National Portrait Gallery, London.
Ch.51   Joseph Wright: Elizabeth Mary Wright, *The Life of Joseph Wright* (London: Oxford University Press, 1932), frontispiece.
Ch.52   Henry Fowler: Jenny McMorris, *The Warden of English* (Oxford: Oxford University Press, 2001), p.125.
Ch.53   George Bernard Shaw: Society of Authors, source unknown.
Ch.55   *Empire Windrush*: Getty Images.
Ch.56   Daniel Jones: University College London.
Ch.57   Survey of English Usage: University College London.

INDEX OF PLACES

The alphabetical order of the index is letter-by-letter.

Wordsmiths and Warriors

Wordsmiths and Warriors

GENERAL INDEX

The alphabetical order of the index is letter-by-letter.

Wordsmiths and Warriors